The Vest Pocket Guide to Information Technology

Second Edition

THE VEST POCKET GUIDE TO

INFORMATION TECHNOLOGY

Second Edition

Jae K. Shim, Ph.D.
Chief Financial Officer
NBRF Incorporated
Professor of Accounting and Finance
California State University, Long Beach

Joel G. Siegel, Ph.D., CPA
Financial Consultant
Professor of Accounting and Finance
Queens College of the City University of New York

John Wiley & Sons, Inc.

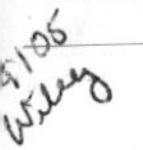

This book is printed on acid-free paper. ♾

Published by John Wiley & Sons, Inc., Hoboken, New Jersey.

Published simultaneously in Canada.

For general information on our other products and services, or technical support, please contact our Customer Care Department within the United States at 800-762-2974, outside the United States at 317-572-3993 or fax 317-572-4002.

Wiley also publishes its books in a variety of electronic formats. Some content that appears in print may not be available in electronic books.

For more information about Wiley products, visit our Web site at http://www.wiley.com.

Library of Congress Cataloging-in-Publication Data:

Shim, Jae K.
The vest pocket guide to information technology / Jae K. Shim, Joel G. Siegel.--2nd ed.
p. cm.
Includes index.
ISBN-13 978-0-471-72500-8
ISBN-10 0-471-72500-5 (pbk.)
1. Information technology—Handbooks, manuals, etc.
2. Management information systems—Handbooks, manuals, etc.
I. Siegel, Joel G. II. Title.
T58.5.S54 2005
658.4'038--dc22

2005043953

Printed in the United States of America

10 9 8 7 6 5 4 3 2 1

About the Authors

Jae K. Shim, Ph.D., is a Professor of Business Administration at California State University, Long Beach. Dr. Shim received his MBA and Ph.D. degrees from the University of California at Berkeley (Haas School of Business). He is the President of the National Business Review Foundation, a management and computer consulting firm. Dr. Shim has published about 50 articles in professional journals, including *Journal of Systems Management, Financial Management, Journal of Operational Research, Omega, Data Management, Management Accounting, Simulation and Games, Long Range Planning, Journal of Business Forecasting, Decision Sciences, Management Science,* and *Econometrica.* Dr. Shim has over 50 books to his credit and is a recipient of the 1982 Credit Research Foundation Outstanding Paper Award for his article on financial modeling. He is also a recipient of a Ford Foundation Award, Mellon Research Fellowship, and Arthur Andersen Research Grant. Dr. Shim has been for over 20 years an industrial consultant in the areas of information systems development and applications, corporate planning modeling, business forecasting, and financial modeling.

Joel G. Siegel, Ph.D., CPA, is a computer consultant to businesses and Professor of Accounting, Finance, and Information Systems at Queens College of the City University of New York. He was previously associated with Coopers and Lybrand, CPAs, and Arthur Andersen, CPAs. He served as a consultant to numerous organizations including Citicorp, International Telephone and Telegraph, Person-Wolinsky Associates, and the American Institute of CPAs. Dr. Siegel is the author of 50 books. His books have been published by Prentice Hall, Richard Irwin, McGraw-Hill, HarperCollins, John Wiley, Macmillan, Probus, International Publishing, Barron's, and the American Institute of CPAs. He has authored approximately 200 articles on business topics including many articles in the area of computer applications to business. His articles have appeared in various journals including *Computers in Accounting, Decision Sciences, Financial Executive, Financial Analysts Journal, The CPA Journal, National Public Accountant,* and *Practical Accountant.*

In 1972, he received the Outstanding Educator of America Award. Dr. Siegel is listed in Who's Who Among Writers and Who's Who in the World. Dr. Siegel is the former chairperson of the National Oversight Board.

How This Book Can Help You

The book covers information systems in all phases of business and in all functional areas to analyze and solve business problems in the real world. The practical and efficient use of computer technology, both software and hardware, is highlighted. All types of business applications are covered. The importance of databases, networking, and telecommunications is clearly presented. Popular accounting, tax, finance, management, manufacturing, and marketing software is explained for easy use. Software for decision support systems (DSSs), executive information systems (EISs), and artificial intelligence (AI) (e.g., financial modeling, budgeting, strategic planning and control, forecasting, data analysis, inventory planning, and optimization software) is covered with real-life examples. What-if analysis and the effects of changing assumptions are discussed.

The purpose of the book is to provide a wealth of current and essential information to managers in all types of organizations so that they may make optimum decisions. It gives the businessperson all he or she needs to know in the computerized financial application and modeling environment. Emerging trends in information technology are anticipated and discussed. In other words, expected developments in computers are presented so that managers can properly plan ahead. The professional success of a business manager depends on keeping abreast of the latest thinking and applications in information technology. This surely gives a competitive edge.

The book is written for business professionals in a practical, reader-friendly manner including clear illustrations. We have simplified difficult computer terminology and usage. Important topics include management information systems (MISs), selection of the best software and hardware for particular applications, business application software (e.g., accounting, finance, management, tax, marketing, and manufacturing), databases, telecommunications and online services (e.g., Internet, AOL, MSN, Dow Jones, Westlaw, AICPA), and computer security and auditing. The latest multimedia trends are covered. New developments in artificial intelligence and expert systems, decision support systems, and executive information systems are covered.

The audience for this book includes accountants, tax preparers, financial managers, general managers, marketing executives, production/operations managers, purchasing managers, personnel managers, business analysts, forecasters, budget analysts, chief financial officers (CFOs), chief executive officers (CEOs), chief operating officers (COOs), chief information officers (CIOs), chief technology officers (CTOs), project managers, consultants, systems analysts, and computer support staff. Businesspeople in large, medium, and small companies will benefit. Private and nonprofit entities will find the material of equal value.

The following are some representative topics, among others discussed in the book, of vital interest to businesspeople:

- Strategic uses of the information system and technology.
- The use of software in planning and control.
- The applications of telecommunication technologies and how digitized computer signals can take advantage of these technologies.
- Accounting and information systems and packages showing how applications can be made to record keeping, reporting, and financial statement presentation.
- The Sarbanes-Oxley compliance software
- An explanation of what a decision support system (DSS) is about and how it is useful to business decision makers to improve the quality of their analysis and evaluation. It improves problem solving.
- The use of artificial intelligence and expert systems in making decisions.
- Computerized security (e.g., protecting files, service contracts, backups, insurance coverage, and security devices). It includes preventing fraud.
- Database management involving organizing and managing information so that it can be retrieved and utilized in an effective and efficient way.
- What a management information system (MIS) is, and what its applications and benefits are.
- The use of online databases (e.g., World Wide Web, Dow Jones, Westlaw, Lexis) in making business decisions.
- The use of the Intranet within a company as an important information source.
- Available accounting and financial software and how they improve financial reporting and analysis.
- The use of networking to operate smarter and be more efficient in a computer environment.
- The use of computer conferencing.
- Financial modeling and what-if analysis in budgeting, forecasting, and general decision making.

- Manufacturing information systems packages to aid in inventory record keeping, inventory management and control, and production planning.
- Executive information systems (EISs).
- Marketing information systems to aid in sales planning, sales forecasting, market research, and advertising effectiveness.
- Selecting the best hardware for the particular application needs and to enhance productivity.
- Value chain management software.

Chapter 1 discusses what management information systems are about and presents MIS techniques. The different types of MISs are explained, including when each type would be most appropriate. Chapter 2 covers MISs in business decision making and explains decision models. Chapter 3 introduces basic hardware components and how to buy the "right" hardware combination for each user's requirements. Chapter 4 presents systems software and explains the functions and terminology of different types of systems software. Chapter 5 covers application software and how such software can be used to improve profitability and enhance productivity. Chapter 6 discusses the use of database software, including query languages. Chapter 7 presents data communications. Chapter 8 discusses the different types of online databases and the information available on them. State-of-the-art communication technologies and popular network applications are also presented. Chapter 9 discusses how to use an Intranet within the business. Chapter 10 presents accounting, audit, and tax software and their business applications. Chapter 11 shows how MISs can be applied to financial management to improve the management of assets and liabilities, and to help plan the financing of debt and equity. The role of the MIS in forecasting is also explained. Chapter 12 discusses manufacturing information systems and packages. It includes applications to production planning so as to improve manufacturing activity and inventory management. Marketing information systems and packages are presented in Chapter 13. The chapter shows how software is used in marketing management, sales planning, and advertising effectiveness. The use of decision support systems (DSSs) to aid in management decision making by making it more accurate and reliable is the subject of Chapter 14. Chapter 15 deals with the use of artificial intelligence software to imitate the human mind process. It aids in managerial analysis and decision making. Chapter 16 is directed toward computer security and auditing. It presents protective data systems and information technology to safeguard the integrity of information. Ways to prevent misappropriation of resources and fraudulent transactions are enumerated.

Chapter 17 deals with wireless technology, which provides businesses with enhanced connectivity and flexibility. Chapter 18 touches upon a strategic issue regarding the economic feasibility study of an Information Technology (IT) project. Finally, Chapter 19 addresses how to manage an IT project. In a project, you usually deal with unique problems, have a set of constraints, and often work with deadlines.

A glossary of MIS terms is included. The presentation is generic in nature. The reader does not need to know programming. There are many checklists, charts, tables, and graphs. In the index, a specific area of interest may easily be found.

In conclusion, the book shows clearly how computers can aid business managers in efficiently performing their functions. Their success depends on being up-to-date in the computer environment and having all information immediately available to make successful decisions.

Contents

CHAPTER 1

WHAT ARE MANAGEMENT INFORMATION SYSTEMS?

WHAT ARE INFORMATION SYSTEMS?

An information system (IS) is a computerized system that processes data (facts) and produces information. This process is defined as an information processing cycle (IPC). The information processing cycle consists of four operations: input, process, output, and storage. Raw data retrieved from the environment and delivered to the computer is called input. After the computer receives data from the input device, it will manipulate, refine, and process the data to produce useful information for users. This step is called processing. After data has been refined and manipulated into useful information, it is displayed to the end users as output. Finally, the information needs to be stored for future uses. All four processes make up the information processing cycle. Input consists of raw facts, while information is a collection of facts organized or processed in such a way that it has additional value for further usage.

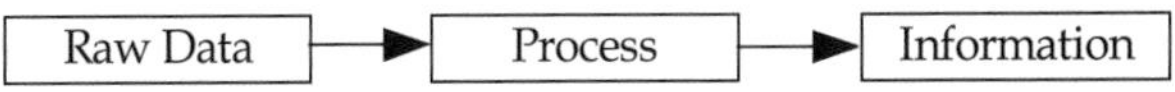

Information itself has value, and commerce often involves the exchange of information, rather than tangible goods. Information is valuable and useful because it can help decision makers. For example, investors are using information to make multimillion-dollar decisions, and financial institutions employ information to transfer millions of dollars. Retailers use information to control inventory and process orders. Information technologies are constantly changing our society, our ways of doing business, and our lives.

To fully understand what an information system is and how it works, it is necessary to examine its components. A complete information system should contain the following elements: hardware, software, data, trained personnel, and procedures.

Computer Hardware

Computer hardware can be classified into five categories: personal computers, servers, minicomputers, mainframe computers, and supercomputers.

Personal Computers

Personal computers are also called microcomputers. Each contains a microprocessor and is designed for individual or personal use. Classifications within this category include nonportable and portable computers.

The most popular type of microcomputer, a desktop computer, is designed to fit on top of a desk. With the same options in the system, desktop models are the least expensive.

Workstations are high-end personal computers, more powerful and expensive than the other personal computers described here. Very often, they are used as the file servers in a network environment. Many engineers use workstations to aid in product design and testing. Workstations are very good in calculations and graphics.

Portable computers include laptop, notebook, subnotebook, and penbased. Laptop computers are the largest portable computers in this category. They weigh between 8 and 15 pounds and have a hard drive, CD-ROM drive, and other equipment. Notebook computers are smaller versions of the laptop computers. They weigh between 4 and 8 pounds. The functions available for notebooks are very similar to those in laptop computers but with a more compact design and smaller screen.

Subnotebook computers are even smaller than notebook computers. They weigh less than 4 pounds and carry fewer optional devices (e.g., CD-ROM drives and regular hard drives). Penbased computers are the smallest computers and use a pen-like device to enter data. This pen-like device can be used to write directly on the screen or can be used as a pointer to make selections from a menu displayed on the screen. The unique feature about penbased computers is the special software designed to allow users to write information into the computer by hand, after several training sessions.

Servers

Server computers are designed to support a computer network that allows users to share files, applications, and hardware resources. A server computer is normally used to serve other computers in the network in terms of file storage and resources management, data communications, printing management, and other computer functions. Characteristics of a server computer include the following:

- It can communicate with other networks.
- It enhances communication speed within the network.
- It has high-end CPU power with a large capacity on the hard drive.
- Some have more than one CPU, providing parallel processing capabilities.
- It has a large memory capacity.

A server computer could be either a high-end microcomputer or a powerful microcomputer with minicomputer-like functions.

MINICOMPUTERS

Minicomputers are more powerful than microcomputers in terms of multiple user environments. In other words, a minicomputer can be used by many operators simultaneously. Many businesses and other organizations use minicomputers for their information processing requirements. The most powerful minicomputers are called super minicomputers.

MAINFRAME COMPUTERS

Mainframe computers are large computer systems that can handle hundreds of users, store large amounts of data, and process transactions at a high speed. Mainframe computers use a very sophisticated computer operating system to manage and control the whole system. Mainframes usually require a specialized environment including air conditioning and raised flooring that allows computer cables to be installed underneath. The price range for mainframes is from several hundred thousand to several million dollars.

SUPERCOMPUTERS

Supercomputers are the most powerful category of computers. Typical applications are scientific calculations, engineering design, space exploration, and other tasks requiring complicated processing. Supercomputers cost several million dollars.

Computer Software

A software program is actually a set of instructions written in various computer languages by programmers. Software contains sequences of operations the computer will follow. Before a program can run or be executed, the program must be loaded into the main memory of the computer. After that, programs can be executed to perform certain functions based on how they are designed. For example, the word processing program allows users to enter their typing and edit the contents. A graphic design program is used to perform graphic designs. Most computer programs are written by people with special training, called computer programmers, who write the necessary instructions in programming languages such as COBOL or BASIC.

System Software

System software consists of programs that are used to control and operate the computer hardware. There are three components in system software: the operating system, utility programs, and language processors. The operating system tells the computer how to perform functions such as how to load, store, and execute programs, how to transfer data between input/output devices, and how to manage resources available (CPU time). The operating system must be loaded in the main memory before the computer can function. Other application software can then be loaded into the computer with the help of the operating system. Utility programs are designed to perform functions that are not available in application software, such as formatting a diskette and creating a directory.

Application Software

Application software consists of programs created to perform a specific user's task. Application software allows a user to prepare a document, design a financial worksheet, or create a useful database. When you think of the different programs that people use to improve the efficiency in the workplace, they can be classified as application software. Most users do not write their own software programs—either system software or application software—because they can buy ready-to-use software.

Data

The term "data" usually refers to the input of a management information system. As the data is processed by the MIS, information is generated. The information can then be used for decision making. Data is normally entered into files or tables, which are then organized into a database. Users can retrieve input data through the application software and produce information as output. If the data is not accurate, the information produced will not be useful. Therefore, the garbage in, garbage out (GIGO) syndrome should be avoided.

Trained Personnel

People who operate an MIS should be properly trained. MIS professionals and programmers are responsible for designing and programming the system, while computer operators use it to generate information. With adequate training, operators can achieve the desired functions designed by MIS professionals. An experienced user can also provide

MIS professionals with valuable suggestions or be involved in MIS development.

Procedures

MIS procedures are designed for users to accomplish certain functions. Well-designed procedures guarantee the quality and the security of information processing.

Information systems that are implemented on a computer can be classified into five different types:

1. Transaction processing systems
2. Management reporting systems
3. Decision support systems
4. Office information systems
5. Executive information systems/executive support systems

The following sections describe these systems.

WHEN TO USE TRANSACTION PROCESSING SYSTEMS (TPSs)

Transaction information systems are designed to process the day-to-day transactions of an organization so that many labor-intensive business activities can be replaced by automated processes. These transactions are characterized by large numbers and routine processes. Each process involves a very simple data transaction, and the TPS is expected to process each one in a very short period of time. Examples include supermarket grocery checkout (i.e., billing systems) or bank transaction processes.

When computers were first used for processing business applications, TPSs were the primary systems implemented to replace the manual systems then in use. Typically, a successful TPS can improve transaction efficiency and customer service, and reduce transaction costs. The first TPS was a batch system. A TPS in batch processing implies that all transactions are collected first and processed at a later time. The disadvantage of batch processing is that information cannot be updated immediately. A TPS with online processing updates information when the transaction is entered. In a business where immediate update is required, an online TPS is necessary. An online TPS requires higher fees for operation than a batch TPS. Today, most TPSs use online processing to achieve better customer satisfaction and current information.

WHEN TO USE MANAGEMENT REPORTING (INFORMATION) SYSTEMS (MRSs)

After a TPS has been implemented, some organizations realize that the results produced do not satisfy higher-level decision making and that the computer's capability to perform rapid calculations and logical functions could be used to produce meaningful information for management. As a result, management reporting systems (MRSs) began to be developed so that managerial reports and summarized data could be produced. These reports helped managers perform their duties and provided middle management with statistical or summarized data for tactical-level decision making. In general, an MRS is usually used with the TPS. The TPS processes daily transactions, updates inventory, and keeps customer information while the MRS uses the data from the TPS to produce daily total sales, inventory ordering lists, and customer lists with different criteria. The output from an MRS provides middle management with printed reports and inquiry capabilities to help maintain operations and management control of the enterprise.

Frequently, an MRS is integrated with a TPS and the input source of the MRS is usually the output of the TPS. For example, a sales transaction can be processed by using a TPS to record the sales total and the customer's information. An MRS can further process this data to generate reports on average sales daily or fast-moving items.

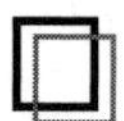

WHEN TO USE DECISION SUPPORT SYSTEMS (DSSs)

Decision support systems (DSSs) are designed to help managers reach a decision by summarizing or comparing data from different resources. They are suitable for semistructured and unstructured problems. DSSs often include query languages, statistical analysis capabilities, spreadsheets, and graphics to help decision makers evaluate the decision. DSSs are a type of MIS expressly developed to support the decision-making process. A DSS facilitates a dialogue between the user, who is considering alternative problem solutions, and the system, with its built-in models and accessible database.

A typical DSS process involves retrieving a model from the model base and allocating proper data from the database. With a model, users can ask if-then questions by changing one or several input variables. The system combines the input data and the model to generate recommendations. The database is managed by a database management system (DBMS), while a model base is managed by a model base management system (MBMS). Some DSSs allow users to create models for better evaluation. For example, the vice president of marketing may want to know the net effect on company profit if the advertising budget decreases. TPSs and MRSs usually do not provide this type of information.

WHEN TO USE OFFICE INFORMATION SYSTEMS (OISs)

Office information systems (OISs) are designed to support office tasks with information technology. Voice mail, multimedia systems, electronic mail, video conferencing, file transfer, and even group decisions can be achieved by an OIS. The final goal for an OIS is to have an office environment where no paper is used (paperless environment).

WHEN TO USE EXECUTIVE INFORMATION SYSTEMS (EISs)

Executive information systems (EISs) are designed to generate information that is abstract enough to present the whole company operation in a simplified version to satisfy senior management. Characteristically, senior managers employ a great variety of informal sources of information, so computerized information systems are able to provide only limited assistance. However, the CEO, senior and executive vice presidents, and board of directors need to be able to track the performance of their company and its various units to assess the business environment and to develop strategic directions for the company's future.

In particular, these executives need a great diversity of external information to compare their company's performance to that of its competitors and to investigate the general trends of the economies in the many countries where the company may be doing business. The EIS is therefore designed to address the information needs for senior management who may not be familiar with computer systems. EISs also provide features that make them easier for executives to use, such as graphical user interfaces that can be mouse or touch-screen oriented. EISs rely heavily on graphic presentation of both the menu options and the data.

WHY DO YOU NEED MISs TO SOLVE YOUR BUSINESS PROBLEMS?

The business environment is changing on a daily basis. The competition is everywhere from cost cutting to marketing strategies. To maintain competitiveness, management must improve the efficiency of operations without sacrificing the quality of products and services. To accomplish this task, managers must make timely and correct decisions. These are the keys to success. Because good decision making requires quality data and up-to-date information, MISs are specifically designed to provide information on a timely basis. MISs also provide different types of information, based on users' needs, to improve effectiveness and efficiency.

WHAT COMPUTER TECHNOLOGIES ARE AVAILABLE FOR BUSINESS?

Information systems are used in all business domains. For example, finance uses information to forecast revenues and maximize investment, make selections on stocks, and even predict bankruptcies. Accounting uses information systems to record transactions, prepare financial statements, manage cash flow, or predict profit or loss. In marketing, information systems are used to develop new merchandise and services, target customer segments, determine the locations for production and distribution facilities (so that the cost can be reduced and more customers will be attracted), formulate price strategies (to maximize total profits), and even develop the promotion policies (so that advertising will be more efficient). In manufacturing, information systems are used to process customer orders, develop production schedules, design new products, and test the quality of products.

In addition, network technologies allow users to share information and other resources. As a result, information retrieval can be more efficient and available. Current Internet technology provides businesses with a variety of external business information. Multimedia information transmissions (with text, graphics, image, and video) are also available on the Internet. With the impact of the Internet, Intranet becomes another new technology popular to business. Intranet is a small version of the Internet within one organization. It provides almost the same services as the Internet, but with better security and privacy. Artificial intelligence technologies are also applied to business functions. Neural networks have been used to predict the stock and bond markets. Expert systems are used to help managers with financial decisions. In the future, more intelligent agents will be used in the business environment to improve the quality of services and products.

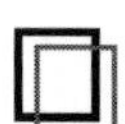

HOW WILL YOU MANAGE YOUR INFORMATION RESOURCES?

Managing these information resources could be a very complicated task due to rapid changes in this field. Generally speaking, there are two options available to managers: in-house operation and outsourcing.

In-house operation requires your own data processing facilities and personnel. This approach allows users to receive MIS services faster and easier. However, it requires the company to use the equipment and employ MIS personnel to assure the facility is fully functional.

A multitude of companies specializing in IS services provide expertise and economies of scale that no single organization can achieve. Outsourcing used to refer only to contracting with an IT company for the development of a system. Currently, outsourcing often means that an organization trusts all the activities associated with its ISs, including development of new systems, to another company. A growing number of businesses turn to IS companies not just for specific hardware or software purchases but for long-term IS services: purchasing and maintaining hardware; developing, purchasing, and maintaining software; installing and maintaining communications networks; developing, maintaining, and operating Web sites; staffing help desks; running the IS daily operation; managing customer and supplier relations; and so on. An organization may use a combination of in-house and outsourced services. It may outsource the development of an IS but then put its own employees in charge of its operation, or it may outsource both the development and operation of the system to another company.

In considering whether to develop systems in-house or to outsource their development, top management should ask the following questions:

- What are our core business competencies? Of the business we conduct, what specialties should we continue to practice ourselves?
- What do we do outside our specialties that could be done better for us by organizations that specialize in that area?
- Which of our activities could be improved if we created an alliance with IS organizations?
- Which of our activities should we work to improve internally?

Outsourcing has come to mean two different things: (1) a short-term contractual relationship with a service firm to develop a specific application for an organization and (2) a long-term contractual relationship with a service firm to take over all or some of an organization's IS functions (see Exhibit 1.1).

Advantages of Outsourcing

Clients contract for IT services to offload in-house responsibility and to better manage risks. When a client outsources, management knows how much the outsourced services will

1. Application development and software maintenance
2. Telecommunications installation and maintenance
3. Hardware purchasing and hardware maintenance
4. Help desk services
5. Web site design and maintenance
6. Staff training

Exhibit 1.1 TYPICAL OUTSOURCED IT SERVICES

cost; thus, the risk of miscalculation is eliminated. But there are additional advantages that make the option attractive:

- *Improved financial planning:* Outsourcing allows a client to know exactly what the cost of its IS functions will be over the period of the contract, which is usually several years.
- *Reduced license and maintenance fees:* Professional IS firms often pay discounted prices for CASE tools and other resources based on volume purchases; they can pass these savings on to their clients.
- *Increased attention to core business:* Letting outside experts manage IT frees executives from managing it.
- *Shorter implementation cycles:* IT vendors can usually complete a new application project in less time than an in-house development team can, thanks to their experience with development projects of similar systems for other clients.
- *Reduction of personnel and fixed costs:* In-house IS salaries and benefits and expensive capital expenditures for items such as CASE tools are paid whether or not the IS staff is productive.
- *Increased access to highly qualified know-how:* Outsourcing allows clients to tap into one of the greatest assets of an IT vendor: experience gained through work with many clients in different environments.
- *Availability of ongoing consulting as part of standard support:* Most outsourcing contracts allow client companies to consult the vendor for all types of IT advice, which would otherwise be unavailable (or only available from a highly paid consultant).
- *Increased security:* An experienced IS vendor is more qualified to implement control and security measures than a client company.

Risks of Outsourcing

Despite its popularity, outsourcing is not a panacea and should be considered carefully before it is adopted. There are conditions under which organizations should avoid outsourcing. The major risks are as follows:

- *Loss of control:* A company that outsources a major part of its IS operations will probably be unable to regain control for a long time.
- *High price:* Despite careful precontract calculations, some companies find out that outsourcing costs them significantly more than they would have spent had they taken care of their own ISs or related services.
- *Risks of losing a competitive advantage:* Innovative ISs, especially those intended to give their owners a competitive advantage, should not be outsourced.

- *First level:* Strategic management is the highest level of management. This level contains fewer decision makers but controls much power over the whole organization. Therefore, the EIS is the most appropriate system available at this level.

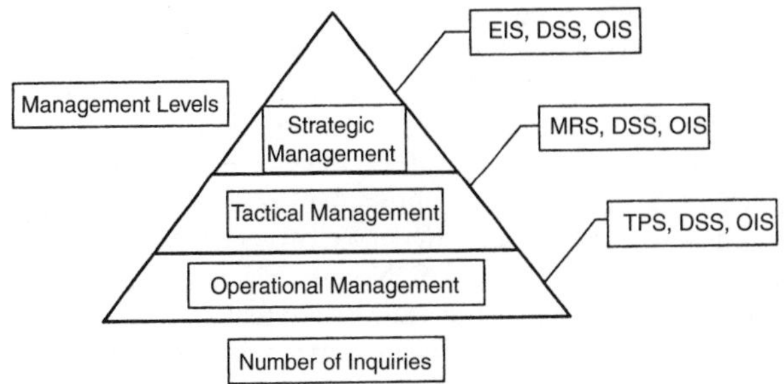

- *Second level:* Tactical management is the middle level of management. Managers at this level very often use MRSs for summarized information and generate management reports for decision making.
- *Third level:* Operational management is the lowest level of management. Foremen and supervisors are at this level. TPSs with large routine processing capability are usually used for this management level.

DSSs and OISs are not specifically designed for any management level. They are appropriate for all three levels of management.

Exhibit 1.2 MANAGEMENT TASK HIERARCHY

- *Loss of experienced employees:* Outsourcing often involves transferring hundreds or even thousands of the organization's employees to the IS vendor.

Different MISs are designed for different management functions. To understand which MIS will serve specific management needs, we categorize management into three levels (see Exhibit 1.2).

WHAT IS THE ROLE OF THE INFORMATION SYSTEMS IN THE DEVELOPMENT OF THE STRATEGIC PLAN?

Strategic planning is the process of selecting the organization's long-term objectives and of setting the strategies for achieving those objectives. This planning process is the responsibility of strategic management and is concerned with the overriding issues facing the organization, such as product lines and profitability. Given the international, competitive, and dynamic environment confronted by an organization, strategic planning is crucial to the survival of that organization.

The IS can play an important role in the development of the strategic plan and in monitoring ongoing operations to measure attainment of the plan. During the strategic planning process, data from the entity-wide database can be compared to data about the competition to determine an organization's relative strengths and weaknesses. For example, this data might include sales trends, gross margin on sales, age of capital assets, skills of existing personnel, debt/equity ratio, and so on. This data can be presented in reports from the existing information systems applications, such as sales/marketing, human resources management, fixed assets, finance and inventory, or via the models incorporated in the DSS and EIS. Note that data from the environment can also be incorporated into the DSS and EIS output. Strategic planners can combine the environmental data with the data obtained internally to assess the organization's competitive position. The demand for such information has been a major driver in the move to enterprise resource planning (ERP) systems, which bring all of the organization's information together into a single entity-wide database and generally provide the associated tools for strategic analysis and decision support.

In addition to assisting in the planning phase, the IS can be used to follow up by reporting certain performance indicators that illustrate the status of processes and critical success factors. For example, the number of franchises along with the level of sales and number of customer complaints for each should indicate the status of an organization's franchise network. Other performance indicators might be the number of new products, the cost to manufacture the products, and their selling price. If the entity-wide database is developed in light of the strategic plan, many of the data for the performance indicators should be readily available.

In addition to an organizational strategic planning process, there must be a strategic planning process for the IS function. That process must be coordinated with the organization's strategic planning process to ensure that the organization's strategic plan is supported and that IT is used to the best advantage of the organization. For example, during the strategic planning process, organizations should seek to achieve strategic advantage over their competitors by utilizing available information technology. This is particularly observable as companies ponder how to deal with the rapidly evolving world of e-business.

CHAPTER 2

MANAGEMENT INFORMATION SYSTEMS AND DECISION-MAKING MODELS

WHAT IS THE MANAGEMENT INFORMATION SYSTEM (MIS)?

A management information system (MIS) is comprised of computer-based processing and/or manual procedures that provide useful, complete, and timely information. This information must support management decision making in a rapidly changing business environment. The MIS must supply managers with information quickly, accurately, and completely. Information systems are not new; only computerization of them is new. Before computers, information system techniques existed to supply information for functional purposes. But what are management information systems? The scope and purpose of the MIS are better understood if each part of the term is defined. See Exhibit 2.1.

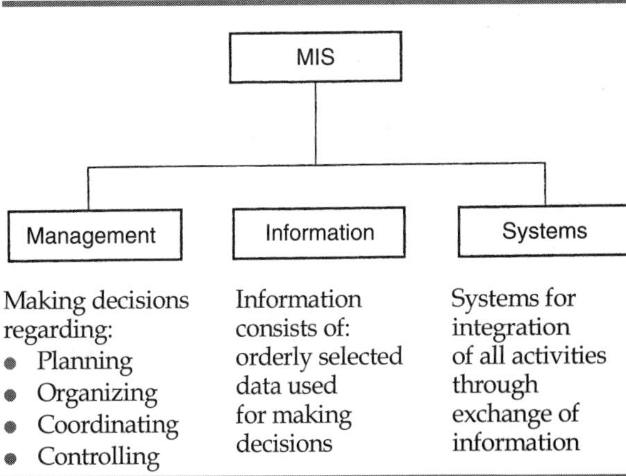

Exhibit 2.1 THE MEANING OF A MANAGEMENT INFORMATION SYSTEM (MIS)

Management

Management has been defined in a variety of ways, but for our purposes it comprises the processes or activities that managers do in the running of their organization: plan, organize, coordinate, and control operations. Managers plan by setting strategies and goals and selecting the best course of action to achieve the plan. They organize the tasks necessary for the operational plan, set these tasks up into homogeneous groups, and assign authority delegation. They control the performance of the work by setting performance standards and avoiding deviations from standard.

Planning

The planning function of management involves the selection of long- and short-term objectives and the drawing up of strategic plans to achieve those objectives. For example, the vice president of marketing must consider numerous factors when planning short-term ad campaigns and promotional activities aimed at opening up new long-term markets.

Organizing and Coordinating

In performing the organization and coordination function, management must decide how best to put together the firm's resources to carry out established plans. For example, senior management must decide on the type and number of divisions and departments in the company and evaluate the effectiveness of the organizational structure. In addition, managers must identify the personnel needs of the company, select the personnel, and ensure proper training of the staff.

Controlling

Controlling entails the implementation of a decision method and the use of feedback so that the firm's goals and specific strategic plans are optimally obtained. This includes supervising, guiding, and counseling employees to keep them motivated and working productively toward the accomplishment of organizational objectives.

Decision Making

Decision making is the purposeful selection from a set of alternatives in light of a given objective. Each primary management function involves making decisions, and information is required to make sound decisions. Decisions may be classified as short term or long term. Depending on the level of management, decisions can be operational, tactical, or strategic.

Information

Data must be distinguished from *information,* and this distinction is clear and important for our purposes. Data consists of facts and figures that are not currently being used in a decision process. It usually takes the form of historical records that are filed without immediate intent to retrieve them for decision making. An example would be the ledgers and other supporting documents that comprise the source material for profit and loss statements. Such material would only be of historical interest to an external auditor.

Information consists of data that has been retrieved, processed, or otherwise used for informative or inference purposes, or as a basis for forecasting or decision making. An example would be any of the supporting documents mentioned above, but in this case the data is used by an internal auditor, the management services department of an external auditor, or by internal management for profit planning and control, or for other decision-making purposes.

Systems

A system can be described simply as a set of elements joined together for a common objective. A subsystem is part of a larger system. All systems are parts of larger systems. For our purposes the organization is the system, and the parts (divisions, departments, functions, units, etc.) are the subsystems. Although we have achieved a very high degree of automation and joining together of subsystems in scientific, mechanical, and factory operations, we have barely begun to apply systems principles to organizational or business systems. The concept of synergism has not generally been applied to business organizations, particularly as it applies to the integration of the subsystems through information interchange. Marketing, production/operations, and finance are frequently on diverse paths and working at cross-purposes. The systems concept of an MIS is therefore one of optimizing the output of the organization by connecting the operating subsystems through the medium of information exchange.

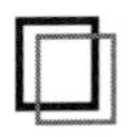

CLASSIFYING MANAGEMENT INFORMATION SYSTEMS IN TERMS OF THE TYPE OF OUTPUT PROVIDED

Another way of classifying MISs depends on the format of the output desired by the users of the system. Three distinctions are made:

1. *MISs that generate reports:* These reports can be income statements, balance sheets, cash flow reports, accounts receivable statements, inventory status reports, production efficiency reports, or any report on the status of a situation of interest to the decision maker. The reports can be historical or refer to the current status of the situation.
2. *MISs that answer what-if kinds of questions asked by management:* These information systems take the information stored in the database and reply to questions asked by management. These questions are in

the form of, "What would happen if this or that happened?" The information system uses its stored information, its comparison and calculation capabilities, and a set of programs especially written for this situation to provide management with the consequences of an action under consideration.

It works like this: The vice president for human resources of an airline wonders what pilot recruiting levels would be necessary if the company changed its retirement age from 65 to 62 at the same time that the Civil Aeronautics Board (CAB) reduced the maximum number of hours a pilot can fly monthly from 80 to 75. The vice president uses a what-if information system approach to answer her question. The computer indicates that monthly recruiting levels would have to be increased from 110 to 185 pilots to meet these two conditions. She realizes this is not feasible and now asks the system the what-if question with the retirement age changed to 63. The reply is now 142 pilots a month need to be recruited. The vice president feels this is an attainable recruiting target. Some what-if systems print out entire financial statements reflecting the financial consequences of actions that are being contemplated. Exhibit 2.2 depicts a what-if scheme.

What-if management information systems combine models (to be discussed later), software, and report-generating capability. The software allows the decision maker to make various inputs to the models

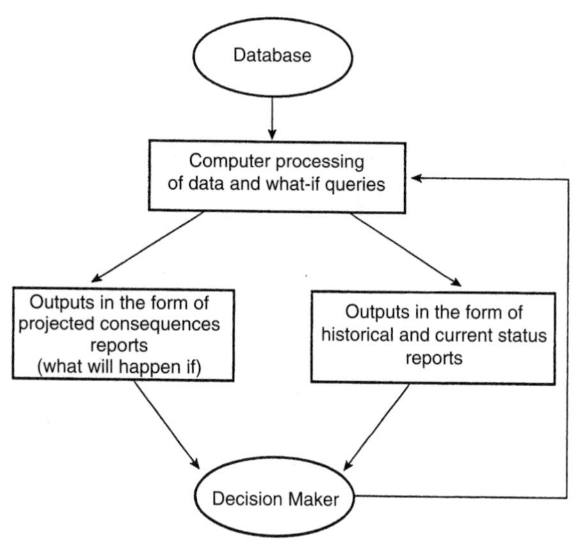

Exhibit 2.2 WHAT-IF MIS

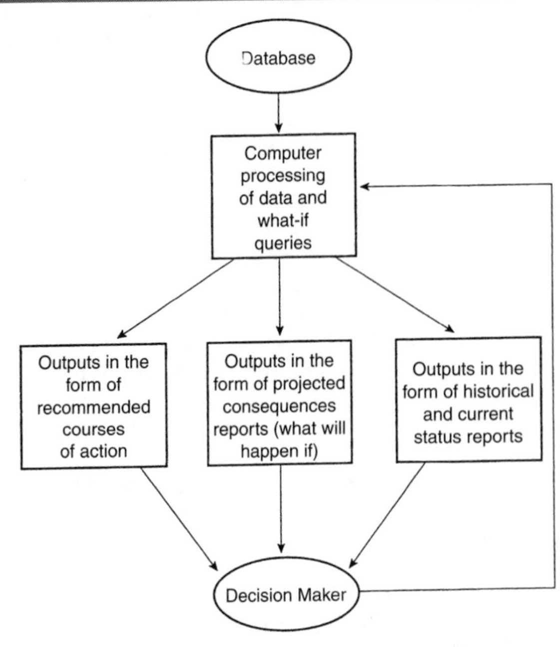

Exhibit 2.3 DECISION MAKER'S WHAT-IF QUESTIONS

and receive outputs. These MISs are generally run on a real-time system that can be online and that can also run on a time-sharing basis.

3. *MISs that support decision making (DSSs):* These advanced systems attempt to integrate the decision maker, the database, and the models being used. A DSS requires a very comprehensive database and the ability to manage that database to provide outputs to the decision maker and to update whatever permanent models are stored in the system. It requires extensive hardware and software. Two features distinguish DSS from other information systems: (1) They actually make a recommended decision instead of merely supplying additional information to the decision maker. (2) They build in the decision maker as an integral part of the system (the software accommodates the person as part of the decision process). Exhibit 2.3 illustrates a DSS management information system.

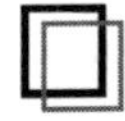

MISs AND ORGANIZATIONAL LEVELS

A management information system should produce useful, accurate, and timely information to management on three levels: low (operational), middle (tactical), and top (strategic). Lower-level managers make day-to-day operational decisions that affect a relatively narrow time frame and that involve details. These decisions are structured. Middle managers are involved with more tactical decisions that cover a broader range of time and involve more experience. Middle managers use summary reports, exception reports, periodic reports, on-demand reports, and event-initiated reports to make semistructured decisions. Top management deals with decisions that are strategic and long term in nature.

The primary objective of the MIS is to satisfy the needs at the various levels. Generally, the information needs to be more summarized and relevant to the specific decisions that need to be made than the information normally produced in an organization. It also has to be available quickly enough to be of value in the decision-making process. The information flows up and down through the three levels of management and is made available in various types of reports.

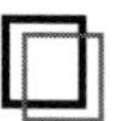

LEVELS OF MANAGEMENT: WHAT KINDS OF DECISIONS ARE MADE?

Each level of management can be differentiated by the types of decisions it faces, the time frame considered in the decisions, and the types of reports needed to make decisions (see Exhibit 2.4).

Lower Management

The largest level of management, lower (operational) management, deals mostly with decisions that cover a relatively narrow time frame. Lower management, also called supervisory management, actualizes the plans of middle management and

Characteristic	Operational	Tactical	Strategic
Frequency	Regular, repetitive	Mostly regular	Often ad hoc (as needed)
Dependability of results	Expected results	Some surprises may occur	Results often contain surprises
Time period covered	Past	Comparative	Future
Level of data	Very detailed	Summaries of data	Summaries of data
Source of data	Internal	Internal and external	Internal and external
Nature of data	Highly structured	Some unstructured data	Highly unstructured (semistructured)
Accuracy	Highly accurate data	Some subjective data	Highly subjective data
Typical user	First-line supervisors	Middle managers	Top management
Level of decision	Task-oriented	Control and resource allocation oriented	Goal-oriented

Exhibit 2.4 COMPARISON OF THE MIS AT THE OPERATIONAL, TACTICAL, AND STRATEGIC LEVELS

controls daily operations—the day-to-day activities that keep the organization humming. Examples of lower-level managers are the warehouse manager in charge of inventory restocking and the materials manager responsible for seeing that all necessary materials are on hand in manufacturing to meet production needs.

Most decisions at this level require easily defined information about current status and activities within the basic business functions—for example, the information needed to decide whether to restock inventory. This information is generally given in detailed reports that contain specific information about routine activities. These reports are structured, so their form can usually be predetermined. Daily business operations data is readily available, and its processing can be easily computerized. Managers at this level typically make structured decisions. A structured decision is a predictable decision that can be made by following a well-defined set of predetermined, routine procedures. For example, a clothing store floor manager's decision to accept your credit card to pay for some new clothes is a structured decision based on several well-defined criteria:

1. Does the customer have satisfactory identification?
2. Is the card current or expired?
3. Is the card number 011 on the store's list of stolen or lost cards?
4. Is the amount of purchase under the cardholder's credit limit?

Middle Management

The middle level of management deals with decisions that cover a somewhat broader range of time and require more experience. Some common titles of middle managers are plant manager, division manager, sales manager, branch manager, and director of personnel. The information that middle managers need involves review, summarization, and analysis of historical data to help plan and control operations and implement policy that has been formulated by upper management. This information is usually given to middle managers in two forms: summary reports, which show totals and trends—for example, total sales by office, by product, by salesperson, and total overall sales—and exception reports, which show out-of-the-ordinary data—for example, inventory reports that list only those items that number fewer than 10 in stock. These reports may be regularly scheduled (periodic reports), requested on a case-by-case basis (on-demand reports), or generated only when certain conditions exist (event-initiated reports).

Periodic reports are produced at predetermined times—daily, weekly, monthly, quarterly, or annually. These reports commonly include payroll reports, inventory status reports, sales reports, income statements, and balance sheets. A manager usually requests on-demand reports when information is needed for a particular problem. For example, if a customer wants to establish a large charge account, a manager might request a special report on the customer's payment and order history. Event-initiated reports indicate a change in conditions that requires immediate attention, such as an out-of-stock report or a report on an equipment breakdown.

Managers at the middle level of management are often referred to as tactical decision makers who generally deal with semistructured decisions. A semistructured decision includes some structured procedures and some procedures that do not follow a predetermined set of criteria. In most cases, a semistructured decision is complex, requiring detailed analysis and extensive computations. Examples of semistructured decisions include deciding how many units of a specific product should be kept in inventory, whether to purchase a larger computer system, from what source to purchase personal computers, and whether to purchase a multiuser minicomputer system. At least some of the information requirements at this level can be met through computer-based data processing.

Top Management

The top level of management deals with decisions that are the broadest in scope and cover the widest time frame. Typical titles of managers at this level are chief executive officer (CEO), chief operating officer (COO), chief financial officer (CFO), treasurer, controller, chief information officer (CIO), executive vice president, and senior partner. Top managers include only a few powerful people who are in charge of the four basic functions of a business: marketing, accounting and finance, production, and research and development. Decisions made at this level are unpredictable, long range, and related to the future, not just past and/or current activities. Therefore, they demand the most experience and judgment.

A company's MIS must be able to supply information to top management as needed in periodic reports, event-initiated reports, and on-demand reports. The information must show how all the company's operations and departments are related to and affected by one another. The major decisions made at this level tend to be directed toward (1) strategic planning—for example, how growth should be financed and which new markets should be tackled first; (2) allocation of resources, such as deciding whether to build or lease office space and whether to spend more money on advertising or the hiring of new staff members; and (3) policy formulation, such as determining the company's policy on hiring minorities and providing employee incentives.

(a) Consumer product business	
Strategic Planning	Competitive
	Industry statistics
Tactical	Sales analysis by customer
	Reorder analysis of new products
	Sales analysis by product line
	Production planning
Operational	Bill of materials
	Manufacturing specifications
	Product specifications
	Order processing
	Online order inquiry
	Finished goods inventory
	Accounts receivable
	General ledger
(b) Bank	
Strategic Planning	Market forecast
	New product development
	Financial forecast
Tactical	Branch profitability
	Product profitability
Operational	Loan billing
	Accounting systems
	Policy issuance and maintenance

Exhibit 2.5 THREE MANAGEMENT LEVELS AND THEIR INFORMATION NEEDS

Managers at this level are often called strategic decision makers. Examples of unstructured decisions include deciding five-year goals for the company, evaluating future financial resources, and deciding how to react to the actions of competitors.

At the higher levels of management, much of the data required to make decisions comes from outside the organization (e.g., financial information about other competitors). Exhibit 2.5 shows the decision areas that the three levels of management would deal with in a consumer product business and a bank.

MODELING A REAL-LIFE SYSTEM

Many MISs are model based. The real world is complex, dynamic, and expensive to deal with. For this reason, we use models instead of real-life systems. A model is an abstraction of a real-life system that is used to simulate reality. Especially in the computing environment we live in, managers and decision makers find it easy to use models to understand what is happening and to make better decisions. There are many different types of models. They include narrative, physical, graphical, and mathematical.

Narrative Models

A narrative model is either written or oral. The narrative represents a topic or subject. In an organization, reports, documents, and conversations concerning a system are all important narratives. Examples include a salesperson verbally describing a product's competition to a sales manager and a written report describing the function of a new piece of manufacturing equipment.

Physical Models

The fashion model is an example of a physical model, as are dolls and model airplanes. Many physical models are computer designed or constructed. An aerospace engineer may develop a physical model of a shuttle to gain important information about how a large-scale shuttle might perform in space. A marketing department may develop a prototype of a new product.

Graphical Models

A graphical model is a pictorial representation of reality. Lines, charts, figures, diagrams, illustrations, and pictures are all types of graphical models. These are used often in developing computer programs. Flowcharts show how computer programs are to be developed. A graph that shows budget and financial projections and a break-even chart are good examples of graphical models. The break-even chart depicts the point at which sales revenues and costs are equal, as shown in Exhibit 2.6.

Mathematical Models

A mathematical model is a quantitative representation of reality. These models are popular for decision making in all areas of business. Any mathematical formula or equation is a model that can be used for simulation or for what-if analysis. Once the models are properly constructed, managers can experiment with them just as physical scientists do a controlled experiment in the laboratory. In a sense, mathematical

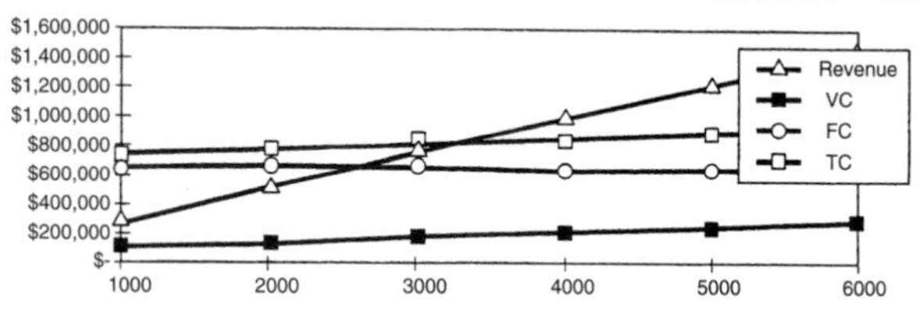

Exhibit 2.6 BREAK-EVEN CHART

models are the managers' laboratory. For example, the break-even formula used to compute the break-even point in Exhibit 2.6 is simply

$$X_{be} = \frac{FC}{(P - V)}$$

where X_{be} = break-even point, P = price or average revenue per unit, V = unit variable cost, and FC = total fixed costs.

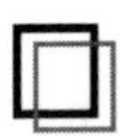

THE MODEL BASE

The purpose of the model base in an MIS is to give decision makers access to a variety of models and to assist them in the decision-making process. The model base can include model management software (MMS) that coordinates the use of models in an MIS. Depending on the needs of the decision maker, one or more of these models can be used.

Financial Models

Financial models provide cash flow, internal rate of return, and other investment analysis. Spreadsheet programs such as Excel are often used for this purpose. In addition, more sophisticated financial planning and modeling programs such as Budget Express can be employed. Some organizations develop customized financial models to handle their own unique situations and problems. However, as spreadsheet packages continue to increase in power, the need for sophisticated financial modeling packages may decrease.

Statistical Models

Statistical models can provide summary statistics, trend projections, hypothesis testing, and more. Many software packages, including Statistical Packages for Social Scientists (SPSS), Statistical Analysis System (SAS), and MINITAB, provide outstanding statistical analysis for organizations of all sizes. These statistical programs can calculate means, variances, correlation coefficients, regression analysis, and can do hypotheses testing. Many packages also have graphics output capability. The following example illustrates the use of SPSS for regression analysis and shows the sample output.

EXAMPLE 2.1 REGRESSION ANALYSIS

Cypress Consumer Products Corporation wishes to develop a forecasting model for its dryer sales by using multiple regression analysis. The marketing department prepared the following sample data:

EXAMPLE 2.1 REGRESSION ANALYSIS *(continued)*

Month	Sales of Washers (x_1)	Disposable Income (x_2)	Savings (x_3)	Sales of Dryers (y)
January	$45,000	$16,000	$71,000	$29,000
February	42,000	14,000	70,000	24,000
March	44,000	15,000	72,000	27,000
April	45,000	13,000	71,000	25,000
May	43,000	13,000	75,000	26,000
June	46,000	14,000	74,000	28,000
July	44,000	16,000	76,000	30,000
August	45,000	16,000	69,000	28,000
September	44,000	15,000	74,000	28,000
October	43,000	15,000	73,000	27,000

SPSS was employed to develop the regression model. Exhibit 2.7 presents the regression output results using three explanatory variables.

* * * * Multiple Regression * * * *

Listwise Deletion of Missing Data

Equation Number 1 Dependent Variable.. SALESDRY

Block Number 1. Method: Enter SALESWAS INCOME

SAVINGS

Variable(s) Entered on Step Number

1.. SAVINGS

2.. SALESWAS

3.. INCOME

Multiple R	.99167
R Square	.98340
Adjusted R Square	.97511
Standard Error	.28613

Analysis of Variance

	DF	Sum of Squares	Mean Square
Regression	3	29.10878	9.70293
Residual	6	.49122	.08187

F = 118.51727 Signif F = .0000

Variables in the Equation

Variable	B	SE B	Beta	Tolerance	VIF	T
SALESWAS	.596972	.081124	.394097	.964339	1.037	7.359
INCOME	1.176838	.084074	.752425	.957217	1.045	13.998
SAVINGS	.405109	.042234	.507753	.987080	1.013	9.592
(Constant)	–45.796348	4.877651			–9.389	

Durbin-Watson Test = 2.09377

Exhibit 2.7 REGRESSION OUTPUT RESULTS

Optimization Models

Optimization models refer to techniques for establishing complex sets of mathematical equations and inequalities that represent objectives and constraints. These models are prescriptive in that they try to provide the best possible solution to the problem at hand. They include mathematical programming such as linear programming (LP) and goal programming (GP) models.

Linear programming (LP) is a mathematical technique designed to determine an optimal decision (or an optimal plan) chosen from a large number of possible decisions. The optimal decision is the one that meets the specified objective of the company, subject to various restrictions or constraints. It concerns itself with the problem of allocating scarce resources among competing activities. The optimal decision yields the highest profit, contribution margin (CM), or revenue, or the lowest cost. A linear programming model consists of two important ingredients:

1. *Objective function:* The company must define the specific objective to be achieved.
2. *Constraints:* Constraints are in the form of restrictions on availability of resources or meeting minimum requirements.

As the name "linear programming" indicates, both the objective function and constraints must be in linear form. If a firm wished to find an optimal product mix, it could use LP techniques. The optimal mix would be the one that maximizes its total CM within the allowed budget and production capacity. Or the firm may want to determine a least-cost combination of input materials while meeting production requirements, employing production capacities, and using available employees.

Applications of LP are numerous. They include:

- Selecting least-cost mix of ingredients for manufactured products
- Developing an optimal budget
- Determining an optimal investment portfolio (or asset allocation)
- Allocating an advertising budget to a variety of media
- Scheduling jobs to machines
- Determining a least-cost shipping pattern
- Scheduling flights
- Gasoline blending
- Optimal manpower allocation
- Selecting the best warehouse location to minimize shipping costs

Formulation of LP

To formulate an LP problem, certain steps are followed. You must define the decision variables that you are trying to solve for, then express the objective function and constraints in terms of these decision variables. All the expressions must be in linear form. In the following example, we will use this technique to find the optimal product mix.

EXAMPLE 2.2 LP PROBLEM

The JKS Furniture Manufacturing Company produces two products: desks and tables. Both products require time in two processing departments: an assembly department and a finishing department. Production time and costs of the two products are as follows:

	Products	Available	
Processing	Desk	Table	Hours
Assembly	2	4	100 hours
Finishing	3	2	90
Contribution Margin Per Unit	\$25	\$40	

The company wants to find the most profitable mix of these two products.

Step 1. Define the decision variables as follows:

A = Number of units of desk to be produced

B = Number of units of table to be produced

Step 2. The objective function to maximize total contribution margin (CM) is expressed as:

Total CM = 25A + 40B

Then formulate the constraints as inequalities:

$2A + 4B \leq 100$ (Assembly constraint)

$3A + 2B\ 90 \leq$ (Finishing constraint)

In addition, implicit in any LP formulation are the constraints that restrict A and B to be nonnegative, i.e.,

$A, B \geq 0$

Our LP model is:

Maximize:	Total CM = 25A + 40B
Subject to:	$2A + 4B \leq 100$
	$3A + 2B \leq 90$
	$A, B \geq 0$

USE OF COMPUTER LP SOFTWARE

We can use a computer LP software package, such as LINDO (Linear Interactive and Discrete Optimization) and What's Best!, to quickly solve an LP problem. Exhibit 2.8 shows a LINDO output by an LP program for the LP model set up in Example 2.2.

EXAMPLE 2.2 LP PROBLEM *(continued)*

Note: The printout shows the following optimal solution:

A = 20 units

B = 15 units

CM = $1,100

Shadow prices are:

Assembly capacity = $8.75

Finishing capacity = $2.50

COMPUTER PRINTOUT FOR LP

INFORMATION ENTERED

NUMBER OF CONSTRAINTS	2
NUMBER OF VARIABLES	2
NUMBER OF <= CONSTRAINTS	2
NUMBER OF = CONSTRAINTS	0
NUMBER OF >= CONSTRAINTS	0

MAXIMIZATION PROBLEM

25 A + 40 B

SUBJECT TO

2A + 4B <= 100

3A + 2B <= 90

RESULTS

VARIABLE	VALUE	ORIGINAL COEFF.	COEFF. SENS.	SOLUTION:
				A = 20
A	20	25	0	B = 15
B	15	40	0	

CONSTRAINT NUMBER	ORIGINAL RHS	SLACK OR SURPLUS	SHADOW PRICE
1	100	0	8.75<— (shadow price of the assembly capacity)

OBJECTIVE FUNCTION VALUE : 1100 = CM

SENSITIVITY ANALYSIS

OBJECTIVE FUNCTION COEFFICIENTS

VARIABLE	LOWER LIMIT	ORIGINAL COEFFICIENT	UPPER LIMIT
A	20	25	60
B	16.67	40	50

Exhibit 2.8 LINDO OUTPUT BY AN LP PROGRAM

RIGHT HAND SIDE			
CONSTRAINT NUMBER	LOWER LIMIT	ORIGINAL VALUE	UPPER LIMIT
1	60	100	180
2	50	90	150

Exhibit 2.8 LINDO OUTPUT BY AN LP PROGRAM *(continued)*

Decision Analysis Models

Decisions are made under certainty or under uncertainty. Decision making under certainty means that for each decision there is only one event and therefore only one outcome for each action. Decision making under uncertainty, which is more common in reality, involves several events for each action with its probability of occurrence. When decisions are made in a world of uncertainty, it is often helpful to make the computations of (1) expected value, (2) standard deviation, and (3) coefficient of variation.

STANDARD DEVIATION

The standard deviation measures the tendency of data to be spread out. Cost analysts and managerial accountants can make important inferences from past data with this measure. The standard deviation, denoted with the Greek letter Σ, read as *sigma,* is defined as follows:

$$\sigma = \sqrt{\frac{\Sigma(x-\bar{x})^2}{n-1}}$$

where x is the mean (arithmetic average).

The standard deviation can be used to measure the variation of such items as the expected contribution margin (CM) or expected variable manufacturing costs. It can also be used to assess the risk associated with investment projects.

EXAMPLE 2.3

One and one-half years of quarterly returns are listed below for United Motors stock.

Time Period	x	$(x-\bar{x})$	$(x-\bar{x})^2$
1	10%	0	0
2	15	5	25
3	20	10	100
4	5	–5	25
5	–10	–20	400
6	20	10	100
	60		650

EXAMPLE 2.3 *(continued)*

From the above table, note that

$$\bar{x} = 60/6 = 10\%$$

$$\sigma = \sqrt{\frac{\Sigma(x-\bar{x})^2}{n-1}} = \sqrt{\frac{650}{(6-1)}} = \sqrt{130} = 11.40\%$$

The United Motors stock has returned on the average 10% over the last six quarters and the variability about its average return was 11.40%. The high standard deviation (11.40%) relative to the average return of 10% indicates that the stock is very risky.

Although statistics such as expected value and standard deviation are essential for choosing the best course of action under uncertainty, the decision problem can best be approached using decision theory. Decision theory is a systematic approach to making decisions, especially under uncertainty. Decision theory utilizes an organized approach such as a *decision matrix* (or *payoff table*).

DECISION MATRIX

A decision matrix is characterized by the *row* representing a set of alternative courses of action available to the decision maker; the *column* representing the state of nature or conditions that are likely to occur and that the decision maker has no control over; and the *entries* in the body of the table representing the outcome of the decision, known as payoffs, which may be in the form of costs, revenues, profits, or cash flows. By computing expected value of each action, we will be able to pick the best one.

EXAMPLE 2.4 DECISION MATRIX EXAMPLE

Assume the following probability distribution of daily demand for a product:

Daily demand	0.0	1.0	2.0	3.0
Probability	0.2	0.3	0.3	0.2

Also assume that unit cost = \$3, selling price = \$5 (i.e., profit on sold unit = \$2), and salvage value on unsold units = \$2 (i.e., loss on unsold unit = \$1). We can stock 0, 1, 2, or 3 units. The question is:

How many units should be stocked each day? Assume that units from one day cannot be sold the next day. Then the payoff table can be constructed as follows:

EXAMPLE 2.4 DECISION MATRIX EXAMPLE
(continued)

	State of Nature				
Demand	0	1	2	3	Expected value
Stock					
(probability)	(.2)	(.3)	(.3)	(.2)	
0	\$0	0	0	0	\$0
Actions					
1	−1	2	2	2	1.40
2	−2	1*	4	4	1.90**
3	−3	0	3	6	1.50

*Profit for (stock 2, demand 1) equals (no. of units sold)(profit per unit) – (no. of units unsold) (loss per unit) = (1)(\$5 – 3) – (1)(\$3 – 2) = \$1

**Expected value for (stock 2) is: −2(.2) + 1(.3) + 4(.3) + 4(.2) = \$1.90

The optimal stock action is the one with the highest expected monetary value. The optimal decision in this case would be to stock 2 units.

DECISION TREE

Decision tree is another approach used in discussions of decision making under uncertainty. It is a pictorial representation of a decision situation. As in the case of the decision matrix approach just discussed, it shows decision alternatives, states of nature, probabilities attached to the state of nature, and conditional benefits and losses. The decision tree approach is most useful in a sequential decision situation.

EXAMPLE 2.5 DECISION TREE EXAMPLE

Assume XYZ Corporation wishes to introduce one of two products to the market this year. The probabilities and present values (PVs) of projected cash inflows are given below:

Product	Initial Investment	PV of Cash Inflows	Probabilities
A	\$225,000		1.00
		\$450,000	0.40
		200,000	0.50
		−100,000	0.10
B	80,000	1.00	
		320,000	0.20
		100,000	0.60
		−150,000	0.20

A decision tree analyzing the two products is depicted in Exhibit 2.9.

	Initial Investment (1)	Probability (2)	PV of Cash Inflows (3)	PV of Cash Inflows (2) × (3) = (4)
Product A		0.40	$450,000	$180,000
	$225,000	0.50	$200,000	100,000
		0.10	–$100,000	–10,000
		Expected PV of Cash Inflows		$270,000
Choice A or B				
Product B		0.20	$320,000	$64,000
	$80,000	0.60	$100,000	60,000
		0.20	–$150,000	–30,000
		Expected PV of Cash Inflows		$94,000

For product A:

Expected NPV = expected PV – I = $270,000 – $255,000 = $45,000

For product B:

Expected NPV = $94,000 – $80,000 = $14,000

Based on the expected NPV, choose product A over product B, however, this analysis fails to recognize the risk factor in project analysis.

Exhibit 2.9 DECISION TREE

Graphical Models

Graphical modeling programs are software packages that assist decision makers in designing, developing, and using graphic displays of data and information. Numerous personal computer programs that can perform this type of analysis are on the market. In addition, sophisticated graphic design and analysis such as computer-assisted design (CAD) is widely available.

Project Planning and Management Models

Project planning and management models are used to navigate and coordinate large projects, and to discover critical paths that could delay or jeopardize an entire project if they are not completed in a timely and cost-effective fashion. Some of these programs can determine the best way to speed up a project by effectively using additional resources, including cash, labor, and equipment. Project management allows decision makers to keep tight control over projects of all sizes and types.

Program evaluation and review technique (PERT) is a useful management tool for planning, scheduling, costing, coordinating, and controlling complex projects such as the following:

- Formulation of a master budget
- Construction of buildings

- Installation of computers
- Scheduling the closing of books
- Assembly of a machine
- Research and development activities

Questions to be answered by PERT include:

- When will the project be finished?
- What is the probability that the project will be completed by a given time?

Simulation Models

The primary use of a simulation model is to respond to what-if questions. These descriptive models can produce large amounts of detailed output because they work by mimicking many parts of the real-world system. One major weakness is that no automatic searching or optimizing is done by the model. (Any such features must be built on top of the simulation model and must be used as a submodel.) In such cases, the simulation may have to be performed many, many times while a search for the best decision parameters is under way. This can be quite expensive if the simulation is complex.

Two major issues in simulation modeling are how long a simulation run must proceed to achieve steady state (typical behavior) and how many different runs must be performed to achieve statistical significance. Inside most simulation models is a pseudo-random number generator. This is a mathematical subroutine that produces numbers that appear to be random. These random numbers are manipulated further to represent parts of the model that are not deterministic. Examples might include the arrival of customers at a ticket counter or the time of failure of an electronic circuit component. These random number generators can be "seeded" with special input parameters to make them produce different streams of random values. Repeating runs with different seed values provides a set of outputs that has a statistical distribution to be analyzed.

Many commercial software packages are available that can be used to build simulation models. Some of these are general-purpose simulation languages that have general but powerful features such as waiting lines and resource pools that ease the modeling task. At the other extreme are tailored simulation models (such as oil refinery models) that are already built but afford the user the ability to specify input parameters to describe the precise configuration under study. In between these extremes are simulation languages that are suited for a large class of models such as networks that are a formalism in which many problems can be represented.

EXAMPLE 2.6
SLAM II SIMULATION MODEL

During a lunch hour, customers arrive at a fast-food restaurant at a rate of three per minute. They require 1.5 minutes to place an order and pay the bill before going to pick up the food. How many cash register stations are needed to ensure that the number of customers waiting in line does not exceed six and that this waiting time does not occur more than 30% of the time during the lunch hour rush?

A simulation language such as the SLAM II can be used to simulate the sequence of the operation in this problem. The language consists of symbols that can be composed on a computer terminal screen into a diagram like the one shown. The first circle represents customer arrivals. The second circle represents the queue, or waiting line. The last circle represents departures from the system.

A random normal probability distribution was chosen to model the customer arrivals. The mean, or average, time between arrivals is set at 20 seconds, and the standard deviation is set to 5 seconds. The simulation model was run for 3,600 seconds for each experiment. The number of servers was changed between runs. The service time was represented by an exponential distribution with a mean of 90 seconds.

The simulation software generates random numbers using mathematical formulas, then computes when customers arrive, how long they require service, and so forth. A clock is simulated to keep track of what should happen next. These performance statistics are collected and reported.

Statistics describing the queue are produced automatically by the simulation software package. Exhibit 2.10 shows that five servers are needed to ensure that the queue will be no longer than six people for 70% of the time. A thorough analysis would involve making more runs to confirm that the above statistics still hold true with different random numbers and longer periods of simulation.

Exhibit 2.10 would serve as a tool for establishing optimal staffing levels for a fast-food restaurant.

Number of Servers								
0	**1**	**2**	**3**	**4**	**5**	**6**	**7**	**8**
4	14	20	24	27	27	28	31	36
5	46	55	60	63	64	68	73	76

Exhibit 2.10 PERCENT OF TIME THAT QUEUE LENGTH IS NO MORE THAN 6

CHAPTER 3

HOW TO SELECT THE BEST MICROCOMPUTER SYSTEM

MICROCOMPUTERS, LARGE-SYSTEM COMPUTING, AND NETWORK COMPUTING

Generally speaking, computers can be classified into five categories: microcomputers, network servers, minicomputers, mainframe computers, and supercomputers.

Microcomputers

Microcomputers are designed for a single-user environment and small business applications. However, more and more businesspeople are using microcomputers for both multiuser networks and business applications. For example, a businessperson can use a microcomputer to organize financial transactions, prepare the corporate tax return (Form 1120 or 1120S), or update the inventory of several supermarkets on a network. Today's microcomputers can be so powerful that they provide solutions for most business applications.

A microcomputer uses a microprocessor as the central processing unit. A microprocessor can be very powerful despite its small size. Currently, there are two major microcomputer systems available on the market. They are the IBM-compatible system and the Apple system. These two systems use different platforms (operating systems) to control the hardware. The IBM-compatible system uses a Windows operating system developed by Microsoft. The Windows operating system provides a graphical user interface (GUI) and a multitasking environment. The Windows operating system—including Windows 98, Windows 2000, and Windows XP workstation—dominates most of the microcomputer market. Apple Macintosh uses a totally different operating system developed by Apple Computer. Newer Apple operating systems are able to run Windows-based applications. However, due to poor market strategy, the Apple system is losing its market share. It is suggested that the businessperson use the IBM system because of greater compatibility, more program availability, and a more opened platform.

Computers on the Go

In today's mobile society, computers are increasingly used outside the office. Notebook or handheld computers are used to record and retrieve data for people on the go.

- *Notebook computer (laptop):* A compact, light, personal computer powered by a rechargeable battery.
- *Personal digital assistant (PDA):* A handheld computer that is small enough to fit in the palm of a hand. Typically a stylus (a penlike pointing and drawing device) is used to enter data through a touch screen, although some handhelds also have a small keyboard or can plug into a folding portable keyboard.
- *Tablet computer (tablet PC):* A full-power PC in the form of a thick writing tablet. It looks like a notebook computer without a keyboard, although it can be connected to a keyboard and a mouse.

Internet Appliances

An increasing number of handheld computers and other electronic devices are manufactured with a capability to link to the Internet. Collectively, such devices are called *internet appliances*. Many of the devices are equipped with circuitry and software that enables them to link wirelessly to the Internet.

Large-System Computing

Large systems consist of mainframe computers, minicomputers, and supercomputers. They are typically multiuser computer systems in which many users share the same computing resources at the same time (time sharing). The computing power of minicomputers or mainframe computers is usually more than microcomputers and so the greater the cost. Mainframe computers and supercomputers are so expensive to purchase and maintain that only large corporations can afford them. The computing power of mainframe computers is usually shared by many users. That means the operating system of a mainframe computer allows many users to participate simultaneously via separate, interconnected terminals. Mainframe computers are typically used for business applications where a large number of transactions are processed. They are fast in processing speed and have large storage capacity.

Supercomputers have the most processing power of all the computers available. They are primarily designed for high-speed computation, especially for scientific research or the defense industry, but their use is growing rapidly in business as prices decrease. Supercomputers are also valuable for large-model simulation and complex mathematical calculations. Weather forecasting agents use supercomputers to model the world's weather system to improve weather predictions in a very short period of time. The computer performance and speed required to achieve that goal needs enormous processing power. To increase the speed of supercomputers, some companies are linking together individual or serial processors into multiple processors or parallel processing systems.

Network Servers

Network servers are used to manage and control computer networks. A network server needs to have larger storage capacity to store network programs and a high-performance CPU to provide timely network functions. Computer networks can be localized or on a worldwide scale. Therefore, computer servers can be designed to manage only several microcomputers in a local area network (LAN) or several hundred computers in a wide area network (WAN).

COMPUTER SYSTEM UNIT

The system unit has components such as the system board (mother board), central processing unit (CPU), main memory (including registers, cache memory, RAM, and ROM), system clock, power supply, expansion slots, ports, and bus lines.

System Board

The system board (or mother board) consists of a flat board that contains the CPU, memory chips, and other devices. A chip has many tiny circuit boards etched on a small square of sandlike material called silicon. Chips are mounted on carrier packages, which then plug into sockets on the system board.

CPU

The central processing unit (CPU) is the center of all computer processing activities. It is here that all processing is controlled, all data is manipulated, and arithmetic/logic computations are performed. The CPU takes data from an input device (keyboard, scanner, or floppy disk) and processes it to generate information so that output devices (the monitor or printer) can display it. Inside the CPU are the arithmetic/logic unit (ALU) and the control unit (CU). The ALU is used to perform the four basic arithmetic operations: addition, subtraction, multiplication, and division. Logic functions are used to compare values. They are >=, <=, =, <, >, and <>. All computer applications—from typing a document to supercomputer simulation—are achieved through these simple operations. The control unit is responsible for managing the traffic of the CPU. It interprets and carries out computer operations contained in computer programs. It moves instructions from the memory to the registers in the control unit. The control unit executes only one instruction at a time and executes it so quickly that the control unit appears to do many different things simultaneously. The CPU capacity is often described in word sizes. A word is the number of bits (such as 16, 32, or 64) that can be processed at one time by the CPU. Therefore, the more bits of the word size, the more powerful is the CPU.

Main Memory

The main memory (or primary storage) consists of registers, cache memory, random access memory (RAM), and read only memory (ROM). Registers are located in the control unit and ALU of a CPU. Registers are special high-speed staging areas that hold data and instructions temporarily during processing. Because the registers are located inside the CPU, their contents can be handled much faster than other main memory.

Cache Memory

Cache, pronounced "cash," memory, is located between RAM and CPU for faster access. It is a special high-speed memory area that the CPU can access quickly. Most frequently used routines are stored in the cache memory to improve performance.

RAM

RAM is the memory used to store temporary data or programs when the computer power is on.

ROM

ROM usually stores very essential information permanently.

System Clock

Part of the computer performance is determined by the speed of system clocks. The system clock controls how often the operation will take place within a computer. The system clock uses fixed vibrations from a quartz crystal to deliver a steady stream of digital pulses to the CPU. The faster the clock, measured in megahertz (MHz), or gigahertz (GHz), the faster the processing. For example, the most recent Intel Pentium IV chip runs at speeds up to 3.8 GHz. (For up-to-date information, visit www.webopedia.com/quick_ref/processor.html.) In February 2005, IBM and partners Sony and Toshiba unveiled a "supercomputer on a chip" that aims to dramatically increase the computing power in video-game systems, TVs, and other computer electronics. This chip is said to run at clock speeds greater than 4 GHz.

Note: Intel® Centrino™ mobile technology is Intel's new technology designed specifically for mobile computing with integrated wireless LAN capability and breakthrough mobile performance. It also enables extended battery life and sleek, easy-to-carry notebook PCs. With Intel Centrino mobile technology, three components work together to enable outstanding mobile performance, extended battery life, and integrated wireless LAN capability in thinner and lighter notebooks. These components are the Intel® Pentium® M processor, the Intel® 855 Chipset Family, and the Intel® PRO/Wireless 2100 network connection. AMD Athlon XP-M is a major competition.

Power Supply

A computer runs on direct current (DC), but the available electricity from a standard outlet is alternating current (AC). The power supply is a device that converts AC to DC to run the computer. Because the power supply can generate lots of heat, a fan in the computer is necessary to keep other devices from becoming too hot. In addition, electrical power drawn from a standard AC outlet can be quite uneven. For example, a sudden electrical surge could burn out the DC circuitry in your computer. Instead of plugging your computer directly into the wall electrical outlet, it is better to plug it into a power protection device. The two principal types are surge protectors and uninterrupted power source (UPS) units. The surge protector is the less expensive device and protects a computer from being damaged by most instances of high voltage. A computer can be plugged into a surge protector, which in turn is plugged into a standard electrical outlet.

Expansion Slots and Boards

Most microcomputers are expandable. Expandability refers to a computer's capacity to add more functions such as more memory or a fax/modem. In other words, when you buy a PC, you can add devices later to enhance its computing power. Expansion slots are sockets on the motherboard into which you can plug expansion cards. Expansion cards (add-on boards) are circuit boards that provide more memory or control peripheral devices. The following are examples of expansion cards:

- *Controller cards:* Controller cards allow your PC to work with the computer's various peripheral devices such as a floppy drive or a hard drive.
- *Graphics cards:* These cards allow you to use different kinds of color monitors with your computer, such as super VGA cards.

Bus Lines

A bus line is an electrical pathway through which bits are transmitted between the CPU and other devices. There are different types of buses. The bus between the CPU and the expansion slots is called a local bus. The bus between RAM and the expansion slots is called an expansion bus. The old 8-bit bus can only transfer 8 bits at a time, while a 32-bit bus can transmit 32 bits at one time.

Ports

A port is a socket on the outside of the system unit that is connected to an expansion board on the inside of the system unit. A port allows you to plug in a cable to connect other devices such as a monitor, a keyboard, or a printer. In general, ports are categorized into three types:

1. *Parallel ports:* A parallel port allows a line to be connected so that many bits can be transmitted at one time. Since many bits can be transmitted, the transmission speed is higher. Printers, monitors, and keyboards use parallel ports.
2. *Serial ports:* A serial (or RS-232) port enables a line to be connected that will send 1 bit at a time. The serial port is usually used for data communication purposes.
3. *USB:* Short for Universal serial bus, a USB is an external bus standard that supports data transfer rates of 12 Mbps. A single USB port can be used to connect up to 127 peripheral devices, such as mice, modems, and keyboards. USB also supports Plug-and-Play installation and hot plugging. It is expected to completely replace serial and parallel ports.

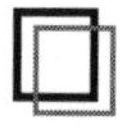

HOW TO SELECT LAPTOPS

Selecting a laptop computer is trickier than buying a desktop PC because laptops are more diverse and more personal. Here are some basics to consider.

1. Get Intel's latest Centrino-brand chip platform, codenamed *Sonoma*, which is faster speeds.
2. Get at least 512 megabytes of memory. Don't worry much about processor speed.
3. Buy as much hard-drive capacity as you can afford.
4. Make sure your computer has multiple USB 2.0 ports, and slots for the memory cards used in cameras.
5. On Windows laptops, security is crucial. Make sure that you get the more secure SP2 version of Windows XP and that you immediately install anti-virus, anti-spam, anti-spyware, anti-popup and firewall software. If you plan to use your laptop in public wireless hot spots, take the time to enable its wireless security features.

Specifically, the following dimensions must be weighed.

- *Size and weight:* There are several classes of laptops. At the light end are machines weighing just 2 pounds to 4 pounds. These models are designed for mobility and are meant to complement a desktop PC. They are very thin and have screens of 12 inches or less. In the middle are laptops weighing from 4 pounds to 7 pounds. These models can serve as desktop replacements but can also be toted on trips. They typically have 14-inch or 15-inch screens.
- *Windows or Mac:* Most laptop buyers will go for Windows machines and Apple's iBooks.
- *Processor:* If you want the best combination of power and battery life from your Windows laptop, get one that uses Intel's power-saving Pentium M processor. These chips are included in models bearing the Centrino label, offered by many manufacturers. But they are also available in some non-Centrino models that use different wireless chips. Don't pay extra for faster processor speeds. Even the slowest laptop processors can handily perform the most common computing tasks.
- *Battery life:* Insist on a laptop that can run for at least three hours on its standard battery. Some models can do much better.
- *Screen and keyboard:* Try to test laptops in stores to ensure you like their screens and keyboards. You don't need a huge screen if you can get one with high resolution.
- *Wireless Networking:* Built-in Wi-Fi networking is a must. Buy a laptop with the newer "g" version. Wireless reception capabilities vary in laptops because of different antenna and case designs. If you plan to use your cell phone as a modem or to synchronize data with a cell phone or PDA, make sure your laptop has another type of wireless networking, called Bluetooth.

HOW DO CPUs AFFECT YOUR COMPUTING POWER?

The CPU is the brain of a computer system. It contains the control unit (CU) and the arithmetic/logic unit (ALU). The power of the CPU can very much determine the performance of the whole system. The CPU is measured by its processing capacity, speed in terms of MHz, word size, and million instructions per second (MIPS). Megahertz (million times per second) is the measurement for computer execution frequency. This frequency is controlled by the system clock. Word size is the number of bits the CPU can process at a time. The larger the word size, the faster the computer

	Transistors	CPU Speed	L2 Cache	Front-Side Bus Speed
Celeron	7,500,000	1.06 GHz - 2 GHz	256 KB, full speed	133 MHz and 400 MHz
Pentium II	7,500,000	233 MHz - 450 MHz	512 KB, half speed	100 MHz
Pentium III	9,500,000	450 MHz - 1 GHz	256 KB, full speed	133 MHz
Pentium III Xeon	28,100,000	500 MHz - 1 GHz	256 KB - 2 MB, full speed	100 MHz
Pentium 4	55,000,000	1.4 GHz - 3.8 GHz	256 KB, full speed	800 MHz
K6-II	9,300,000	500 MHz - 550 MHz	N/A	100 MHz
K6-III	21,300,000	400 MHz - 450 MHz	256 KB, full speed	100 MHz
Athlon (K7)	22,000,000	850 MHz - 1.2 GHz	256 KB, full speed	200 MHz and 266 MHz
Athlon XP	37,500,000	1.67 GHz	384 KB, full speed	266 MHz
Duron	N/A	700-800 MHz	64 KB, full speed	200 MHz
PowerPC G3	6,500,000	233 MHz - 333 MHz	512 KB, 1 MB, half speed	100 MHz
PowerPC G4	10,500,000	400 MHz - 800 MHz	1 MB, half speed	100 MHz
Athlon 64	105,900,000	800 MHz	1 MB, half speed	1.6 GHz
G5	58,000,000	2.5GHz	512 KB	900MHz - 1.25GHz

Exhibit 3.1 COMPARISON OF POPULAR MICROCOMPUTER CPUS

Source: An update on this chart can be found at www.webopedia.com/quick_ref/processor.asp. For more in-depth technical specifications on these chips, visit www.SandPile.org.

can process data. MIPS is used to measure how many millions of instructions can be processed within a second. For microcomputers, CPU can be classified into two categories: Apple/Macintosh system (developed by Motorola) and IBM-compatible system (manufactured by Intel). Exhibit 3.1 illustrates the comparison of popular Microcomputer CPUs.

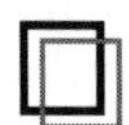

INPUT TECHNOLOGIES

Input devices are used to collect data (raw facts) from the environment. The data source could be a document, picture, speech, movie, or even the temperature of a certain location. Most current input technologies are designed to capture data and send it to the computer system. The following are some of the input technologies available:

Keyboard

Keyboards are conventional input devices. Microcomputer keyboards have all the keys that typewriter keyboards have plus others unique to computers. People who always thought typing was an overrated skill will find themselves slightly behind in the Digital Age, since learning to use a keyboard is still probably the most important way of interacting with a computer. Users who have to use the hunt-and-peck method waste a lot of time. Fortunately, there are software programs available that can help you learn to type or improve your typing skills.

You are probably already familiar with a computer keyboard. As the use of computer keyboards has become widespread, so has the incidence of various hand and wrist injuries. Accordingly, keyboard manufacturers have been giving a lot of attention to ergonomics, which is the study of the physical relationships between people and their work environment. Various attempts are being made to make keyboards more ergonomically sound in order to prevent injuries.

Mouse

A mouse is a device that is rolled about on a desktop pad and directs a pointer on the computer's display screen. The pointer may sometimes be, but is not necessarily, the same as the cursor. It may be an arrow, a rectangle, or even a representation of a person's pointing finger. The pointer may change to the shape of an I-beam to indicate that it is a cursor showing the place where text may be entered. The mouse has a cable that is connected to the microcomputer's system unit by being plugged into a special port. The taillike cable and the rounded "head" of the instrument are what suggested the name "mouse." On the bottom side of the mouse is a ball (trackball) that translates the mouse movement into digital signals. On the top side are one, two, or three buttons. Depending on the software, these buttons are used for such functions as clicking, dropping, and dragging. Gently holding the mouse with one hand, you can move it in all directions on the desktop (or on a mouse pad, which may provide additional traction). This will produce a corresponding movement of the mouse pointer on the screen.

Trackball

Another form of pointing device, the trackball, is a variant of the mouse. A trackball is a movable ball on top of a stationary device that is rotated with the fingers or palm of the hand. In fact, the trackball looks like the mouse turned upside down. Instead of moving the mouse around on the desktop, you move the trackball with the tips of your fingers. Trackballs are especially suited to portable computers, which are often used in confined places, such as on airline tray tables. Trackballs may appear on the keyboard centered below the space bar, as on the Apple powerboat, or may be built into the right side of the screen. On some portables they are a separate device that is clipped to the side of the keyboard.

Bar Code Readers

Bar code readers are designed to read Universal Product Code (UPC) or similar bar codes. You can find this type of device in the supermarket or in the library when you check out a book.

Penbased Input

This type of device uses handwriting as the input. People's handwriting can be converted into typed letters for further processing. This technology makes the keyboard an optional device and reduces the computer size a great deal.

Image Scanner

This device allows users to store a picture as a computer file. Images can be modified by the computer software after they are digitized and saved as a file.

Voice Recognition Device

Users can issue a command or text by speaking into a microphone, making typing or mouse input optional. A training session may be required to let the computer understand and recognize your voice and accent.

Magnetic Ink Character Recognition (MICR)

MICR is used by banks to read the magnetic ink on checks and deposit slips. MICR is a form of data entry device.

Video Capture

A video can be digitized as a computer file. This file can be further modified or edited for special effects.

Touch Screens

A touch screen is a video display screen that has been sensitized to receive input from the touch of a finger. Because touch screens are easy to use, they can convey information quickly. You'll find touch screens in automated teller machines and tourist directories in airports. Touch screens are also available for personal computers, consisting of an overlay that mounts with adhesive to the front of a monitor.

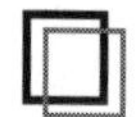

WHAT INPUT DEVICES DO YOU NEED?

A keyboard and a mouse are the most useful input devices for most software. However, if you need to use multimedia software or have a variety of information sources stored in different media, you might need devices such as image scanners, the microphone for your voice input, or a digital camera. Digitized files require lots of disk space for storage. Before you upgrade your system with advanced input devices such as video and audio input, ample secondary storage devices will be needed.

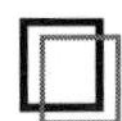

OUTPUT TECHNOLOGIES

The types of output generated from the computer depend on the needs of users and on the hardware and software equipment. In general, output can be classified into two categories based on how output is displayed:

1. *Hard copy:* Printed output by printers or plotters.
2. *Soft copy:* Displayed output by monitors or other devices.

Output can also be classified based on the way output is presented: text, graphical, video, or audio formats.

Text Format

Text format was the original output when computers were first created. Text output can be numbers, alphabetic, and other symbols found on the keyboard. It has a great limitation in terms of presenting charts and images. Today, very few computer systems use text format as the only output display.

Graphical Format

Graphical format allows users to view output by the images it contains. By using a graphical format, computer-user interfaces can be dramatically improved.

Video Format

Video output is designed to display movies that have been digitized. This type of output provides a movielike image to the user. However, digitized movies require lots of capacity to store and transmit digital signals. This limitation keeps video format from being widely used.

Audio Format

Voice can also be digitized into computer files. This audio file can be stored or transferred just like a regular computer data file. With a sound card, speakers, and a microphone, users can use an audio format to communicate with another party by voice.

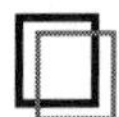

WHAT OUTPUT TECHNOLOGIES DO YOU NEED?

Depending on the task you would like to achieve, the output devices you need vary.

Regular Computer Users

A computer with a multimedia system can provide you with many ways of presenting information. This system should contain speakers, the video capture board, the digital camera, and a microphone. With the necessary software, the user is able to create a picture, a movie, or a voice message.

Retailers

A retailer requires inventory update and pricing display when merchandise is checked out. A bar code reader allows cashiers to scan the Universal Product Code (UPC) and retrieve current price as well as update the inventory.

Cartoon/Movie Makers

To be able to modify videos or animation, special software for graphics is needed. This type of software allows users to create special effects and modify videos, as desired.

Information Help Center

The information center is designed to provide users with a self-guided information resource. For example, a state welcome center usually has information terminals with touch-screen monitors that allow visitors to touch the screen for menu selection and receive information.

Publishers

Desktop publishing software allows users to edit magazines, newspapers, or other publications on a computer. This can dramatically improve the efficiency of publication.

Video Conferences

A meeting can be held without all participants attending the meeting physically. Users can use the video conference technology to conduct a meeting from remote locations and still see the other participants.

Architect

By using computer-aided design (CAD) software, users are able to generate architectural drawings more efficiently. Some CAD software allows users to create a three-dimensional image.

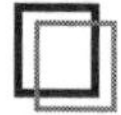

SECONDARY STORAGE

Compared with the primary storage devices, secondary storage is a type of storage device that is generally less expensive and slower in terms of data retrieval speed. Information on secondary storage devices is also permanent. We classify secondary storage devices into three categories: magnetic tape, magnetic disk, and optical disk. Exhibit 3.2 summarizes characteristics of storage media for business consideration.

Medium	Storage Capacity	Transfer Rate	Cost (per 1 MB)
Magnetic Hard disk	High	Fast	Moderate
Magnetic tape	Moderate	Slow	Very low
Optical tape	Very high	Very slow	Low
CD	High	Very slow	Low
DVD	Very high	Moderate	High
Flash memory	High	Moderate	Very high

Exhibit 3.2 CHARACTERISTICS OF STORAGE MEDIA

Magnetic Tape

Magnetic tape is thin plastic tape that has been coated with a substance that can be magnetized; data is represented by the magnetized or nonmagnetized spots. Magnetic tapes are the original secondary storage device of computer systems. Since the sequential access method is used, magnetic tape devices are slow in data retrieval but are the least expensive secondary device. For large storage and low performance requirements such as backup or duplicate storage, magnetic tapes are the ideal choice. The two principal forms of tape storage of interest to us are magnetic-tape units used with mainframes and minicomputers and cartridge tape units used on microcomputers.

Magnetic Disk

There are two types of magnetic disk devices: floppy disk and hard disk. They both are random access devices. Therefore, they are faster and more expensive than magnetic tape.

Floppy Disk

A floppy disk drive is a device that holds a diskette, which spins inside. The drive reads data from and writes data to the diskette. A diskette is inserted into a slot, called the drive gate or drive door, in the front of the disk drive. On a diskette, data is recorded in rings called tracks. Each track is divided into eight or nine sectors. Sectors are invisible wedge-shaped sections used for storage reference purposes. Unformatted disks are manufactured without tracks and sectors in place. The operating system writes tracks and sectors onto the diskette to make formatted disks.

Hard Disk

A hard disk is a disk made out of metal and covered with a magnetic recording surface. Hard disk drives read and write in much the same way that diskette drives do. However, hard drives can handle thousands of times more data than diskettes. In addition, they are faster than floppy disk drives in terms of reading and writing data. Hard disks are one or more platters sealed inside a hard disk drive that is built into the system unit and cannot be removed. The operation speed and the capacity of a hard drive are much more than a floppy disk because a hard disk can store data 30 to 2,000 times and spins several times faster than a diskette. For example, a 2.1-gigabyte hard disk will spin at 7,800 revolutions per minute compared to 360 rpm for a diskette drive. The disadvantage of a hard drive is that the read/write head rides on a cushion of air about 0.000001 inch thick over the disk surface. A head crash happens when the surface of the read/write head, or particles on its surface, come into contact with the disk surface, causing the loss of some or all of the data on the disk.

Optical Disk

Optical disks are removable disks on which data is written and read through the use of laser beams. A single optical disk of the type called CD-ROM can hold up to 700 megabytes of data. This is equivalent to about 270,000 pages of text. Other optical devices are write once read many (WORM) and erasable optical disks.

CD-ROM

Compact disk read only memory (CD-ROM) is an optical disk format that is used to read prerecorded text, graphics, and sound. Since CD-ROM is a read-only disk, CD-ROM cannot be written on or erased by the user.

CD-RW

Short for CD-rewritable disk, CD-RW is a type of CD disk that enables you to write onto it in multiple sessions.

DVD-R, DVD-RW

DVD media can accommodate an astonishing 9.4 GB of data.

USB Keychain Hard Drives

Also called pen drives, thumb drives, jump drives, or flash drives, USB keychain hard drives are changing the way we store and transport data. The days of small and inconvenient media are gone. Capacities range from 128 MB to 2 GB.

CHAPTER 4

WHAT IS SYSTEMS SOFTWARE?

THE OPERATING SYSTEM, UTILITY PROGRAMS, AND LANGUAGE TRANSLATORS

Systems software is used to control the computer hardware so that all computer devices can interact with application software smoothly. It creates a layer of insulation between the computer hardware and application software, which can greatly help simplify the design of application software. Generally speaking, systems software consists of three components: operating systems, utility programs, and programming language processors (language translators).

The Operating System (OS)

The operating system (OS) consists of the master system of programs that manage the basic operations of the computer. These programs provide the control and use of hardware resources, including disk space, memory, CPU time allocation, and peripheral devices. They are also the interface between computer hardware and application programs so that end users can concentrate on their own tasks or applications rather than on the complexities of managing the computer. To be more specific, the operating system is used to control the hardware memory, schedule the execution of programs, and schedule input/output traffic between the CPU and other devices.

A good operating system can dramatically improve the effectiveness and the efficiency of program execution performance. Many different operating systems are available for computers. For example, Cray supercomputers use UNICOS and COS, IBM mainframes use MVS and VM, Data General minicomputers use AOS and DG, and DEC minicomputers use VAX/VMS.

Some operating systems are designed for a microcomputer single-user environment and others for multiple users. The complexity is much higher in a multiple-user OS due to the management of computer memory and CPU time shared by many users. Today, many computers use an operating environment that provides end users with a user-friendly interface. Some operating systems have a graphical user interface (GUI) that provides visual clues such as icons and objects to help the users. Each icon represents a folder, an application package, or a file. By clicking icons, users can open a folder or use an application package.

Windows XP is the latest version of the IBM-compatible operating system, which is widely used by most IBM-compatible microcomputers. Common features of Windows operating systems include support for the use of a mouse, icons, pull-down menus, and the capability to open several applications at the same time.

Booting

Booting refers to the process of loading an operating system into a computer's main memory from the hard disk. This loading is accomplished by a program that is stored permanently in ROM.

Housekeeping Tasks

Housekeeping tasks provide end users with functions that don't require application programs. One example is the Format command.

User Interface

This function allows users to communicate or interact with the OS. Three types of user interfaces are common: command, menu driven, and graphical user interface (GUI).

Managing Computer Resources

Computer resources include the CPU, main memory, the printer, the monitor, and other peripheral devices. This activity manages and controls the resources available to the user so that each user's task can be accomplished.

Managing Files

This function allows users to find, copy, erase, and manipulate computer files from the hard disk and the floppy disk. For example, you can copy files from one disk to another, make a duplicate copy of a disk for backup, or erase a file from a disk.

Managing Tasks

Operating systems are designed to run user tasks more efficiently. They can be classified into three types: multitasking, multiprogramming (time sharing), and multiprocessing.

- Multitasking is the execution of two or more programs by one user concurrently on the same computer with one CPU.
- Multiprogramming is the execution of two or more programs on a multiuser operating system. The CPU

time is shared by many users in the management of the OS.

- Multiprocessing uses multiple CPUs to perform work simultaneously. In other words, tasks can be broken down into several subtasks, and each subtask is assigned to a CPU for processing.

Utility Programs

Utility programs are used to help end users with a "tool box" to fine-tune hardware components or modify system software functions, and they are normally associated with the operating system. The utility programs for large computer systems (e.g., mainframe computers and supercomputers) are designed for professional system programmers to either modify or repair the system software. However, the utility programs for microcomputers are very often used by end users. They are user-friendly and designed for end users to format a diskette, change the monitor's background pattern, or install computer hardware. Some vendors provide utility programs that can enhance the performance of the computer (such as a RAM disk), install virtual memory, or check for viruses. Some of the principal utility programs include the following:

- *Data recovery:* A data recovery utility is used to "undelete" a file or information that has been accidentally deleted. By this function, users are able to undo the last delete operation that has taken place.
- *Screen saver:* A screen saver prevents a monitor's display screen from being etched by an unchanging image (burn-in).
- *Backup:* The backup utility allows users to make a backup, or duplicate, copy of the information on the hard disk.
- *Data compression:* Data compression removes redundant elements, gaps, and unnecessary data from a computer's storage space so that less space is required to store or transmit data.
- *Virus protection:* A virus consists of hidden programming instructions that are buried within an application or system program. Viruses can reproduce themselves and cause damage to computer programs.

Programming Language Processors

A program language processor can be either a compiler or an interpreter. A compiler translates programming codes into machine code all at once so that an executable file will be created. An interpreter translates a program line by line for each execution. Interpreters are usually used by business researchers or software developers who frequently modify their software and make lots of changes. It is easier to diagnose the programming errors line by line after the execution. An example is the BASIC interpreter.

A compiler has the advantage of being able to generate an executable file for later execution. This file, called the object code, is represented in binary code (machine code). The original program is called the source code. Users only need the object code to execute the program. Therefore, they do not have to compile the program every time they need to run it. The drawback is that if there are any programming errors, it is very hard for the program designers to tell what went wrong. Therefore, compilers are best used for programs that are fully developed and ready for the user.

IBM-COMPATIBLE OPERATING SYSTEMS

IBM-compatible operating systems are listed in Exhibit 4.1. The latest version of Windows, Windows XP, is described below.

Windows XP

Windows XP is an operating system introduced in 2001 from the Microsoft Windows family of operating systems, the previous version of Windows being Windows Me. Microsoft called the release its most important product since Windows 95. Along with a redesigned look and feel to the user interface, the new operating system is built on the Windows 2000 kernel, giving the user a more stable and reliable environment

Name	OS Developer	Runs on
OS390 (formerly MVS)	IBM	IBM mainframes
OS400	IBM	IBM AS/400 computers
MS-DOS	Microsoft	PCs
Windows 95, 98, Me, NT, 2000, XP	Microsoft	PCs
MacOS X	Apple Computer	Macintosh PCs
Solaris	SunSoft, Inc.	Sun computers
UNIX	AT&T (originally) and other software companies	Various versions for IBM, Macintosh, Sun, and other computers
Linux	Linus Torvalds and other software companies	PCs, mainly servers
NetWare	Novell	Usually network servers
PalmOS	Palm	Handheld computers (PDA)
Windows CE	Microsoft	Handheld computers (PDA)

Exhibit 4.1 POPULAR OPERATING SYSTEMS

than previous versions of Windows. Windows XP comes in two version: Home and Professional. Where as the Professional edition focuses on reliability and security, the Home edition includes extensive digital photography, digital music, digital video, home networking, and communications features. The company has also focused on mobility for both editions, including plug and play features for connecting to wireless networks. The operating system utilizes the 802.1x wireless security standard.

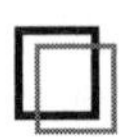

MACINTOSH OPERATING SYSTEMS

Although IBM system platforms traditionally use microprocessors made by Intel and use DOS or Windows in terms of OS, Apple computers typically use Motorola processors and a proprietary Apple operating system such as System 7. Macintosh had a very successful experience in designing graphical user interfaces in the 1980s. A multitasking environment was also available in the 1980s. However, at the time, IBM-compatible computers only used DOS operating systems, which have very poor user interfaces. However, this advantage was eliminated after Microsoft launched a Windows serial operating system that has a graphic user interface and multitasking environment similar to the Macintosh version.

Earlier versions of the Macintosh operating system, Mac OS for short, were called System x.x, where x.x were the version numbers. With the release of Mac OS 8, however, Apple dropped the System moniker. The newest version, Mac OS X Tiger, features breakthrough search technology known as *Spotlight,* outstanding graphics and media, unparalleled connectivity, an intuitive user interface and a virtual toolbox chock full of cleverly integrated features—all atop a rock-solid UNIX foundation—and gives you the most innovative, stable, and compatible desktop operating system. *Note:* **Microsoft's** next-generation operating system for Windows, code-named *Longhorn,* is Windows' answer to Mac OS X Tiger. However, its graphics capabilities make the Macintosh a popular choice for people working in commercial art, desktop publishing, multimedia, and CAD/CAM applications.

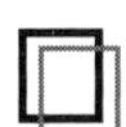

OTHER OPERATING SYSTEMS

Other operating systems, including UNIX, are designed for minicomputers or mainframe computers.

Unix

UNIX is a powerful operating system developed by AT&T for minicomputers. At the time of UNIX development in the

1970s, AT&T was not permitted to market the operating system due to federal regulations that prohibited the company from competing in the computer marketplace. In the 1970s, when AT&T was divided into many small companies, many federal regulations were removed. Since then, UNIX has increased in popularity. Today, UNIX is the leading portable OS. It can be used on many computer system types and performs on personal computers to mainframe systems, because it is compatible with different types of hardware. Users have to learn only one system.

Netware

NetWare is a local-area network (LAN) operating system developed by Novell Corporation. NetWare is a software product that runs on a variety of different types of LANs, from Ethernets to IBM token-ring networks. It provides users and programmers with a consistent interface that is independent of the actual hardware used to transmit messages.

Linux and the Open-Source Revolution

The great majority of business and individual software is proprietary—that is, software that is developed and sold for profit. The developer retains the rights to the software. In most cases you do not actually own the copies of applications that you "purchase"; you only purchase licenses to use those applications. In contrast to proprietary software, there are growing numbers of computer programs that have been developed by many unrelated programmers not for profit. The advantages of open-source software over proprietary software are clear: the software has fewer bugs because thousands of independent programmers review the code, and it can offer more innovative features by incorporating ideas from a diverse set of experts from different countries and cultures who collaborate. However, the concept of open source is probably best known for its application in the development of Linux, a popular variant of UNIX.

Linus Torvalds developed it for his own use, but he has never claimed rights to the software. So far, more than 200 programmers have contributed code to Linux. Linux has become the OS of choice of many Internet service providers to run their Internet servers. While many versions of Linux can be downloaded free of charge from the Web, most firms prefer to purchase a packaged version. Companies such as Red Hat, Ximian, SCO, and VA Software sell the software and promise technical support. Usually, contracts also include updates.

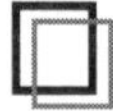

SINGLE-USER VERSUS MULTIUSER SYSTEMS

Single-user operating systems can allow only one user to work at a time. This kind of OS has a relatively simple design and usually has fewer graphic user interfaces. Most microcomputers have a single-user OS. (DOS and Windows are good examples.) A multiuser OS allows many users to share the same computer. It is normally a mini or a mainframe computer. A multiuser OS has a more complicated design, since many users have to access the same resources at the same time. This could create tremendous traffic and management problems among different users. UNIX is a good example of a multiuser system.

SINGLE-TASKING SYSTEMS VERSUS MULTITASKING SYSTEMS

Single Tasking

Single tasking implies that only one job or task can be executed at one time. DOS is a typical example of a single-tasking system, since only one job can be executed. However, a multitasking system allows more than one job (task) to be executed at the same time. With multitasking, you can work on your word processing program while your printer manager software is running the functions that control the printer. This is usually conducted by opening several windows. Microsoft Windows and Macintosh OS are good examples.

Multitasking

The multitasking environment allows users to perform several computer tasks at one time. Each task occupies a window. By swapping between windows, users are able to use different software packages as they wish.

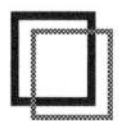

EVOLUTION OF PROGRAMMING LANGUAGES

Programming languages can be classified into five generations in terms of the history of development.

First-Generation Programming Language

Machine code is represented as binary data. All programming is represented by 1s and 0s, since inside the computer only 1 or 0 (on or off) had any meaning within the circuits. To see how hard this is to understand, imagine having to read this:

```
00010101001110111001110000011111101000001111
```

Machine languages also vary according to the make of the computer, another characteristic that makes for difficulty. However, machine codes are very efficient from a hardware point of view because no additional processing procedures are required.

Second-Generation Programming Language

Assembly language is designed to simplify the coding process of machine codes. Instead of binary code, all addresses are coded in a hexadecimal system and all operators are represented in English abbreviations. For example,

```
ADD 43(9, 2), B4(10, A)
```

is a piece of assembly code, which is still pretty obscure. Therefore, assembly language is also considered a low-level language. Both first- and second-generation programming languages are hardware dependent, which means programmers must know the hardware structure and configuration in order to write codes properly.

Third-Generation Programming Language

Third-generation programming languages are designed to let programmers develop codes without the knowledge of computer memory configuration. Examples include COBOL, PASCAL, FORTRAN, and many popular languages. One drawback of a third-generation language is that it could be too complicated to code. A good programmer usually requires a couple of years of training and experience.

BASIC

Short for Beginner's All-purpose Symbolic Instruction Code, BASIC is a popular microcomputer language. It is widely used on microcomputers and easy to learn. It is suited to both beginning and experienced programmers. It is also interactive—users and computers communicate with each other directly during the waiting and running of programs.

Another version created by the Microsoft Corporation is Visual BASIC, which has been hailed as a programming breakthrough. Visual BASIC makes it easier for novice programmers, as well as professionals, to develop customized applications for Windows.

PASCAL

Another language that is widely used on microcomputers and easy to learn is PASCAL. It is named after Blaise Pascal, a seventeenth-century French mathematician. Pascal has become quite popular in computer science programs. One advantage is that it encourages programmers to follow structured coding procedures. It also works well for graphics.

C/C++

C is a general-purpose language that also works well with microcomputers. It is useful for writing operating systems, spreadsheet programs, database programs, and some scientific applications. Programs are portable: They can be run without change on a variety of computers. C++ is a version of C that incorporates object-oriented technologies. It is popular with some software developers and promises to increase programmer productivity.

COBOL

COBOL—which stands for Common Business-Oriented Language—is one of the most frequently used programming languages in business. Though harder to learn than BASIC, its logic is easier for a person who is not a trained programmer to understand. Writing a COBOL program is sort of like writing the outline for a business research analysis. The program has four divisions, which in turn are divided into sections, which are divided into paragraphs, then into statements.

FORTRAN

Short for FORmula TRANslation, FORTRAN is a widely used scientific and mathematical language. It is very useful for processing complex formulas. Thus, many scientific and engineering programs have been written in this language.

ADA

Ada is named after Augusta Ada, the English Countess of Lovelace, who is regarded as the first programmer. Ada was developed under the sponsorship of the U.S. Department of Defense. Originally designed for weapons systems, it has commercial uses as well. Because of its structured design, modules (sections) of a large program can be written, compiled, and tested separately before the entire program is put together.

Fourth-Generation Programming Language

Fourth-generation programming language is designed for people who need a simplified and powerful tool to conduct programming processes. Tens of third-generation language codes can usually be compacted into several lines. However, this language requires a lot of hardware power to translate into machine code and perform the execution.

QUERY LANGUAGES

Query languages enable nonprogrammers to use certain easily understood commands to search and generate reports from a database.

APPLICATION GENERATORS

An application generator contains a number of modules—logically related program statements—that have been preprogrammed to accomplish various tasks. An example would be a module that calculates overtime pay. The programmer can simply state which task is needed for a particular application. The application generator creates the program code by selecting the appropriate modules.

Fifth-Generation Programming Language (Natural Language)

Natural languages are designed to give people a more human connection with computers. The language used to communicate is basically the language we use on a daily basis such as English, Chinese, and French. This kind of language allows users to speak or type in human language command to execute the function. This language provides a computer novice with a handy tool.

Generation	Sample Statement
First	1000011101110011
Second	ADD 32(4, B), 8AB(5, 9)
Third	Counter: = 20
Fourth	Select name FROM Executive
Fifth	Update the inventory file by transaction file

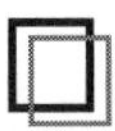

WHAT ARE OBJECT-ORIENTED LANGUAGES (OOLs) AND COMPUTER-AIDED SOFTWARE ENGINEERING (CASE) TOOLS?

Object-oriented languages have a different way to code. They allow the interaction of programming objects. This approach to programming is called object-oriented programming (OOP). In OOP, data, instructions, and other programming procedures are grouped together. The items in a group are called an object. The process of grouping items into an object is called encapsulation. Encapsulation means that functions or tasks are captured into each object, which keeps them safer from changes because access is protected. Objects often have properties of polymorphism and inheritance. Polymorphism allows the programmer to develop one routing that will operate or work with multiple objects. Inheritance means that objects in a group can take on or inherit characteristics of other objects in the same group or class of objects. This helps programmers select objects with certain characteristics for other programming tasks or projects. Professional MIS programmers are consistently looking for ways to make the programming development process easier, faster, and more reliable. CASE tools provide some automation and assistance in program design, coding, and testing. Some CASE tools can even convert your design into real codes.

CHAPTER 5

PRACTICAL GUIDE TO APPLICATION SOFTWARE

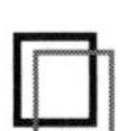

FINDING OUT WHAT IS AVAILABLE

Before you decide to buy a piece of software, you should decide what functions are to be achieved. For example, if you just want to have a simple word processing system for your resume preparation, a simple word processing package would be enough. However, if you need to edit magazines for publication, professional desktop publication software would be required. If the computer functions are common, packaged software is suitable. If, however, your requested function is rare or in a large scale so that no existing packaged software is available, you may have to develop your own software from scratch. This is called customized software. In general, customized software is more time-consuming and costs more money to develop, but it is more efficient in operation due to the special design of functions. You can buy packaged software from many computer software stores or through mail order. However, if you decide to design from scratch, you then have to choose a programming language to do the coding. This designing process is known as systems analysis and design cycle.

Versions

A version is a major upgrade in a software product. Versions are usually represented by numbers such as 1.0, 2.0, 3.0, and so forth. The higher the number, the more recent the version.

Release

A release is a minor upgrade. The number after the decimal point indicates releases: for example, 3.1, 3.12, 3.121, and so on.

Yearly Version

Microsoft used "Windows 95" instead of "Windows 4.0" for its new operating system, since it was launched in 1995.

Most software is upward compatible (forward compatible). That means the document created under an earlier version or release can be processed on a later version or release. Downward compatible means that the document created under a later version can be run on older versions or releases. Software can be classified into three categories in terms of software copyright.

Proprietary Software

Proprietary software is the software whose rights are owned by an individual or business. Therefore, the ownership of the software is protected by the copyright. There are two types of licenses of the ownership:

1. *Single-user licenses:* Users can buy one copy of the software license and use this software in a single machine.
2. *Site licenses:* Users can buy multiple usage in a certain area such as a company.

Public Domain Software

Public domain software is software that is not protected by copyright law and may be duplicated by anyone. Examples are government-developed programs for the general public and programs donated by the original creator. Public domain software can normally be downloaded from the Internet or from the bulletin board of network service providers such as America Online, CompuServe, Prodigy, and so on.

Freeware

Freeware is software that is available free of charge through the Internet or computer user groups. Sometimes software developers promote their product by giving away free software for a trial period, usually a 30-day trial. To create a standard for software on which managers are apt to agree, the developers want to see how users respond so that they can make improvements in a later version. This is one of the reasons why there is no need to pay for it. The software distributed is free of charge but usually with limited functions. Freeware developers often retain all rights to their programs, so technically you are not supposed to duplicate and distribute it. An example of freeware is Mosaic.

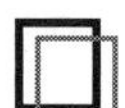

SEVEN MAIN TYPES OF SOFTWARE AND HOW THEY OPERATE

There are seven major types of application software on the market. They are presentation software, word processing software, spreadsheet software, database software, communication software, desktop publishing, and graphics software.

Presentation Software

Presentation software is designed to generate graphical presentation slides for communicating or making a presentation of data to others. Good presentation software provides managers with graphical user interface and lots of utilities to make transparencies. Some presentation graphics packages provide artwork, drawing function, and even multimedia utilities to make the presentation more attractive.

Word Processing Software

Word processing software allows users to create, edit, format, save, and print documents such as letters, memos, reports, and manuscripts. Some word processing software also includes artwork, drawing functions, spreadsheet utilities, and graphics. Others provide users with spelling checkers, grammar checkers, and thesaurus functions.

Spreadsheet Software

A spreadsheet allows managers to create tables and financial schedules with mathematical functions by entering data in prepared tables; spreadsheets can calculate entered data and provide solutions. The major spreadsheets are Microsoft Excel, Lotus 1-2-3, and Quattro Pro.

A spreadsheet contains many cells, each of which can be used to store a number (such as 34), a formula (such as = A4 + B4), or a label (1996 Sales Report). A cell is where a row and a column intersect. For example, C4 is the address of the cell where column C and row 4 intersect. A cell pointer indicates where data is to be entered. The cell pointer can be moved around like a cursor in a word processing program. The cell pointer moves to activate that cell and allows the user to input or update the content of that cell.

Because a cell contains numbers, labels, and formulas, users can design a template with formulas and labels so that other users will type in collected data and receive the answer. Today's spreadsheets are more sophisticated. They very often have drawing facilities, artwork library, database interface, and a good graphics generator. Spreadsheets have become the most popular program for business.

Database Software

Database software is a program that controls the structure of a database and access to the data. A database is any electronically stored collection of data in a computer system. These computer-based files are organized according to their common elements so that data can be retrieved easily. The following is a description of database elements:

- File. A collection of related records
- Record. A collection of related fields
- Field. A unit of data consisting of one or more characters

A database management system (DBMS) is software that controls and manipulates the structure of a database. Popular database software includes Oracle, Paradox, and Access. Principal uses of database software are as follows:

1. *Create a database.* Managers can create a database by creating files (or tables). Each table has several fields, which is a type of attribute consisting of one or more characters. A field can have the attribute of text, data, numbers, or even objects. After the format of a table is created, managers can input records into the database. A record is a collection of related fields. An example is an employee's name, address, and phone number.
2. *Select and display a database file or a report.* After a database (consisting of several files) is created, users can manipulate this database through queries. The function of a query is to screen all records by defined criteria.
3. *Update a database.* Users can also delete, add, or change a record in a data file.
4. *Calculate and format a database.* Some DBMSs contain built-in mathematical formulas. This feature can be used to find the average number of a selected group. An example is to find the average age of all customers who live in California.

Major database manipulation languages are Structured Query Language (SQL) and Query By Examples (QBE). Generally speaking, SQL is more powerful than QBE. Most professional database administrators are required to know SQL. Generally speaking, database software is much better than the old file managers because it can access several files at one time (also known as flat-file management systems).

Communication Software

Computers are often networked so that information can be shared. In order to transfer information between different computers, communication software is required. Communication software allows computers to exchange data over a private network such as a local area network (LAN) or over a public network such as a wide area network (WAN). When communication software exists in both sending and receiving units, computers are able to establish and relinquish electronic links, code and decode data transmissions, verify transmission errors, compress data streams for more efficient transmission, and manage the transmission of documents. Communications software provides functionality far beyond numeric computation, textual editing, and graphics. It provides access to a virtually unlimited amount of information from anywhere in the world.

Desktop Publishing

Desktop publishing involves using a microcomputer and peripherals to mix text and graphics to produce high-quality printed output. Magazines or newspapers usually use the final product of desktop publishing. Major desktop publishing programs are Aldus PageMaker, QuarkXpress, and Ventura Publisher.

Graphics Software

This presents pictorial descriptions including diagrams and charts to understand business relationships and trends.

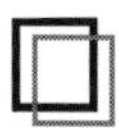

PACKAGED, CUSTOMIZED, OR SEMICUSTOMIZED SOFTWARE

There are three approaches to acquire software depending on the purpose of usage, the cost, and the duration of development.

Packaged Software

Large software corporations (such as Microsoft) target for a large number of end users and for general purposes, so they usually design packaged software. In other words, the software functions available are common and popular to the general public. This enables a large population to share the development cost and pay much lower prices for well-designed software. However, they may not fit into every user's particular needs. Since software packages are developed to satisfy most end users, the user interface and software documentation are very well prepared.

Customized Software

Customized software requires intensive development efforts. It usually takes a longer time and costs more money to develop. Typically, only large corporations can afford the development cost. The major reason for customized software is that similar software is not available on the market or the user group is so small that it would not be worthwhile for any software company to develop it. Customized software requires more time and effort to develop a system that is tailored to customers' needs. In other words, the functions available in customized software are more flexible and powerful. Two system development methodologies are available: (1) system analysis and design life cycle and (2) prototyping.

System Analysis and Design Life Cycle

The system development life cycle consists of seven steps:

1. Identify problems and opportunities.
2. Analyze and document existing systems.
3. Determine information requirements.

4. Design technology and personnel requirements.
5. Develop, test, and validate the system.
6. Implement the system.
7. Evaluate and maintain the system.

PROTOTYPING

This method involves building a working model and modifying it to fit the manager's requirements. A working model (system) may only cover a subset of the whole system or only some functions. A complete system can then be built by including more functions or expanding to other subsystems.

Semicustomized Software

The trade-off between customized software and packaged software is to have software that provides a general structure. Customers can modify this software by customizing the functions. For example, lots of database software provides a general database structure. Based on different individual needs, users can develop different applications for different environments.

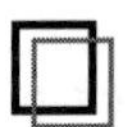

WHERE TO GET SOFTWARE ASSISTANCE

There are several places where you can receive software assistance, including the following:

- *Software vendors:* Software producers usually provide buyers with telephone assistance. Managers can call the technology support department helpline.
- *Software online help:* Most software programs come with online help. Online help contains instructions or explanations that can be retrieved right from the program. Users can get immediate responses from the help menu. One drawback for online help is that users may not be able to get the answers they are looking for.
- *Network:* On the Internet (or other networks), there are many software users' bulletin boards. Many ideas and problems are posted on the bulletin board. Users can certainly exchange ideas or find answers through these resources.
- *Professional consulting firms:* Most software consulting firms provide software assistance for a fee. Services provided by consulting firms can be very expensive.
- *Software training facilities:* Schools or training institutes give seminars or courses for different types of software.
- *Vendors' seminar:* Most vendors provide seminars for new software releases. Users (or buyers) can attend

these seminars for more information and help. Most seminars are free to users.

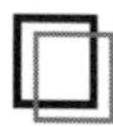

PRESENTATION SOFTWARE

Presentation software offers users a wide choice of presentation effects. These include three-dimensional displays, background patterns, multiple text fonts, and image libraries that contain illustrations of objects such as people and cars. Using graphics software as a presentation tool allows you to effectively create professional quality graphics that can help you communicate information more effectively. Persuasion, Harvard Graphics, and PowerPoint are popular presentation graphics packages. Multimedia has significant business applications.

WORD PROCESSING SOFTWARE

Word processing is the most widely used general application. If you need to create documents such as letters or memos, you can make the process much easier with a word processing tool. Some of the most popular software programs are Microsoft Word and Word Perfect. Word processing software allows you to enter text on the computer keyboard in the same manner as you create documents on a typewriter. As you enter the characters, they are displayed on the screen and stored in the computer's main memory. You can then edit this document electronically. "Editing" includes such functions as delete, insert, move, or copy words or sentences. You can also use format function to specify the margin, page length, character size, and font. Good word processing software also includes a spelling checker, thesaurus, and grammar checker.

GUIDELINES IN PREPARING SPREADSHEET SOFTWARE

Spreadsheet software allows you to organize numeric data in a worksheet or table format called a spreadsheet. Within a spreadsheet, data is organized horizontally in rows and vertically in columns. The intersection where a row and column meet is called a cell. Cells are named by their location in the spreadsheet. Each cell may contain three types of data: labels (text), values (numbers), and formulas. The text (label) identifies the data and documents the spreadsheet. The numbers are values, which can be calculated. The formulas perform calculations on the data in the spreadsheet and display the resulting value in the cell containing the formula.

DATABASE SOFTWARE

A database refers to a collection of data that is stored in files. Database software allows you to create a database and to retrieve, manipulate, and update the data that you store in it. In a manual system, data might be recorded on paper and stored in a filing cabinet. In a database on the computer, data will be stored in an electronic formation on an auxiliary storage device such as a disk. A file is defined as a collection of related data organized in records. Each record contains a collection of related facts called fields. For example:

Name	Employee File SS#	Phone Number
Robert Jones	365-98-6509	909-675-9842
Mary Smith	876-92-1425	818-837-2897
Jim Lee	987-26-3833	909-824-2225
John Doe	873-22-2998	818-827-9988

The employee file contains four records and each record has three fields.

Database software can organize data in a certain way that allows users to retrieve, update, delete, or create data almost immediately. Managers can therefore greatly improve productivity.

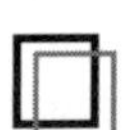

DATA COMMUNICATIONS SOFTWARE

Data communications software is used to transmit data from one computer to another. It gives users access to databases such as stock prices and delivery schedules. There are two kinds of data communication software: network operating systems and network browsers. The network operating system is the software used to manage network communications. A network operating system (OS) can be very powerful, managing several hundred workstations or even network servers in a wide area network. A network OS can also be designed to handle only a handful of PCs in a local area network. A network browser is used to access the network. Network users can access the network and retrieve information from the network through the network browser. For example, Novel and Windows NT are two popular local network OSs. Navigator and Mosaic are popular network browsers.

WHEN TO USE INTEGRATED SOFTWARE PACKAGES

Integrated software packages combine the features of several popular applications such as word processing, spreadsheets, database, presentation, and data communications software. Since different software is combined together as a single package, users do not have to pay the full price of each individual software program. In addition, the functions available for each different software program are more consistent than for individual applications bought separately. Three major integrated software packages are Microsoft Office, Lotus SmartSuite, and Corel Perfect Office Select.

CHAPTER 6

DATA AND DATABASES

WHAT IS A DATABASE?

A database is a system where data is organized in a certain way so that accurate and timely information can be retrieved. The information systems used to manage databases are called database management systems (DBMSs). A database management system is software that allows managers to create, maintain, and report the data and file relationships. A file management system is software that allows users to manipulate one file at a time. DBMSs offer many advantages over file management systems, as discussed in the following sections:

- *Reduced data redundancy:* Data redundancy means the same data field appears in different tables sometimes in a different format. For example, a customer's name, address, and phone number can be stored in both the checking account file and the receivables account file. This would cause problems in terms of maintenance and update. It requires more time and money to maintain files with redundant records.
- *Improved data integrity:* Data integrity means that data is accurate, consistent, and up-to-date. If the same data is stored in different files, data updating may not cover all data elements in different files. Some reports will be produced with erroneous information.
- *Improved data security:* Database management systems allow users to establish different levels of security over information in the database. This guarantees that data will be retrieved or updated by authorized users only. For example, the sales manager can only read employee payroll information, not modify it. A nonmanagement employee probably has no access privilege to the payroll data and can neither inquire nor modify the data.
- *Reduced development time:* Since database management systems organize data in a better way, this enables the

database administrator (DBA) to improve the efficiency and productivity of database development. For example, instead of creating a new file, the DBA can add new fields into existing files and still maintain data integrity.

WHAT IS A DATABASE FILE (TABLE)?

A database file is a collection of related records that describe a subject by using a set of fields. Exhibit 6.1 shows a file with three records used to describe a student by using fields of "Name," "GPA," and "Major."

Most organizations have many files that have from hundreds to hundreds of thousands of records. Files that are stored on secondary storage devices can be organized in several different ways, and there are advantages and disadvantages to each of these types of file organizations.

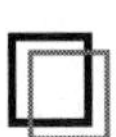

TYPES OF FILE ORGANIZATION

Three types of file organization are used on secondary storage devices. They are sequential, indexed sequential, and direct file. Files stored on tape are processed as sequential files. Files on disk are usually direct or indexed-sequential files.

Sequential File

Sequential files can be stored on a sequential access device such as magnetic tape or a random access device such as a disk. In a sequential file, records are arranged one after another in a predetermined order. For example, an employee file can be organized by employee ID number. If this file is stored on a disk or tape, the employee record with the smallest ID number would be the first record in the file.

Indexed-Sequential File

An indexed-sequential file allows both sequential and direct access to data records. Thus, files must be on a direct access storage device such as a disk. In indexed-sequential files, records are usually physically arranged on a storage medium by their primary key just as they are with sequential files. The difference is that an index also exists for the

Name	Student GPA	Major
Robert Smith	3.2	IS
Mary Lee	3.5	ACCT
Jim Shaw	2.9	IS

Exhibit 6.1 TYPICAL DATA FILE

file; it can be used to look up and directly access individual records. Files set up to allow this type of access are called ISAM (indexed-sequential method) files. Many DBMSs use ISAM files because of their relative flexibility and simplicity. This is often the best type of file for business applications that demand both batch updating and online processing.

Direct File

A direct file provides the fastest possible access to records. ISAM also provides users with direct access to individual records. Direct file is typically the best when access time is critical and when batch processing is not necessary. A direct file uses a formula to transfer the primary key to the location of each record. This formula is called a hashing algorithm. Therefore, no index is needed to locate individual records. Many hashing algorithms have been developed. One popular procedure is to use prime numbers in the formula process. In general, the primary key value is divided by a prime number that corresponds to the maximum number of storage locations allocated for the records of this file. The reminder obtained in this division is then used as the relative address of a record, but relative address can be translated into physical locations on the storage medium.

DATA MODELS (RELATIONAL, HIERARCHICAL, AND NETWORK)

Relational Databases

The relational database relates or connects data in different files through the use of a key field, or common data element (see Exhibit 6.2). In this arrangement, data elements are stored in different tables or files made up of rows and columns. In database terminology, tables are called relations, rows are called tuples, and columns are called attributes. In a table, a row resembles a record—for example, a student's GPA record has a field of "student name," a field of "GPA," a field of "address," and a field of "phone number." In this table, a student is described by a record or a combination of

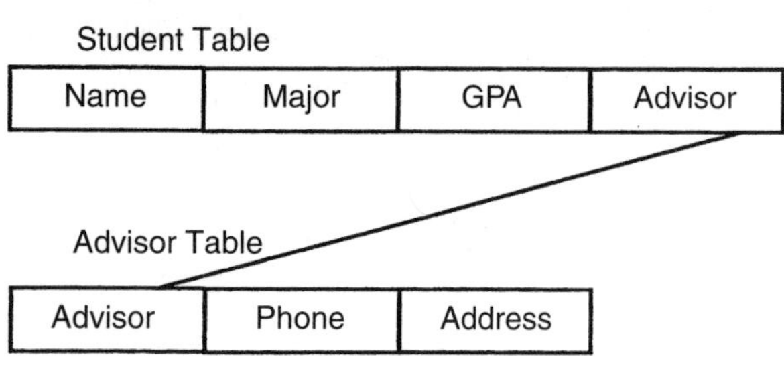

Exhibit 6.2 A RELATIONAL DATABASE

fields. The advantage of a relational database is that the manager does not have to be aware of any data structure or data pointer. Managers can easily add, update, delete, or create records using simple logic. However, a disadvantage is that some search commands in a relational database require more time to process compared with other database models.

Hierarchical Databases

In a hierarchical database, fields and records are arranged in a family tree, with lower-level records subordinate to higher-level records (see Exhibit 6.3). In a hierarchical database, a parent record may have more than one child, but a child always has only one parent. This is called a one-to-many relationship. To locate a particular record, you have to start at the top of the tree with a parent record and trace down the tree to the child. Hierarchical databases are the oldest of the four data models and are still used in some reservation systems. In addition, accessing or updating records is very fast since the relationships have been predefined. The drawback of hierarchical data models is that the structure is quite rigid and adding new records to the database may require that the entire database be redefined.

Network Databases

A network database (see Exhibit 6.4) is similar to a hierarchical database except that each child can have more than one parent record. In other words, a child record is referred to as a member and a parent record is referred to as an owner. The advantage of the network database is its ability to establish relationships between different branches of data records and thus offer increased access capability for the manager. However, like the hierarchical database, the data record relationships must be predefined prior to the use of the database and must be redefined if records are added or updated.

Object-Oriented Databases

An object-oriented database uses objects as elements within database files. An object consists of text, sound, images, and

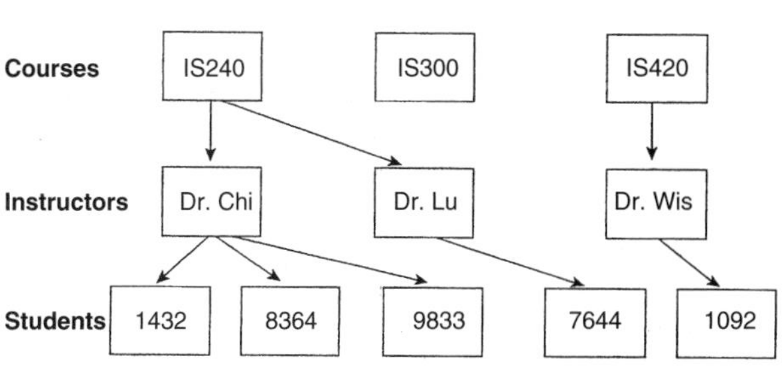

Exhibit 6.3 A HIERARCHICAL DATABASE

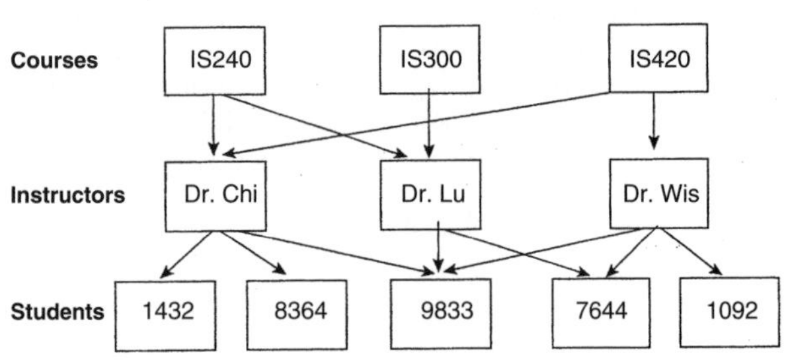

Exhibit 6.4 A NETWORK DATABASE

instructions on the action to be taken on the data. For example, traditional data models such as hierarchical, Network, and relational data models can contain only numeric and text data of an instructor. An object-oriented database might also contain the instructor's picture and video. Moreover, the object would store operations, called methods, that perform actions on the data—for example, how to calculate this person's pension fund based on his or her age and contributions.

PRIMARY KEYS, SECONDARY KEYS, AND FOREIGN KEYS

In a database, data records are organized and identified by using the key field. A key field contains unique data to identify a record so that it can be easily retrieved and processed. There are three types of key fields used for database management.

Primary Keys

The primary key can be a single field or a combination of several fields. It is the most important identifier to retrieve records. It is unique and can have only one in each table. For example, the social security number is a good primary key to identify each person, while age may not be useful since many people may have the same age.

Secondary Keys

Secondary keys can be any field or the combination of several fields. A secondary key does not have to be unique and many of them can exist in a table. For example, we can use major as a secondary key to allocate students majoring in information systems.

Foreign Keys

The foreign key is the field or a combination of several fields that can be used to relate two tables. A foreign key must be a primary key in one table. This primary key can thus be

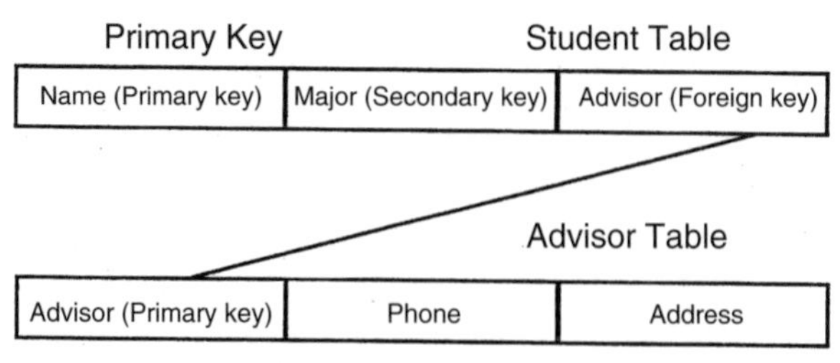

Exhibit 6.5 KEY FIELDS

connected to another table. For example, a student table contains social security number, major, and advisor's name. The advisor table has advisor's name, phone number, and address. The "advisor's name" is the foreign key to connect the student table with the advisor table (see Exhibit 6.5).

DATABASE DESIGN

Database design is an intuitive and artistic process. There is no strict algorithm for it. Typically, database design is an interactive process: During each iteration, the goal is to get closer to an acceptable design. Thus a design will be developed and then reviewed. Defects in the design will be identified, and the design will be redone. This process is repeated until the development team and users are satisfied with what is available. A well-designed database enables managers to perform efficient and useful tasks. In other words, a poorly designed database may cost lots of money and time without any significant contribution to a company's operation. Database design procedures are therefore very important and crucial to the success of a database system. Procedures for database design are listed in the following sections:

Current System Analysis and Survey

This process involves surveying and observing current manual data processes and potential benefits from computerized database systems. Usually, both decision makers and process operators are interviewed to collect information on potential problems and opportunities. After the system analysis has been conducted, a feasibility report is prepared for evaluation. The suggestion of the feasibility report can be either positive or negative. The main reasons for a suggestion of infeasibility are financial and managerial problems.

Logical Database Design

A logical database design specifies the logical format of the database. The records to be maintained, their contents, and relationships among those records are specified. It is sometimes called the conceptual schema, or the logical schema. There is a technique called normalization that was developed to improve the structure of files in a relational database. By using this method, data can be organized into the most efficient and logical file relationships.

Physical Database Design

The logical schema is transformed into the particular data constructs that are available with the DBMS to be used. Whereas the logical design is DBMS independent, the physical design is DBMS dependent. Logical schema specifies general database design that can be implemented in any database management software, while physical schema is designed based on the real database management software and cannot be transferred from one to another.

Implementation

After physical schema is designed, the database implementation will be conducted. This process involves lots of coding and programming. This process can be done with a DBMS such as ORACLE, FOXBase, Microsoft SQL Server, and a front-end tool for user interface development such as Visual Basic or Power Builder.

Testing and Debugging

This process involves testing the system and making sure that it is ready to operate. In this stage, both program developers and end users should get involved in the process.

Training, Evaluation, and Documentation

If both the end-user group and development team are satisfied with the system, the training session should proceed. The purpose of the training session is to teach managers how to use this new system and perform simple troubleshooting functions. The development team should also prepare system documentation for the managers for reference purposes.

OTHER FEATURES IN A DATABASE MANAGEMENT SYSTEM

Data Dictionary

The data dictionary stores the data definitions or a description of the structure of data used in the database. This information could be stored in a dictionary-like document or on a text file. Managers can check the data dictionary and retrieve necessary information about the properties and nature of the database. Some data dictionaries can also monitor the data being entered into the database management system to be sure it conforms to that definition, such as field name, field size, and type of data (text, numeric, date, logic, and so on). The data dictionary can also help the database administrator (DBA) and other database designers with security concerns such as who has the right to access what kind of information.

Database Utilities

The database needs to be maintained to ensure that the data are properly organized. Database utility programs provide the DBA with functions that can fine-tune the database functionality, such as removing redundant or nonused records, assigning priorities to different users, and monitoring resource allocation. A good database utility program can improve the productivity and efficiency of a DBA.

Database Recovery

Situations such as systems failure, computer malfunctioning, disk head crash, program bugs, and so on may cause a database management system to crash. Unfortunately, when systems fail, business does not stop. Customers continue to buy and pay, return merchandise, and obtain servicing. Therefore, system failures must be recovered as soon as possible. Furthermore, business demands that transactions that were in processing when the failure occurred be recovered in such a way that their outputs are identical to what would have been produced. In other words, failure should be transparent in their effects on data. Recovering from a database system failure is getting more difficult due to the complexity of modern database management systems. It is impossible to simply fix the problem and resume program processing where it was interrupted. Even if no data is lost during a failure, the timing and scheduling of computer processing is too complex to be accurately recreated. Some techniques have been developed to recover from a system failure:

- Recovery via reprocessing
- Recovery via roll-back/roll-forward
- Transaction logging
- Write-ahead log

The details of these techniques are beyond the scope of this book. Readers can check database books for more information.

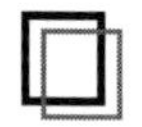

THE DATABASE ADMINISTRATOR (DBA)

What Is a Database Administrator?

The DBA is the person who manages all activities related to the database. A qualified DBA should be able to understand the hardware configuration (such as the client/server environment) and take advantage of existing hardware capability to improve the performance of the database management system. He or she should have expertise in terms of database engines (such as SQL) and front-end tools (such as Visual Basic and Power Builder) to create a good user interface. A DBA should be able to do limited troubleshooting in both the application area and system level, since a database crash may involve both application and system software.

Major Functions of a Database Administrator

The responsibilities of a DBA are the following:

Database Design

The database administrator helps determine the design of the database including fields, tables, and key words. Later, he or she determines how resources are used on secondary storage devices, how files and records may be added and deleted, and how losses may be detected and remedied.

System Backup and Recovery

Because loss of data or a crash in the database could vitally affect the organization, a database system must be able to recover if the system crashes. The DBA needs to make sure the system is regularly backed up and should develop plans for recovering data in case of a failure.

End User Service and Coordination

A DBA should determine user access privileges and arrange resources allocation for different user groups. If different users conflict with each other, the DBA should be able to coordinate to make sure an optimal arrangement is agreed upon.

Database Security

The DBA can specify different access privileges for different users of a database management system to protect the database from unauthorized access and sabotage. For example, one kind of user is allowed to retrieve data, whereas another might have the right to update data and delete records.

Performance Monitoring

The database system should maintain a certain standard of services for all users. The DBA monitors the system and uses different database tools to make sure that the system is set up to satisfy managers' performance requirements.

QUERY LANGUAGES

What Is a Query Language?

A query language is a simple English-like language that allows managers to specify what data they are looking for either on a printed report or on the screen. Generally speaking, there are two types of query language: structured query language and query by examples.

Structured Query Language

Structured query language (SQL) is the most widely used database query language. In 1985, the American National Standards Institute formed a committee to develop industry standards for SQL. Today, most database management systems support this standard. Exhibit 6.6 shows an example of the SQL statements.

Query by Example

Query by example (QBE) helps the manager construct a query by displaying a list of fields that are available in the files from which the query will be made.

```
SELECT name, gpa
FROM student
WHERE gpa >= 3.0
ORDER BY name
```

Exhibit 6.6 Structured Query Language

CHAPTER 7

DATA COMMUNICATIONS

Data communication has become more and more important in business. The ability to instantly communicate information is changing the way people do business and interact with each other. New data communication technologies allow voice, image, and even video to be transmitted through the network. Many business applications are available because of new data communication technologies. Examples are electronic mail, voice mail, teleconferencing, fax, electronic data interchange (EDI), online services, and others. As a matter of fact, more and more new services will become available through the network because of the information superhighway.

DIGITAL SIGNALS VERSUS ANALOG SIGNALS

Digital signals are individual voltage pulses that represent the bits that are grouped together to form characters. This type of signal is usually used inside the computer to transmit data between electronic components and close-range devices. Digital signals have the characteristics of short-range transmission (at most several hundred feet) and are represented by on/off binary systems. Local area networks (LANs) usually use digital signals for transmission. This transmission is normally restricted to a certain area such as a room or a building.

Analog signals are continuous electromagnetic waves. They are able to travel long distances, and most long-distance transmissions are carried out by analog signals. For example, voice transmission through the telephone lines and data transmission between computers use analog signals.

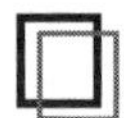

DIGITAL DATA VERSUS ANALOG DATA

Data can be defined as raw facts. To transfer data between devices, data must be represented in a certain format. There are generally two types of data representations. One is called digital data; the other is analog data. Digital data representation uses a binary system (i.e., 1 and 0) to represent any data. A number, a letter, an image, or even a video can be represented in a binary system.

Analog data representation uses continuous signals. Voice, pictures, and video are normally represented as analog data. The videotape records video in analog signals and a cassette records audio signals in analog form. The same data or information can be represented by both digital and analog representations. For example, audiocassettes use analog representation to record voice, while compact disks have digital representation. In general, digital data representation is more accurate and durable for repetitive usage than analog data representation. However, digital data representations require more storage space for voice and video than analog representations.

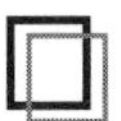

DIGITAL TRANSMISSION VERSUS ANALOG TRANSMISSION

Digital transmission uses either digital signals or analog signals to transmit information in digital format. That means all data or information must be converted into digital representation prior to transmission. For example, an image can be converted into a digital file and transmitted by analog signals to the destination. Digital transmission uses repeaters instead of amplifiers for long-distance transmission. It is considered the best way for information transmission. Analog transmission uses analog representation by analog signals. For example, a telephone conversation can be transmitted in analog representation and uses analog transmission.

	Digital Representation	**Analog Representation**
Digital transmission	Integrated services digital network (ISDN)	Not available
Analog transmission	Using modem to transmit computer files	Traditional telephone calls

TYPES OF WIRED COMMUNICATION MEDIA

There are three types of wired transmission media: twisted-pair wire, coaxial cable, and fiber-optical cable. The following sections describe them in more depth.

Twisted-Pair Wire

Most telephone lines consist of cables made up of hundreds of copper wires called twisted-pair wire. TPW has been the standard transmission medium for years for both voice and data. However, they are now being phased out by more technically advanced and reliable media (such as fiber-optic cables). TPW consists of two or more strands of insulated copper wire twisted around each other in pairs. They are then covered in another layer of plastic insulation. Since so much of the world is already served by twisted-pair wire, it will no doubt continue to be used for years, both for voice messages and for modern-transmitted computer data. However, it is relatively slow and does not protect well against electrical interference.

Coaxial Cable

Coaxial cable, commonly called "coax," consists of insulated copper wire wrapped in a solid or braided metal shield, then in an external cover. Coaxial cable has a larger bandwidth than TPW. Bandwidth represents the number of communications that can be transmitted at one time. A coaxial cable has about 80 times the transmission capacity of TPW. Coaxial cable is often used to link parts of a computer system in one building. In addition, coaxial cable is much better at resisting noise than twisted-pair wiring.

Fiber-Optical Cable

A fiber-optic cable consists of hundreds of thin strands of glass that transmit not electricity but rather pulsating beams of light. These strands, each as thin as a human hair, can transmit billions of pulses per second, each "on" pulse representing 1 bit. When bundled together, fiber-optic strands in a cable 0.12 inch thick can support a quarter- to a half-million voice conversations at the same time. In other words, fiber-optic cable has the largest bandwidth. In fiber-optic cable, signals in the form of light waves are transmitted through tubes of glass. In general, FOC has 26,000 times the transmission capacity of TPW. In addition, FOC has the following advantages over both TPW and CC: Such cables are immune to electronic interference, which makes them more secure. They are also lighter and less expensive than coaxial cable and are more reliable at transmitting data.

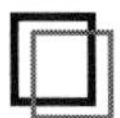

WIRELESS COMMUNICATION MEDIA

Major wireless transmission media are the microwave system and the satellite system. In addition, there are other systems such as the global positioning system, pager, and cellular phone systems.

Microwave System

Microwaves are high-frequency radio waves that travel in straight lines through the air. Because of the curve of the earth, they must be relayed through amplifiers or repeaters

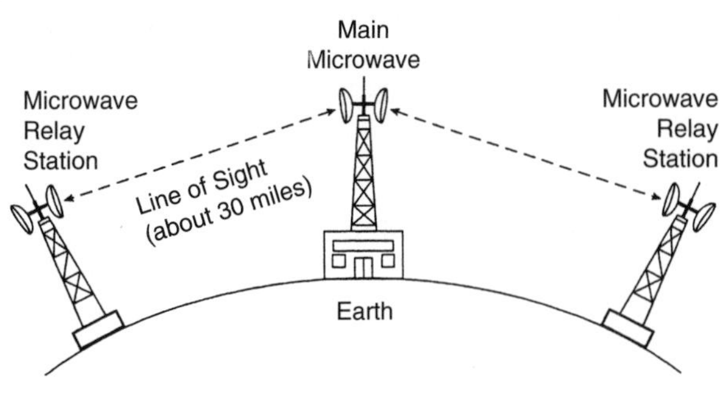

Exhibit 7.1 A MICROWAVE SYSTEM

to regenerate signals. They can be installed on towers, high buildings, and mountaintops. Satellites can be used as microwave relay stations (see Exhibit 7.1). Many of these rotate at a precise point and speed above the earth. This makes them appear stationary and can transmit signals as a relay station in the sky. The drawback is that bad weather can affect the quality of transmission.

Satellite System

Satellite systems use a sky station to transmit signals between two locations on earth. Communication satellites are microwave relay stations in orbit around the earth (see Exhibit 7.2). Typically the orbit is 22,300 miles above the earth. Since the satellite travels at the same speed as the earth, it appears to be stationary in space. The power for a satellite comes from

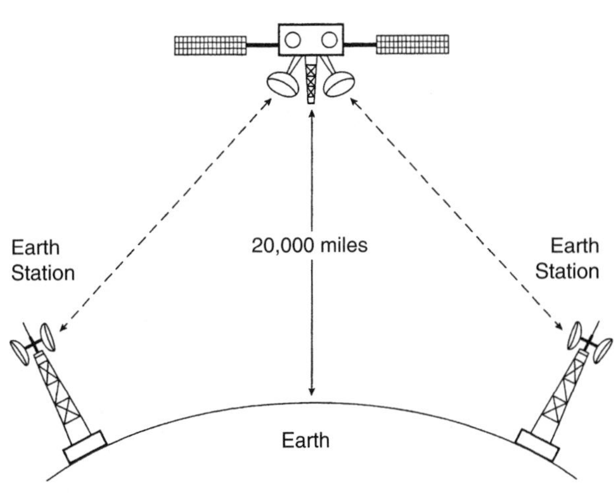

Exhibit 7.2 A SATELLITE SYSTEM

solar panels. When the satellite receives signals from one station on earth, it will then transmit them to another station on earth. Each satellite contains many communication channels and receives both analog and digital signals from earth stations. Sometimes, it can take more than one satellite to deliver a message.

Global Positioning System (GPS)

The original design of GPS was for military purposes. The project cost about $10 billion and consisted of 24 earth orbiting satellites that consistently transmit signals to identify earth locations. A GPS receiver can then pick up the signals from four satellites, calculate the signals, and generate the longitude, latitude, and altitude with the accuracy of a few feet. Although the system was designed for military usage, business applications have been implemented. Examples are tracking a delivery truck or a salesperson's automobile.

Pagers and Cellular Phones

Pagers or beepers are designed to receive another party's phone number so that the owner of a pager can call back immediately. This is a one-way communication device and does not provide response to the calling party. Paging services include SkyTel, PageNet, and EMBARC. Some pagers can transmit full-blown alphanumeric text and other data.

Cellular phones are designed primarily for communicating by voice through a system of cells. Each cell is hexagonal in shape, usually 8 miles or less in diameter, and is served by a transmitter-receiving tower. Calls are directly transmitted to a mobile telephone switching office (MTSO), then connected to the regular telephone network. If the caller is moving from one cell to another, the ongoing call will be "handed off" to another MTSO. Newer technologies allow digital signals to be transmitted by cellular phones.

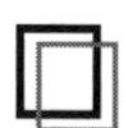

MODEMS AND OTHER DEVICES

Current communication networks use voice-graded media. Digital signals, being voltage pulses, do not travel a long distance. To send digital signals from the computer into the networks, a special device is needed to convert digital signals into analog signals so that analog signals can carry the information and travel a long distance. Modems are the device for this purpose. A modem can convert digital signals to analog signals when transmitting data and convert analog signals to digital signals when receiving data. In other words, computer digital signals can be converted into analog signals and transmitted through current telephone networks.

LOCAL AREA NETWORK (LAN) AND ITS APPLICATIONS

A local area network (LAN) is a privately owned communications network that covers a limited geographic area such as a company computer laboratory, an executive's office, one building, or a group of buildings close together. The range is typically within a mile or so. The topologies of LANs are Star, Ring, Bus, and Hybrid.

Components of a LAN

Microcomputer (Workstation)

A LAN consists of many workstations, each of which can be used as a server, a terminal, or a microcomputer. A server in a LAN stores network management software and performs management functions. There are different types of LAN servers depending on the major functions assigned in a client/server environment. A printer server provides printing services to other workstations, while a file server stores network and application software for the network. Other devices may include a fax machine, a scanner, or a printer.

Network Interface Card

A network interface card is the interface between the network and the computer. This card provides the communication protocol recognized by the network architecture. For example, an ethernet card is used to connect a PC with the network in a BUS network.

Network Operating System

A network operating system (NOS) is software that allows a user to manage the resources of a computer network. The NOS runs on the server computer in addition to the client operating systems, such as Windows or OS/2. The functions provided by NOS are:

- *Administration:* To add, delete, or organize client users and perform maintenance tasks such as backup.
- *File management:* To store and transfer software to client computers.
- *Printer management:* To prioritize printing jobs and direct reports to specific printers on the network.
- *Network security:* To control the access and usage of the network.

Types of LANs

- *Peer to peer:* All workstations on the network have the same priority and equal status. Workstations can exchange data or information through the network.

- *Client server:* Server computers are used to provide certain functions for other client computers. Each server computer is dedicated to a specific function.

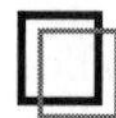

WIDE AREA NETWORK (WAN) AND ITS APPLICATIONS

Wide area networks are communication networks covering a large geographical area. A WAN uses telephone lines, microwaves, satellites, or a combination of communication channels to transmit signals. A WAN that is limited to the area surrounding a city is referred to as a metropolitan area network (MAN).

Integrated Services Digital Network (ISDN)

ISDN is an international standard for the digital transmission of both voice and data. Using ISDN lines, data can be transmitted over one or more separate channels at up to 2.2 billion bits per second if fiber-optic cables are used. This higher 64,000-bit transmission system allows full-motion video images to be transmitted.

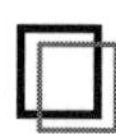

NETWORK TOPOLOGIES

Generally speaking, three basic LAN topologies and a hybrid topology are recognized:

- *Star:* A star network is one in which all microcomputers and other communication devices are connected to a central server. Electrical messages are routed through the central node to their destinations. The central node monitors the flow of traffic.
- *Ring:* A ring network is a network in which all workstations are connected in a continuous loop. Ring networks use a broadcast topology. Messages pass from node to node in one direction. The computer scans the message from the preceding node for an address that it recognizes. If the message contains the proper address, it is read. Otherwise, it is sent ahead to the next node.
- *Bus:* The bus topology is a linear channel with many connected nodes. There is no central server. Each node transmits messages to all other devices. If a node receives a message that was not sent to this node, this message will be discarded. Otherwise, it is read. Advantages of a bus are that it may be organized as a client/server or peer-to-peer network and it is easier to maintain than other networks. The bus topology is often called a broadcast topology, since every message or set of data sent on the bus goes to every node.

- *Hybrid:* Hybrid networks are combinations of star, ring, and bus networks. For example, a bus network may connect with a ring topology, which communicates with another star network.

Selection of the proper topology configuration depends on three primary criteria: the distance between points, the amount of time permissible for transmissions, and the amount of data to be transmitted from one point to another.

INTERNET AND E-COMMERCE

The Internet is the largest and best-known wide area network in the world. Because of its tremendous size and number of users, most businesses have taken advantage of its powerful and convenient features for many business applications and opportunities. Often called electronic commerce, business transactions can be made electronically. Consumers can browse the Internet virtual shopping mall and place orders for the company's merchandise. Investors can trade securities over the Internet. Telephone calls can also be connected via the Internet. Other services available on the Internet are:

- *Electronic mail:* E-mail can be sent anywhere in the world to users with an Internet address. Loss of confidentiality is a major risk of an e-mail system. Thus, inability to encrypt messages going between network gateways is a major security issue. A gateway is a means of connecting otherwise incompatible networks, nodes, or devices. It performs this function by converting one set of communication protocol to another. Accordingly, even if all systems are secured, an unsecured gateway can be a security exposure.
- *File transfer and software downloads:* The Internet can transfer different files all over the world. Software can also be downloaded from the Internet.
- *Database search:* The Internet can be used to access different databases.
- *Discussion and news group:* Thousands of discussion topics can be discussed in the bulletin board of the Internet. Information can be shared within this business group.

The Internet is an international network connecting approximately 36,000 smaller networks that link computers: commercial institutions and businesses. There are about 100 million Internet users, and the number is increasing exponentially. The reason the Internet is getting more popular is its power and practicality. The potential and utilization of the Internet for business is unlimited. Exhibit 7.3 presents examples of e-commerce top-level domains.

Top-Level Domain Name	Typical Holders	Restricted?	Example
.com	Commercial organizations	No	www.yahoo.com
.org	Not-for-profit organizations	No	www.aicpa.org
.net	Telecommunication companies	No	www.comcast.net
.edu	Higher education institutions	Yes	www.berkeley.edu
.gov	Government agencies	Yes	www.sob.gov
.mil	U.S. military installations	Yes	www.army.mil
.aero	Aviation organizations	Yes	www.cathaypacific.aero
.biz	Businesses of all kinds	Yes (only commercial entities)	www.websitesnow.biz
.coop	Cooperatives	Yes	www.coopscanada.com
.info	Any organization or individual	No	www.wcet.info
.museum	Museums	Yes	icom.museum
.name	Individuals	No	www.john.name
.pro	Professionals and professional associations	Yes	Schwartz.law.pro
Two-letter country codes: .uk (U.K.), .de (Germany), .cn (China), .il (Israel), .fr (France), .nz (New Zealand), etc.	Any organization or individual	Usually not restricted to sites within the country	www.imj.il www.sap-ag.de bv.airfrance.fr www.hol.gr

Exhibit 7.3 EXAMPLES OF INTERNET TOP-LEVEL DOMAINS

Electronic Commerce

The term electronic commerce emerged only several years ago when people started to understand the powerful tool of the Internet. The basic idea of electronic commerce is to let businesspeople conduct business transactions over the Internet. For example, a shopper can browse the Internet, look at the merchandise on the Internet, and place an order. This transaction can be completed by sending a company's purchase order number to the vendor and receiving a confirmation number. The advantage of electronic commerce is that business transactions can be very efficient and fast through the Internet. Entrepreneurs can use the Internet as the marketplace rather than huge retail channels. However, there are some other issues that need to be researched, such as how to police the transactions over the network, how to certify the accuracy of each transaction, and how to prevent transaction fraud.

Internet Development Tools

To design an Internet application, proper tools are required. HyperText Markup Language (HTML) is designed to implement home page design. This language requires certain programming training, and many people may not like to learn a new language. Recently, more Internet development tools have been released. Microsoft FrontPage is a tool that provides users with a graphical user interface (GUI) and word processing type of user friendliness. Netscape Navigator and Internet Explorer 3.0 also provide an Internet development tool. In addition, JAVA by Sun Microcomputers provides sophisticated functions for Internet application development.

INTRANET

Intranets are internal corporate networks that use the infrastructure and standards of the Internet and the World Wide Web. In other words, an Intranet is a small version of the Internet, which is basically developed and used by a single corporation. Customers or employees can access the database of information in a company through Web browsers to reduce operating costs. One of the greatest considerations of an Intranet is security, preventing unauthorized people from accessing a company's data through the Internet. To prevent this from happening, security software called firewalls has been developed. It blocks unauthorized traffic from entering the Intranet.

NETWORK SOFTWARE

Network System Software

Popular network system software for LANs are Novell's NetWare, Microsoft's Windows New Technology (NT) Server, and Apple's Apple Talk. Most network system software for WANs is custom-made and usually requires mainframe computers to operate.

Network Application Software

Most application software for individual computers has a network version. To share the same software on the network, a site license is required.

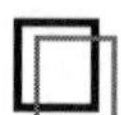

COMPUTER CONFERENCING

Another application developed based on telecommunication technologies is the computer conference. It can be either voice communication through the network or voice plus video communications. This technology is also available on LANs, WANs, and even on the Internet. The benefit of the computer conference is to reduce travel cost and improve efficiency.

MULTIMEDIA

Multimedia refers to technology that presents information in more than one medium, including text, graphics, animation, video, music, and voice.

Multimedia Components

To have a multimedia computer, which is able to deliver sound, video, image, and voice, a sound card is required. The function of a sound card is to digitize voice or sound into a computer data file. This data file can then be transmitted and converted back to sound or voice. In addition, a video capture card is needed in order to convert a video from a regular video device, such as a VCR, to a digital file. This file can be converted back to a regular video. A digital camera can be useful when a picture is taken and needs to be transferred into a digital file. Pictures can also be digitized through a scanner.

Since Multimedia information (such as video) requires lots of storage space, a device called a CD-ROM is necessary. CD-ROM stands for compact disk read-only memory, which is an optical disk that is used to hold prerecorded text, graphics, and sound. Like a music CD, CD-ROM is a read-only disk, which means the disk cannot be written on or erased by the user. A CD-ROM drive allows users to receive input information from a CD-ROM, which typically can store up to 650 megabytes of memory. Short for CD-ReWritable disk, CD-RW is a type of CD disk that enables you to write onto it in multiple sessions. DVD media (DVD-R and DVD-RW) can accommodate an astonishing 9.4 GB of data.

Multimedia Applications

Multimedia provides businesspeople with a better way of communicating. Managers can deliver a better presentation or lecture by including animation and voice. Productivity can therefore be improved by using multimedia. Some applications are discussed below.

Encyclopedias, Large Databases

A large database that is not time sensitive can be stored in a CD-ROM for later retrieval. For example, the encyclopedia and business article collections can be stored on a CD-ROM.

Training

A lecture can be given by interactive multimedia systems over the Internet. As a result, employees can go to virtual educational instruction on corporate business areas.

Presentations

There are presentation software packages designed to include animation, voice, and pictures. By using these tools, presenters can deliver important messages more effectively than using traditional presentations.

Animation

Corporate visual presenters use multimedia techniques to produce special effects to aid corporate employee learning. Business presentations may use lots of multimedia techniques in the business education process.

CHAPTER 8

NETWORK AND TELECOMMUNICATIONS

WHAT IS TELECOMMUNICATION?

Telecommunication means using computers to communicate over a distance. To communicate properly, two computers must use the same standard transmission procedure (protocols). Telecommunication is a popular application of personal computers. The future trend is toward increased use of telecommunications. There are several types of online systems:

- *Commercial online services* offer both general-interest services that appeal to a wide variety of people and specialized services that appeal to special interests such as stock market research or marketing research.
- *Bulletin board systems* (BBSs) are often set up by special-interest groups to provide the public with specialized services. Many BBSs have nothing more than a single telephone input line and a large hard disk. They may be managed by only a single owner or system operator.
- *Direct connection* is another common use of telecommunication, in which you dial another computer directly. For example, you can connect directly to the computer of a customer or supplier. To connect, you only need the permission of the operator of the remote computer and its modem number. You incur no charges, except perhaps for any long-distance calling changes. With specialized software, it is possible for you to control the other computer from a remote location.

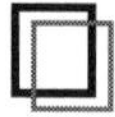

GOING ONLINE

To access any online service, you will need an account number and a password. You will also need a modem and communication software. Most service providers have their own communication software and it is generally free. To access other online services, you will need your own communication software.

Modem

You will need a modem to connect your computer to the telephone line. Most modems also provide faxing capabilities. You can purchase either an internal or an external modem. There is no difference in performance between internal and external modems. Internal modems plug into expansion slots inside your computer; this means an internal modem will not occupy any extra space on your desk. Internal modems are also less expensive, since they do not require an external case or a separate power supply.

The most important consideration in selecting a modem is its speed, or baud rate. You should select a modem with a minimum speed of 28,800 bits per second (bps). A high-speed modem is compatible with lower-speed modems. A 28,800 bps modem can communicate with a 14,400 bps or a 2,400 bps modem. Other considerations in selecting a modem are available software support, reliability (minimal errors), versatility, message buffering, call duration logging, error correction ability, and voice data switching.

An intelligent modem can perform many functions more complicated than receiving and transmitting characters over the telephone lines. It allows for dialing, answering, or hanging up the phone on command, redialing last number called, and recalling a series of phone numbers. A "dumb" modem does not possess internal instructions for dialing or hanging up. It does not recognize if it is starting the call or answering it (a person usually has to put the modem switch manually to either "originate" or "answer"). It has to be instructed on the operating speed.

Automatic features are available for different types of modems, including:

- *Auto/log on:* Log-on information is provided automatically.
- *Auto/answer:* Modem is able to get calls and data without the computer operator's intervention.
- *Auto/dial:* Modem can automatically place a call.
- *Auto/redial:* This feature keeps calling a number that is busy until the call goes through.
- *Directory dialing:* This feature allows dialing from a directory of numbers that have been saved in a smart telecommunications software program.
- *Number chaining:* Allows for responding to a busy signal by dialing other numbers.
- *Line test:* Modem tests the telephone line.
- *Answer-back strings:* The modem responds to an incoming call by giving identification codes or messages.

- *Self-test:* The modem verifies its own reliability.
- *Software disconnection:* Capability of modem to hang up the phone.
- *Dial tone connection:* The modem listens for a dial tone, dials 9 to get an outside line, then waits for a second dial tone.
- Line-sound monitoring.

Types of Telecommunications

There are several different ways you can use telecommunications; most people tend to use the following types of activities:

- *Electronic mail* (e-mail) is available on most systems and it allows you to send and receive messages in your mailbox. Your e-mail messages may be private or public. You can send a private message to another user who has an electronic mailbox. You can also send a public message that can be read by everyone on the system.
- *Real-time conferencing* takes you one step beyond e-mail. As soon as you type your message, the recipient is able to get the message immediately and can then respond. Real-time conferencing (also called "chatting") is similar to talking to someone on the telephone; however, instead of talking, you type your messages. Real-time conferencing offers at least two advantages over telephone conferencing. First, a large number of users can communicate simultaneously. Second, a written record can be kept of all statements. Problem situations may be solved more quickly.
- *File transfer* is frequently used in telecommunications. You can either download or upload files. Downloading involves copying files from an online system to your own computer. Uploading is the reverse process; that is, you send a copy of files from your computer to the online system. Most commercial online services and BBSs have software that can be downloaded. Some services also allow you to upload software. Generally, the software that is downloadable is either public domain or shareware. You can try this software for free; however, if you continue to use shareware software, you are expected to pay a small registration fee. *Note: A buffer* is a temporary storage area holding information such as that downloaded from an online service.
- *Online research* is possible on almost any topic. There are specialized databases for stock market data, accounting and tax information, marketing data,

management updates, production information, legal cases, computer information, and a wide variety of other topics. There are also databases that provide indexes and abstracts of business and financial articles from thousands of publications.

- *Online transactions* are now becoming the norm in many industries. It is possible to do banking and order merchandise online. It is easy to check the cash balance, find out what checks have cleared, or contact your bank's service online. Everything from financial specifics to economic data is online. Businesses can place orders with suppliers and receive orders from customers.

COMPUTER NETWORKS

A computer network is simply a set of computers (or terminals) interconnected by transmission paths. These paths usually take the form of telephone lines; however, other media such as wireless and infrared transmission, radio waves, and satellite are possible. The network serves one purpose: exchange of data between the computers and/or terminals.

The considerations in selecting a network medium are:

- Technical reliability
- Type of business involved
- The number of managers who will need to access or update data simultaneously
- Physical layout of existing equipment
- Frequency of updating
- Number of micros involved
- Compatibility
- Cost
- Geographic dispersion
- Type of network operating software available and support
- Availability of application software
- Expandability in adding additional workstations
- Restriction to PCs (or can cheaper terminals be used?)
- Ease of access in sharing equipment and data
- Need to access disparate equipment like other networks and mainframes
- Processing needs
- Speed
- Data storage ability
- Maintenance

- Noise
- Connectability mechanism
- Capability of network to conduct tasks without corrupting data moving through it
- Appearance
- Fire safety

Advantages of Networks

Computer networks provide several advantages. Most organizations are geographically dispersed, with offices located all over the world. Computers at each site need to transfer and exchange data, frequently on a daily basis and sometimes even in real time. A network provides the means to exchange such data.

Even if the organization is not geographically dispersed and has only one office, networks can serve useful functions. Networks permit efficient sharing of resources. For example, if there is too much work at one site, the network allows the work to be transferred to another computer in the network. Such load sharing enhances productivity by allowing a more even utilization of an organization's resources.

Backup capability is an especially important feature of networks. For instance, if one computer fails, another computer in the network can take over the load. This might be critical in certain industries such as financial institutions.

Networks can be used to provide a very flexible work environment. An organization can allow its employees to connect to the network and work from home, or telecommute. A network makes it easier for employees to travel to remote locations and still have access to critical data such as sales for last week or research data from a project.

Data Flow

Data flows between computers in a network using one of three methods. *Simplex* transmission is in one direction only. An example of simplex transmission is radio or television transmission. Simplex transmission is rare in computer networks due to the one-way nature of data transmission. *Half-duplex* transmission is found in many systems. In a half-duplex system, information can flow in both directions. However, it is not possible for the information to flow in both directions simultaneously. In other words, once a query is transmitted from one device, it must wait for a response to come back. A *full-duplex* system can transmit information in both directions simultaneously; it does not have the intervening stop-and-wait aspect of half-duplex systems. For high throughput and fast response time, full-duplex transmission is frequently used in computer applications.

Data switching equipment is used to route data through the network to its final destinations. For instance, data switching equipment is used to route data around failed or busy devices or channels.

In designing the network, three factors must be considered. First, the user should get the best response time and throughput. Minimizing response time entails shortening delays between transmission and receipt of data; this is especially important for interactive sessions between user applications. Throughput involves transmitting the maximum amount of data per unit of time.

Second, the data should be transmitted along the least-cost path within the network, as long as other factors such as reliability are not compromised. The least-cost path is generally the shortest channel between devices and involves the use of the fewest number of intermediate components. Furthermore, low-priority data can be transmitted over relatively inexpensive telephone lines, while high-priority data can be transmitted over expensive high-speed satellite channels.

Third, maximum reliability should be provided to assure proper receipt of all data traffic. Network reliability includes not only the ability to deliver error-free data but also the ability to recover from errors or lost data in the network. The network's diagnostic system should be capable of locating problems with components and perhaps even isolating the component from the network.

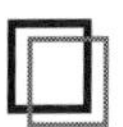

NETWORK TOPOLOGIES

The network configuration or topology is the physical shape of the network in terms of the layout of linking stations. A *node* refers to a workstation. A *bridge* is a connection between two similar networks. Network protocols are software implementations providing support for network data transmission. A *server* is a microcomputer or a peripheral device performing tasks such as data storage functions within a local area network (LAN).

Network servers are of several types. A *dedicated server* is a central computer used only to manage network traffic. A computer that is used simultaneously as a local workstation is called a *nondedicated server*. In general, dedicated servers provide faster network performance, since they do not take requests from both local users and network stations. In addition, these machines are not susceptible to crashes caused by local users' errors. Dedicated servers are expensive and cannot be disconnected from the network and used as stand-alone computers. Nondedicated servers have a higher price-performance ratio for companies that need occasional use of the server as a local workstation. The most common types of network topologies are shown in Exhibit 8.1.

Hierarchical

The hierarchical topology (also called vertical or tree structure) is one of the most common networks. The hierarchical topology is attractive for several reasons. The software to control the network is simple and the topology provides a concentration point for control and error resolution. However, it also presents potential bottleneck and reliability problems. It is possible that network capabilities may be completely lost in the event of a failure at a higher level.

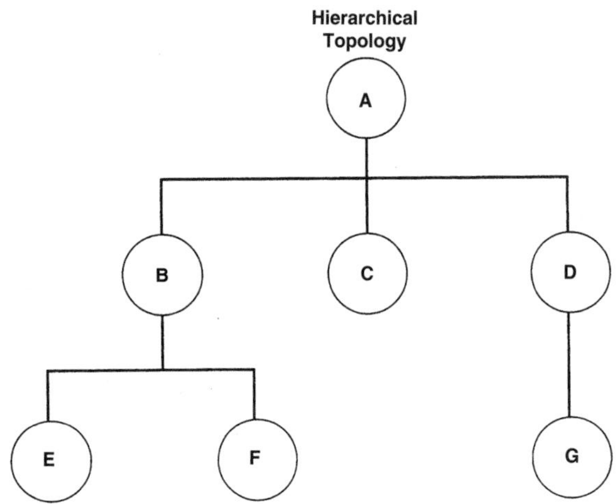

Horizontal

The horizontal topology (or bus topology) is popular in local area networks. Its advantages include simple traffic flow between devices. This topology permits all devices to receive every transmission; in other words, a single station broadcasts to multiple stations. The biggest disadvantage is that since all computers share a single channel, a failure in the communication channel results in the loss of the network. One way to get around this problem is through the use of redundant channels. Another disadvantage with this topology is that the absence of concentration points makes problem resolution difficult. Therefore, it is more difficult to isolate faults to any particular component. A bus network usually needs a minimum distance between taps to reduce noise. Identifying a problem requires the checking of each system element. A bus topology is suggested for shared databases but is not

Exhibit 8.1 COMMON TYPES OF NETWORK TOPOLOGIES

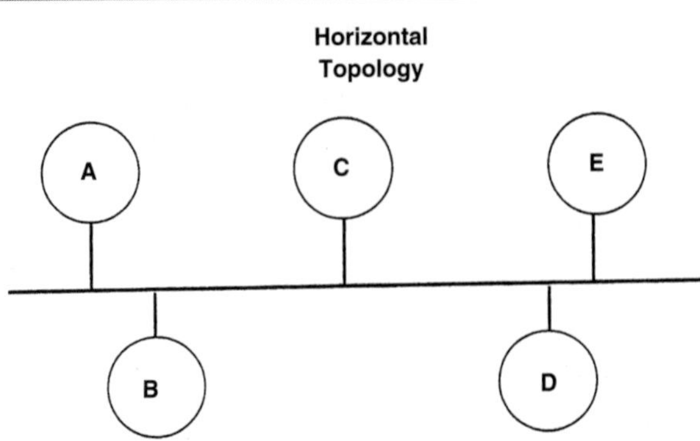

good for single-message switching. It employs minimum topology to fill a geographic area, while having complete connectivity.

Star

The star topology is a very popular configuration and it is widely used for data communication systems. The software for star topology is not complex, and controlling traffic is simple. All traffic emanates from the hub or the center of the star. In a way, the star configuration is similar to the hierarchical network; however, the star topology has more limited distributed processing capabilities. The

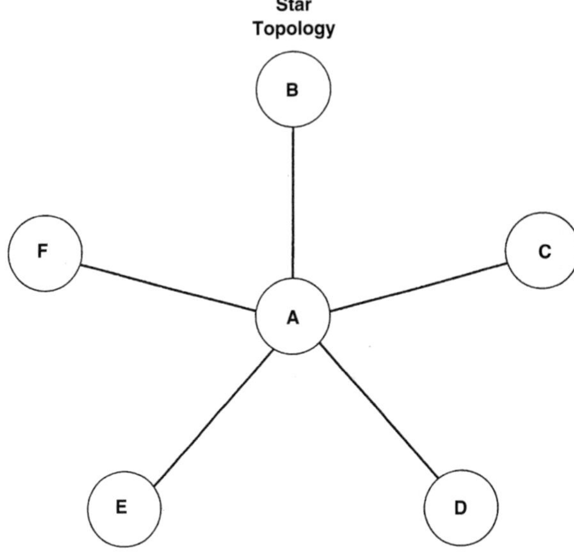

Exhibit 8.1 COMMON TYPES OF NETWORK TOPOLOGIES *(continued)*

hub is responsible for routing data traffic to other components. It is also responsible for isolating faults, which is a relatively simple matter in the star configuration. The star network, like the hierarchical network, is subject to potential bottleneck at the hub, which may cause serious reliability problems. One way to minimize this problem and enhance reliability is by establishing a redundant backup of the hub node. A star network is best when there is a need to enter and process data at many locations with day-end distribution to different remote users. Here, information for general use is sent to the host computer for subsequent processing. It is easy to identify errors in the system, since each communication must go through the central controller. While maintenance is easily conducted, if the central computer fails, the network stops. There is a high initial cost in setting up the system because each node requires hookup to the host computer in addition to the mainframe's cost. Expansion is easy, as all that is needed is to run a wire from the terminal to the host computer.

Ring

The ring topology is another popular approach to structuring a network. The data in a ring network flows in a circular direction, usually in one direction only. The data flows from one station to the next station; each station receives the data, then transmits it to the next station. One main advantage of the ring network is that bottlenecks, such as those found in the hierarchical or star networks, are relatively uncommon. There is an organized structure. The primary disadvantage of the ring network is that a single channel ties all of the components in a network. The entire network can be lost if the channel between two nodes fails. Establishing a backup channel can usually alleviate this problem. Other ways to overcome this problem are using switches to automatically route the traffic around the failed node, or installing redundant cables. A ring network is more reliable and less expensive when there is a minimum level of communication between micros. This type of network is best when there are several users at different locations who have to access updated data on a continual basis. Here, more than one data transmission can occur simultaneously. The system is kept current on an ongoing basis. The ring network permits managers within the firm to create and update shared databases. With a ring, there is greater likelihood of error incidence compared to a star because data is handled

Exhibit 8.1 COMMON TYPES OF NETWORK TOPOLOGIES *(continued)*

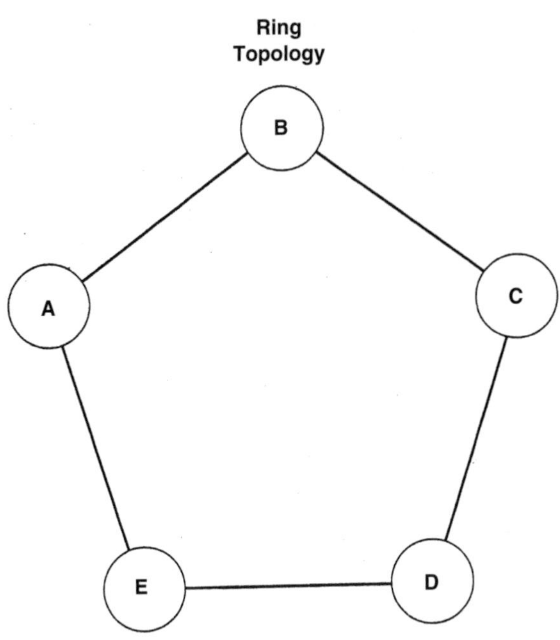

by numerous intervening parties. In light of this, the manager should recommend that data in a ring system make an entire circle before being removed from the network.

Mesh

The mesh topology provides a very reliable though complex network. Its structure makes it relatively immune to bottlenecks and other failures. The multiplicity of paths makes it relatively easy to route traffic around failed components or busy nodes.

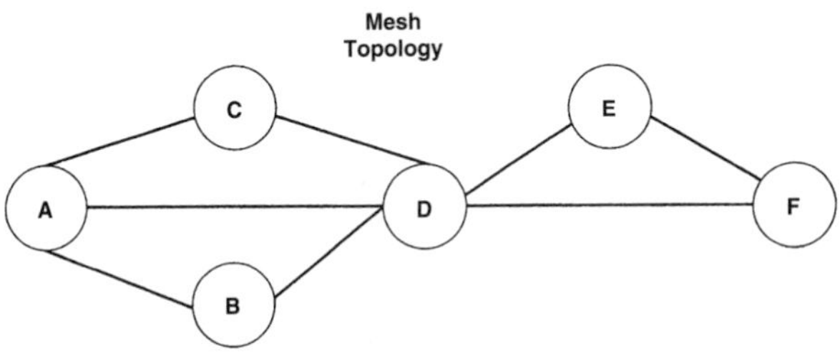

Exhibit 8.1 COMMON TYPES OF NETWORK TOPOLOGIES *(continued)*

Wide Area Networks and Local Area Networks

Networks may be broadly classified as either wide area networks (WANs) or local area networks (LANs). The computers in a WAN may be anywhere from several miles to thousands of miles apart. In contrast, the computers in a LAN are usually closer together, such as in a building or a plant. Data switching equipment might be used in LANs, but not as frequently as it is in WANs.

The channels in WANs are usually provided by an interchange carrier, such as AT&T or MCI, for a monthly fee plus usage cost. These channels are usually slow and relatively error-prone. In contrast, the channels in a LAN are usually fast and relatively error-free; the user organization usually owns these channels.

The major difference between WANs and LANs is that their topologies usually take on different shapes. A WAN structure tends to be more irregular. Since an organization generally leases the lines at a considerable cost, an attempt is usually made to keep the lines fully utilized. To keep the lines fully utilized, data is often routed for a geographical area through one channel; hence, the irregular shape of the WAN network.

The LAN topology tends to be more structured. Since the channels in a LAN network are relatively inexpensive, the owners of a LAN are generally not concerned with the maximum utilization of channels. Furthermore, since LANs usually reside in a building or a plant, such networks tend to be inherently more structured and ordered. LANs are flexible, fast, compatible, maximize equipment utilization, reduce processing cost, reduce errors, and provide ease of information flow. LANs use ordinary telephone lines, coaxial cables, fiber optics, and other devices like interfaces. Fiber optics result in good performance and reliability, but they are expensive. LAN performance depends on physical design, protocols supported, and transmission bandwidth. *Bandwidth* is the frequency range of a channel and reflects transmission speed along the network. Transmission speed is slowed down as more devices become part of the LAN.

Two or more LANs may be interconnected. Each node becomes a *cluster* of stations (subnetworks). The LANs communicate with each other.

Advantages of Interfacing Networks

- Total network costs are lower.
- There is flexibility in having individual subnetworks to meet particular needs.
- More reliable and higher-cost subnetworks can be used for critical activities and vice versa.
- If one LAN fails, the other LAN still functions.

Disadvantages of Interfacing Networks

- Complexity is greater.
- Some network functions may not be able to go across network boundaries.

ELECTRONIC DATABASES

There has been a tremendous growth in the online database industry throughout the world in terms of the number and type of databases, producers, and vendors. Never before has management had real-time access to such a vast amount of information resources. Online business databases improve decision making and analysis, allow management to add value by creating new products and services through information exchange and processing, and improve the bottom line. Online databases are a resource to be converted to useful information for decision-making purposes. The real measure of the industry, however, is its actual use as measured by the number of online searches. Estimates produced by the major word-oriented database vendors show that the number of online searches increased from fewer than one million in 1974 to almost 100 million in 2004. These figures do not include financial transaction databases, such as databases for stocks, electronic ordering, and so on. If they did, the total searches would be many times higher.

One way to classify databases is according to the presentation methodology. The methodologies include text, number, image (video), audio, electronic services, and software. The earliest public databases were text based, and they still are the predominant type of database. The user performs searches using text phrases in order to find specific information. Text-based databases include bibliographic, directory, dictionary, full text, and others.

Numeric databases are used primarily for transactions and for obtaining statistical information. They actually represent a declining proportion of all database types. One application of a multimedia database is in the real estate industry, where clients can be taken on a "virtual visit" of a particular property without leaving the office. Bulletin board services (BBSs) are another form of online database that have a wide variety of downloadable data.

Commercial online services, such as America Online, CompuServe, Prodigy, Microsoft Network, and Netzero have extensive access to various business database providers. Their primary function is to be a conduit for delivering databases developed by these providers.

The World Wide Web (Web) portion of the Internet has a rapidly increasing series of online business databases. These databases use multimedia graphical and audio features with hypertext links to other data and resources. Users need a

Web browser to read a graphical Web database. Web online business databases are a valuable resource because they link to all other Internet resources including text files, Telnet (standard Internet protocol for remote terminal connection service), Gophers (a distributed information service that makes hierarchical collections of information available across the Internet), Usenet newsgroups (a collection of thousands of topically named newsgroups and members associated with them on the Internet), and other portions of the Internet as required.

Another form of a multimedia database is the development of a vast number of CD-ROM business databases that interrelate audio, video, and text and allow the user search and download capabilities.

Faxback services are becoming popular and are a major source of timely business information. They are easy to use and provide a wide variety of information by just using a fax machine or a fax modem.

Finally, there are many online U.S. government databases. These high-quality databases contain extremely useful information and are often free of charge.

COMMERCIAL ONLINE SERVICES

These services are steadily increasing in popularity, are designed to be user friendly, and normally have graphical user interface (GUI) software with access to the Internet including the Web. Pricing options vary widely, and each service should be consulted directly. A partial listing of the most popular services is given below:

- *America Online (AOL) (800-827-6364):* AOL is user-friendly and utilizes an excellent GUI software and Web browser. It has a news and finance section, which includes stock quotes, business news, public discussion forums, and extensive business databases including Morningstar. America Online's information content is primarily news oriented. News services such as Reuters, ABC, *Time* magazine, the *New York Times*, CNN, and UPI are available on AOL. You can obtain financial news and stock quotes, and make stock purchases on AOL. Stock portfolios can also be valued automatically with updated stock quotes. *Business Week, Worth,* and *Investor's Business Daily* are also available online. A wide assortment of business software is available for downloading. AOL has several forums on taxes, personal finance, and business strategy.
- *CompuServe (800-848-8199):* This service can be accessed by using any standard communications software and it also provides its own GUI CompuServe Information Manager. CompuServe provides access to a wide

variety of business databases, program packages, encyclopedia references, legal advice, stock quotes, news and e-mail services. Extensive news is provided by the Associated Press (AP) and the information is updated continuously. Over 700 forums on a wide variety of subjects are available online. The Easy Sabre's Bargain Finder can be used to search for the lowest available airfare. CompuServe's Fundwatch allows investors to search for mutual funds most suitable to their criteria from a database of 4,800 funds. CompuServe has a huge library of business and general-interest software available for downloading.

- *Dialog (800-3-Dialog):* It is an online business information service that has searchable company information databases, bibliographic references, newsletters, and related publications. Dialog provides access to more than 450 databases including TRW, Moody's *Corporate Profiles*, and D&B Donnelly.
- *Dow Jones News Retrieval (609-452-1511):* This service can be accessed by using any standard communications software as well as its own Dow Jones Link GUI software. This service provides access to the *Wall Street Journal, Barrons*, the *Washington Post*, and Dow Jones News Service.
- *Hoover's Online (866-635-9715):* This service provides comprehensive company, industry, and market intelligence that drives business growth. It has a database of 12 million companies, with in-depth coverage of 40,000 of the world's top business enterprises.
- *LEXIS/NEXIS (800-346-9759):* This service uses its own research software for searching in specific industries including public relations and law. It is the most popular database of legal information including case decisions and previous testimony of expert witnesses. Besides case records, files of state and federal codes and regulations are available on everything from banking to hazardous wastes. This includes law review and journal articles. It has a collection of U.S. patents and public records data including real estate transactions, and corporate reports filed with government agencies. Individual libraries exist on *LEXIS* such as a bankruptcy library. This approach ensures the user is in the right place, pulling together relevant filings and cases from all jurisdictions, along with applicable codes and reference materials. There are also electronic editions of basic legal reference tools such as the *Martindale-Hubbell Law Directory* for locating practicing attorneys by state or by specialty, or verifying the credentials of the opposing counsel. Also, *LEXIS* contains the *American Law Reports*, which is a useful legal research tool. *LEXIS* contains thousands

of unpublished decisions that are not available in any library. The *LEXIS* online database includes the *Department of State Bulletin*, the *Federal Judiciary Almanac*, the American Maritime Cases, Model Rules of Professional Conduct, Opinions of the American Bar Association Committee on Ethics and Professional Responsibility, the *Environmental Law Reporter*, the National Insurance Law Service, the legislative history of securities acts, the RIA Federal Tax Coordinator 2d, and the Interstate Commerce Commission decisions, opinions, and orders. The *LEXIS* online service allows you to search geographically and narrow down by state or country. The *LEXIS* online service is organized into libraries and files facilitating information searches. Examples of important libraries (you select a library as a means of narrowing down the files in which the searching will be done) include GENFED (files containing federal cases and other federal materials), MEGA (case law from a different jurisdiction), CODES (statutes of a particular jurisdiction), and STATES (files, cases, and other materials from a particular state). Once a library is selected, one or more files is selected. The *LEXIS* online is easy to use and can perform searches that are not only time-consuming by conventional methods but unimaginable.

- *Microsoft Network (MSN):* MSN offers content similar to America Online and CompuServe.
- *Total Online Tax and Accounting Library (TOTAL) (800-862-4272):* An online service available to the members of American Institute of Certified Public Accountants (AICPA). TOTAL allows access to a variety of online services including LEXIS (Legal Information Services), NEXIS (News Information Services), and NAARS (National Automated Accounting Research System).
- *West Law Tax:* It provides legal and tax information.

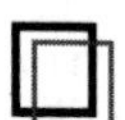

U.S. GOVERNMENT'S STAT-USA ONLINE SERVICE

The U.S. government has moved aggressively to provide extensive online database access. The Economics and Statistics Administration of the U.S. Department of Commerce has created STAT-USA for providing U.S. government online databases. It has several databases on the Internet at http://www.stat-usa.gov (see World Wide Web) with an Internet mail address at statmail@esa.doc.gov. STAT-USA received the National Performance Review's Hammer Award, which recognizes those federal agencies leading the way in "creating a government that works better, and costs less."

STAT-USA publishes the most timely business and economic information that the federal government has to offer. It eliminates the need to call from agency to agency to find the report that you need. STAT-USA gathers the most crucial, timely business and economic information from over 50 federal agencies and distributes them from a central source, saving countless hours in research time.

STAT-USA/Internet provides over 300,000 reports and statistical series (the equivalent of seven sets of encyclopedias) online, including press releases, trade leads, and reports that are released on a daily or weekly basis. Searching is done using Inquery, an award-winning natural-language search and retrieval software program that greatly simplifies locating files.

Access to the Economic Bulletin Board/Lite Edition (EBB/LE) is included as part of a STAT-USA/Internet subscription. Quarterly, annual, and Class C subscription group rates are available. For more information on the EBB/LE or to place an order, call 202-482-1986 or send e-mail to stat-usa@doc.gov. Companies interested in obtaining access for multiple users should call 202-482-1986 for information on the available pricing options. STAT-USA/Internet databases include:

- *Budget of the United States:* STAT-USA offers budget files free of charge in ASCII and in Adobe's™ Portable Document Format, and makes them searchable using Inquery. The Budget contains the budget message of the president, the president's budget proposals, analytical perspectives, and historical tables.
- *Bureau of Economic Analysis (BEA) Economic Information:* An authoritative online news release source for Survey of Current Business issues, and for detailed data files from BEA's national, regional, and international economic accounts.
- *Bureau of Economic Analysis, U.S. Department of Commerce:* GDP press release (complete) with corporate profits; economic indicators summary text file; leading, coincident, and lagging indexes release (text and tables in text format); and personal income and outlays.
- *Bureau of the Census, U.S. Department of Commerce:* New construction, durable goods, shipments and orders, new home sales, housing starts, manufacturing and trade inventories and sales, advance retail sales, shipments, inventories and orders, and U.S. international trade in goods and services—formerly merchandise trade (complete release).
- *Bureau of Labor Statistics, U.S. Department of Labor:* The Employment Situation (complete release), Consumer Price Index (full release), Producer Price Index (text/tables), and Productivity and Cost Preliminary (complete release).

- *Daily Economic Press Releases:* State and local government bond rates, trade opportunities, 10:00 A.M. and 12:00 P.M. daily foreign exchange rates, the daily treasury statement, treasury rate quotations, and yield curve points.
- *Economic Bulletin Board/Lite Edition:* The Economic Bulletin Board/Lite Edition is a comprehensive Internet source for government-sponsored economic releases and business leads. The EBB/LE offers a small subset of the files available on STAT-USA's modem-based Economic Bulletin Board (EBB) system; thus its title "Lite Edition." Economic news and business leads are available the minute they are released on the EBB/LE as well as in-depth analyses of markets, products, and economic trends. The EBB/LE provides searchable databases containing export promotion information; the Trade Opportunity Program (TOPS) and market research reports with daily updates and three months of archives; and the U.S. Department of Agriculture's Agricultural Trade Leads.
- *Federal Reserve Board (FRB):* Summary of commentary on current economic conditions by the Federal Reserve District, industrial production and capacity utilization, FRB bank credit, FRB consumer credit report, FRB foreign exchange rates, FRB selected interest rates, FRB money stock data, and FRB aggregate reserves.
- *Global Business Opportunities Service (GLOBUS):* GLOBUS is an international marketplace for U.S. businesses, providing billions of dollars in procurement opportunities from all over the world. Currently, GLOBUS contains the Commerce Business Daily, and Small Purchase Opportunities from the Defense Logistics Agency.
- *Census Bureau's Merchandise Trade Export and Import Statistics:* These are available on a commodity level as well as a country level.
- *Economic Bulletin Board (EBB):* This is the world's leading source of government-sponsored business data. Begun in 1985, it helped launch the era of electronic reporting and is still the most used bulletin board of its kind. On the EBB, late-breaking business developments are reported within 30 minutes after they are received from contributing federal agencies. In-depth analyses of markets, products, and economic trends are also provided. The EBB has a vast collection of files. The list of available files alone is 471 pages. The EBB collects, collates, and publishes data from more than 35 federal agencies.

ONLINE BUSINESS DATABASES

The following online business databases are a selected listing of the numerous databases available. For complete online business database listings, you are urged to consult the *Gale Directory of Databases* (Detroit: Gale Research, Inc.):

- *ABA Banking Journal:* A database of the complete text of the *ABA Banking Journal* covering the commercial banking industry. It is updated monthly, and it is available through LEXIS/NEXIS. Produced by the Simmons-Boardman Publishing Corporation, New York, NY 10014 (212-620-7200).
- *ABEL:* A bibliographic database containing more than 15,000 citations to items listed in the *Official Journal of the European Communities* covering legislation enacted by the Commission of the European Communities. It is available online from the Commission of the European Communities (CEC), and it is updated daily. Produced by the Commission of the European Communities, Office for Official Publications, Luxembourg (phone: 0352-499282563).
- *ABI/INFORM:* A service with more than 675,000 citations, with abstracts, to articles appearing in more than 1,200 international periodicals. It is available on a wide number of commercial services and is updated weekly or monthly depending on the service. Produced by UMI/Data Courier, Louisville, KY 40202-2475 (502-583-4111).
- *ACBAS:* A directory of over 1,400 publicly available French, German, and English-language online business databases. It is updated monthly. Produced by Yves Balbure, Malmaison, France (phone: 01-47518431).
- *Access Business Online:* This is your all-in-one business center. It offers business executives headline news, press releases, classifieds, links to financial markets, company profiles, upcoming trade shows and seminars, search capability of vendors in various industries, and much more. Exec-U-Net is an excellent tool for business executives to communicate with other business executives and senior professionals. Some examples of topics included on the information matrix are Market News and Business Connections, Independent Business, Wall Street and World Wide Finance, GeoPolitical Strategist, and Import/Export Exchange.
- *Advertising and Marketing Intelligence (AMI):* A bibliographic database abstracting articles from 75 advertising, marketing, and media publications. It includes information on products and services. It is updated

daily and is available on LEXIS/NEXIS. Produced by the New York Times Company, Parsipanny, NJ 07054 (201-267-2268).

- *FASAB:* The Federal Accounting Standards Advisory Board provides up-to-date information on issues in public financial management and accounting matters. In addition to available newsgroups and mailing lists, FASAB offers much more. Publications, legislation, exposure drafts, and newsletters are among many of the available topics to sift through at this Web site. For those involved with the FASAB, there is a calendar of events listed as well as the latest meeting minutes and highlights.
- *Internal Auditing World Wide Web:* Comprehensive Web sites for internal auditors.
- *Kaplan's Audit Net Resource List:* A monthly updated directory of accounting and auditing resources.
- *Moody's Investors Service, Inc.:* A corporate and municipal bond financial service. It is available online through Dialog (212-553-0546).
- *NAARS (National Automated Accounting Research System):* NAARS contains the full text, including footnotes and the auditor's report, of the financial statements of over 4,200 company annual reports for each year on file. NAARS also includes the complete text of a wide variety of authoritative accounting literature, such as Statements on Auditing Standards (SAS), Accounting Research Bulletins (ARB), and Accounting Standards Executive Committee (ASEC) position papers and issue papers.
- *Netsurfer Focus:* Computer and network security. Contains guidance on computer security.
- *New York State Society of CPAs' Luca Online:* A database of accounting, auditing, and tax information.
- *Rutgers Accounting Web:* One of the most comprehensive accounting indexes available. There is a link to nearly every accounting-related site on the Internet. The Rutgers Web server serves as a Web site for the American Institute of CPAs (AICPA), Institute of Management Accountants (IMA), Institute of Internal Auditors (IIA), Financial Accounting Standards Board (FASB), and American Accounting Association (AAA), just to mention a few. You can access numerous publications and documents from the AICPA site. There is also a database on "Improving Business Reporting" that can be accessed through the AICPA Web site. Another feature of the AICPA Web site is the "AICPA Documents on Call via Fax." The code numbers for each of the documents are given. The Institute of Management Accountants offers case studies in management accounting practices and techniques such as

implementing activity-based costing. Its research publications are listed in an annotated bibliography in chronological order. The Institute of Management Accountants displays upcoming events. The FASB site contains a listing of everything having to do with the FASB. All of its statements and interpretations are listed. Hundreds of accounting firms, including the "Big 4," can be accessed at this Web site.

CHAPTER 9

THE INTRANET

Intranet utilization in corporate America is rapidly growing. Because Intranets use Internet technology, there is ready access to external data. In effect, Intranets are internal Web sites. An Intranet is an important tool to use in business and is developed and used by the company itself. An Intranet is easy to install and flexible (what is developed for one platform may be used for others).

Corporate managers must have a knowledge of Intranet structure and organization because it relates to accounting, tax, audit, control, and security issues. Managers, customers, employees, stockholders, potential investors, creditors, loan officers, government agent representatives (SEC, IRS), and other interested parties can access the database or information in a company through Web browsers (interfaces) such as Netscape Navigator and Microsoft's Internet Explorer. Management may set up an Intranet to improve operating efficiencies and productivity and to reduce operating costs (e.g., distribution expenses), time, and errors. Of course, keeping information on the Intranet current takes time and resources. Proper controls must be established to guard against unauthorized access of the company's data through the Internet. One security device is the use of firewalls (barriers) to protect the company's Intranet by unauthorized access and to prevent misuse of the Intranet by outsiders who might otherwise be able to alter accounting and financial information, steal property, obtain confidential data, or commit other inappropriate or fraudulent acts. Further, add-on security tools are available to restrict users by preventing them from performing certain acts or from viewing certain "restricted" information.

In an Intranet, one protocol connects all users to the Web server. Intranets run on standard protocols supported by any computer.

INTRANET EXPLOSION

Information system (IS) and functional department managers quickly saw the power of this new communications medium as a resource to be leveraged on the corporate network as well. The Intranet is a powerful tool to make information more readily available within and outside the company.

With businesses under significant pressure to empower employees and to better leverage internal information resources, Intranets furnish a very effective communications platform that is both timely and extensive. A basic Intranet can be set up in days and can eventually act as an information hub for the whole company, its remote offices, partners, suppliers, customers, investors, creditors, consultants, regulatory agencies, and other interested parties.

Intranets provide the following features:

- Easy navigation (internal home page provides links to information)
- Ability to integrate distributed computing strategy (localized web servers residing near the content author)
- Rapid prototyping (can be measured in days or even hours in some cases)
- Accessibility via most computing platforms
- Scaleable (start small, build as requirements dictate)
- Extensible to many media types (video, audio, interactive applications)
- Ability to be tied in to "legacy" information sources (databases, existing word processing documents, groupware databases)

The benefits of these features are many, including:

- An Intranet is inexpensive to start, requires minimal investment in dollars or infrastructure.
- Open platform architecture means large (and increasing) numbers of add-on applications.
- A distributed computing strategy uses computing resources more effectively.
- An Intranet is much more timely and less expensive than traditional information (paper) delivery.

CALENDAR-DRIVEN VERSUS EVENT-DRIVEN STRATEGY

One of the key drivers in the Intranet adoption curve is they allow businesses to evolve from a calendar- or schedule-based publishing strategy to an event-driven or needs-based publishing strategy. In the past, businesses published an employee handbook once a year, whether or not policies changed to coincide with that publication date. Traditionally, even though these handbooks may have been outdated as soon as they arrived on the users' desks (and were promptly misplaced), they would not be updated until next year.

With an Intranet publishing strategy, information can be updated instantly. If the company adds a new mutual fund to the 401K program, content on the benefits page can be immediately updated to incorporate that change, and the company internal home page can have a brief announcement about the change. Then when employees refer to the 401K program, they have the new information at their fingertips. Content can be changed or updated to reflect new rules at any time.

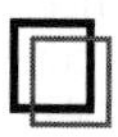

INTRANETS REDUCE COST, TIME TO MARKET

Intranets dramatically reduce the costs (and time) of content development, duplication, distribution, and usage. The traditional publication model includes a multistep process including creation of content, migration of content to desktop publishing environment, production of draft, revision, final draft production, duplication, and distribution.

The Intranet publishing model includes a much shorter process, skipping many of the steps involved in the traditional publication model. In the Intranet model, revision becomes part of the updating process while the original content is available to end users, thus dramatically reducing the time it takes for the information to become available to the user. As the information is centrally stored and always presumed to be current, the company will not have to retrieve "old" information from employees, thus saving updating expenses.

This new publishing model significantly reduces both costs and the time frame. Assuming that the corporate local area network (LAN) environment can support Intranet activities (and most can), the information technology (IT) infrastructure is already in place. Further, most popular Intranet Web servers can run on platforms widely found in most companies (Pentium class computers, Apple Macintosh, Novell NetWare, etc.), so little if any additional infrastructure is required.

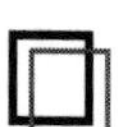

PRACTICAL APPLICATIONS

The uses of Intranets (internal Webs) by companies are unlimited, including:

- Furnishing outside CPAs with accounting, audit, and tax information.
- Providing marketing and sales information to current and prospective customers or clients.

- Providing information to salespersons in the field and managers at different branches (e.g., sales and profit reports, product tracking, transaction analysis).
- Furnishing resource needs and reports to suppliers.
- Communicating corporate information to employees, such as company policies and forms, operating instructions, job descriptions, time sheets, human resource data and documents, business plans, newsletters, marketing manuals, phone directories, schedules, and performance reports.
- Assisting in employee training, development, and technical support.
- Transferring information to government agencies (e.g., Department of Commerce, SEC, IRS).
- Furnishing current and prospective investors with profitability, growth, and market value statistics.
- Providing lenders and creditors with useful liquidity and solvency data.
- Providing project, proposal, and scheduling data to participating companies in joint ventures.
- Providing press releases and product/service announcements.
- Giving legal information to outside attorneys involved in litigation matters.
- Providing trade associations with input for their surveys.
- Accessing and searching databases and rearranging information.
- Furnishing information to outside consultants (e.g., investment management advisors, pension planners).
- Providing insurance companies with information to draft or modify insurance coverage.
- Allowing for collaborative workgroups such as letting users access various drafts of a specific project document interactively and add annotations and comments. For example, Ford's Intranet links design engineers in the United States, Europe, and Asia
- Furnishing economic statistics about the company to economic advisors.
- Facilitating database queries and document requests.
- Providing spreadsheets, database reports, tables, checklists, and graphs to interested parties.
- Displaying e-mail.

Site maps (e.g., Table of Contents) should be included so that users may easily navigate from each note (element) and are visible through frames or panels.

An Intranet requires Web application development for its internal network such as appropriate Web servers. For quick response time, there should be a direct connection to the server. Web browsers may be used to achieve cross-platform viewing and applications for a wide variety of desktops used within the company. The use of Web technology (e.g., Web servers) allows each desktop having a Web browser to access corporate information over the existing network. Therefore, employees in different divisions of the company located in different geographic areas (e.g., buildings) can access and use centralized and/or scattered information (cross-section).

There are many client/server applications within and among companies such as cross-platform applications. The major element in an Intranet is the Web server software, which runs on a central computer and serves as a clearinghouse for all information. Web servers for the Intranet are available from many vendors including:

- IBM (800-426-2255): Internet Connection Server for MVS.
- Microsoft (800-426-9400): Internet Information Server (comes with Microsoft's NT Server).
- Netscape (415-528-2555): Fast Track and Commerce Server for Windows.
- Lotus (800-828-7086): InterNotes Web Publisher.
- CompuServe (800-944-9871): Spry Web Server for Windows NT.

We believe that advantages of the Microsoft's Windows NT Server are higher security and easier capability to upgrade to more powerful hardware at a later date as application needs increase.

Further, there are many Intranet tool vendors such as Illustra Information Technologies (http://www.illustra.com; 510-652-8000) and Spider Technologies (http://www.w3spider.com; 415-969-7149). For example, we recommend as an Intranet tool Frontier Technologies' Intranet Genie, which includes a fairly secure Web server, HTML authoring instructions and guidelines (discussed below), Web browser, and e-mail functions. Regardless of the operating system used (e.g., Windows, UNIX, Macintosh), many Intranet tools are available.

HYPERTEXT MARKUP LANGUAGE (HTML)

We recommend the use of a Hypertext Markup Language (HTML) in developing Intranets because it is an easier graphical user interface (GUI) to program than windows environments such as Motif or Microsoft Windows. HTML is a good integrating tool for database applications and information systems. It facilitates the use of hyperlinks and search engines, enabling the easy sharing of identical information among different responsibility segments of the company. Intranet data usually goes from back-end sources (e.g., mainframe host) to the Web server to users (e.g., customers) in HTML format.

COMMON GATEWAY INTERFACE (CGI)

The majority of Web applications run through a mechanism in the Web server referred to as the common gateway interface (CGI). CGI is used to connect users to databases. Most CGI programs are written in TCL or Perl (a scripting language). However, due to the fact that these languages involve printing a source code of the Web server, there is an unsecured situation from a control and security standpoint. Other deficiencies are relative slowness in applications, nonexistence or inadequate debuggers, and maintenance problems. We suggest considering other languages for the CGI such as C or C++.

We recommend the following for CGI business applications:

1. In developing Web applications for Intranets, code management tools are needed to enable different participants in a corporate project or activity to communicate and work together. You must also use tools for database design, modeling, and debugging. In this connection, the following Web sites, among others, provide helpful information to corporate managers:
   (a) Basic HTTP (http://www.w3.org/TR/REC-html40/types.html)
   (b) HTML Browser List (http://www.w3.org/MarkUp/)
   (c) Web Server Comparison Chart (http://www.orphanage.com/products/compare.html)
   (d) HTML Specs from the WWW Consortium (http://www.w3.org/hypertext/www/markup/markup.html) or (http://www.macronimous.com/resources/web_servers_demystifyed.asp)
   (e) Introduction to CGI (http://hoohoo.ncsa.uiuc.edu/cgi/overview.html)
2. Do not commit to a particular server or browser because new technological developments require flexibility on your part. Therefore, you should set up your system so that it may accommodate many servers and browsers.
3. Make sure your HTML user interface is separate from the database and application logic.

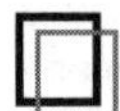

SETTING UP AN INTRANET

Intranet applications are scaleable—they can start small and grow. This feature allows many businesses to try out an Intranet pilot—to publish a limited amount of content on a single platform and evaluate the results. If the pilot looks promising, additional content can be migrated to the Intranet server.

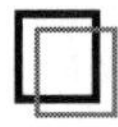

PROPOSED CONTENT

Companies must ascertain if data should be made available via a Web server, via e-mail, or by some other means. If the data is of general import, such as company travel guidelines or mileage reimbursement, it can be posted on a Web server so that when employees and travel agents, among others, require this information, they click on Travel Guidelines from the human resources page and obtain the most current information.

Many businesses find building Web interfaces to legacy information as a key application. With tools such as Purveyor's Data Wizard, HTML Transit, and WebDBC, end users can build simple point-and-click access to this legacy information without any programming, making it available to nontechnical users through their Web browser. Key database applications include customer records, product information, inventory, technical problem tracking, call reports, and so on. In addition, individuals can quickly set up seminar or training registration forms for short-term usage, loading the registrants' information into an easily manipulated database.

Conversely, interoffice e-mail may be more appropriate for interrupt-driven time-sensitive information, especially for a focused group of recipients: "Our most important customer is coming in March 2, so please attend the briefing at 9 A.M." In this case, the Web server can be used as an extended information resource: "Before the meeting, check the internal Web server link for Current Customers for updated information concerning this account."

ENHANCEMENTS

Intranets can provide efficient access to other external information resources including group access to mailing lists, threaded discussion groups, and stock/bond quotes. In this way, the oft-accessed information can be aggregated at the firewall and efficiently dispersed within the company, thus reducing external bandwidth and connectivity requirements.

Multithreaded discussion group software, or conferencing applications, can run on the same platform as the Intranet application, providing further chances to discuss company issues and the content that resides on the server.

INTRANETS COMPARED TO GROUPWARE

Intranets and groupware are not mutually exclusive. Many companies find that groupware (work flow, collaborative computing, etc.) is appropriate for certain focused applications, while Intranets are suitable for migrating existing content to online delivery. Others find a powerful combination in groupware and a Web server (Lotus InterNotes engine for publishing Notes databases on the Web, for example).

Ultimately, each application strategy has its merits. Beyond this, Intranet applications and Web servers make an excellent foundation for Web-based groupware, allowing businesses to employ a Web-centric Intranet system strategy and leverage the nearly ubiquitous Web browser and the powerful navigational aids provided by HTML.

CHAPTER 10

ACCOUNTING PACKAGES

This chapter discusses several software applications of particular interest to accountants. The discussion includes the major players in the area and some important features to look for when considering a particular type of software.

There are many factors that must be weighed when selecting a computer software package. Besides determining the software features currently needed and required in the future, the buyer must have a thorough understanding of the firm's existing system and whether proposed software will integrate with all areas of that system and business. Some of the basic considerations include features and capabilities, compatibility and integration, ease of customization, ease of use, written documentation and technical support, price, and vendor's reputation and stability.

In the DOS world, vendors tried to top each other by constantly enhancing features. With the advent of Windows, they are competing by concentrating on improving integration and customization. With Windows interfaces, data can more easily be linked and exchanged with all types of applications, such as spreadsheets, databases, and even e-mail. Thus, compatibility with existing systems and data is an extremely important consideration when selecting new software. Likewise, customization of input screens and reports to conform to a firm's needs can more easily be done, and capabilities vary between packages.

Although the price of a system is an important consideration, it should never be the deciding factor. Often the cost of software is relatively insignificant when compared to the costs of implementation, training, ongoing maintenance, and support. Training costs can be reduced if the program has good context-sensitive online help. Installation will be much simpler if the program has a checklist or "wizard" that actually walks the user through the installation procedure.

Before buying any package, try calling the customer support department of the vendor. Customer support can give you detailed information about the features of a package. Vendors typically offer a demo or a free or low-cost trial of their computer software product. You might also get information about specials or discounts available to professionals such as practicing accountants.

ACCOUNTING SOFTWARE

The fundamental task of accounting software is to automate the routine chore of entering and posting accounting transactions. This information is organized in an electronic format so as to produce financial statements, and it can be accessed immediately to assist in the management of the firm.

An accounting software package consists of a series of highly integrated modules. Each module corresponds to a specific accounting function (e.g., payroll, accounts receivable and accounts payable). After the details of the transaction are entered in one of the modules in an integrated system, the chart of accounts from the general ledger is "read." The transaction is then automatically posted to the accounts in the general ledger. For example, when a sale on an account is entered in the accounts receivable module, a debit is automatically made to the accounts receivable account in the general ledger and an offsetting credit made to the general ledger sales account.

Synex Systems' F9 software does financial reporting including variance and ratio analysis. Activity Financial's Actuity package also prepares financial statements.

In *Peachtree Accounting,* the user has the ability to enter data or perform tasks within a module by use of navigation aids. These aids, which are a graphical representation of the task flow of a module, can appear on the bottom of each screen. For example, in the navigation aid for payables, the user can directly enter purchases or record payments, print checks, and maintain vendor information and the general ledger.

Module Descriptions

The basic modules typically required by a firm and often integrated in an accounting software package include the following: general ledger, accounts receivable and invoicing, accounts payable and purchase order processing, inventory, payroll, job costing, and fixed assets.

General Ledger

The general ledger is the heart of the accounting system. It contains the chart of accounts of the business. A general ledger module should contain a sample chart of accounts that can be customized to a particular business. In addition, it should contain predefined reports that support budget data and prior year comparisons that can be tailored to a firm's specific needs. Other essential features include the capability to generate automatic reversing and recurring journal entries, having at least 13 periods open at one time, and the ability to make prior period adjustments or post entries to another year without closing the current year.

Accounts Receivable and Invoicing

The accounts receivable and invoicing functions are often combined in the same module. This module allows you to enter sales data and permits extensive sales analysis. It provides customer receivables management by tracking customers' balances, generates invoices and/or monthly statements, as well as aging reports. It should allow for setting up credit limits for each customer, provide for flexible billing options, and provide for the ability to apply partial payments to specific invoices or to the oldest balance. For faster processing, online inquiry should show the complete customer record at a glance including balances and unpaid invoices, and allow you to make changes "on the fly."

Accounts Payable and Purchase Order Processing

Accounts payable and purchase order processing can be combined in a single module. The module tracks obligations to vendors and determines a best payments schedule, prints checks, and provides for the distribution to accounts. It should allow for enhanced management of order processing by tracking orders from the start to the receipt of goods. It should be able to detect supply problems and thus permit early planning for alternate sources. To analyze vendor performance, it must track the complete purchase and delivery history of vendors and allow for easy access to this information.

Inventory

This module automatically tracks inventory as purchases or sales are made and maintains cost and price data for each inventory item. In an integrated system, the Inventory main file, which stores the product's number, is checked when a sales invoice is created in the accounts receivable module. If sufficient inventory is on hand, the amount of the sale is reduced from the balance. Likewise, when inventory is purchased, the inventory quantity is automatically increased. The module should help improve inventory management by alerting the user when to reorder, identifying slow-moving items, and analyzing performance by item and category.

Payroll

The payroll module maintains default information for each employee (e.g., rate of pay and income tax withholding information). The module calculates the wages to be paid, prints checks, and keeps track of deductions, sick and vacation days, and other such information. It maintains information for government reporting (e.g., 941, W-2, unemployment, and state tax forms). For cost control, it should be able to provide for expense distribution or integrate with a costing module.

JOB COSTING

A job costing module allows you to track and report on the costs, income, and profitability of individual jobs or projects. This is done by assigning a job ID number to purchases, sales, and employee hours. A job cost module should provide for an accurate audit trail, detailed income, expenses and committed costs, as well as the tracking of other user-defined categories. For example, Maxwell Business Systems' JAMIS is a job costing accounting package that tracks costs by project, contract, or organization over multiple years.

FIXED ASSETS

Fixed assets usually represent a significant investment by a firm; thus, it is essential to keep track of them, but it is extremely tedious to do so. Tracking fixed assets and the repetitive calculation of depreciation is well suited for the computer. Most accounting software packages include a fixed-asset module or capabilities to control fixed assets. It is also possible to purchase dedicated stand-alone fixed-asset packages.

Fixed-asset software can handle large amounts of data and a variety of depreciation methods for financial accounting and tax purposes. It should be able to maintain detailed information about each asset, including a description of the asset, its location, date placed in service, and estimated useful life. It should also be able to track additions and disposal, as well as basis adjustments. An example of a fixed-asset package is Decision Support Technology's BASSETS Fixed Asset System.

Before purchasing an accounting package, check if it has a fixed-asset module, or capabilities sufficient for your needs. If not, ask if the vendor produces a stand-alone version or would recommend a third-party vendor. Before purchasing a stand-alone fixed-asset software package, make sure that it allows for easy sharing of information with your general ledger, tax packages, and other data repositories.

Market Leaders

There are a number of accounting software products. They can conveniently be categorized as low-end, midlevel, and high-end packages. TechRepublic (http://techrepublic.com.com/) provides a list of these packages.

HIGH-END PACKAGES

High-end applications serve midsize regional companies and large multinational corporations. They are flexible, easy to implement, and can be modified to meet the users' needs. Although this category of software is not inexpensive, high-end packages are not in the same league as AS/400 or ERP installations and therefore do not enter the $100,000 range.

- AccountMate Software: Visual AccountMate
  (http://www.accountmate.com/EN/products/)
  Client/server software available to almost any size business
- ACCPAC International: ACCPAC for Windows Corporate Series
  (http://www.accpac.com/products/finance/accwin/cs/default.asp)
  Multitier business management system, multicurrency and multilingual support, e-business and sales force automation capabilities, customization options
- Damgaard: Axapta
  (http://www.damgaard.com/)
  Internet-enabled, object-oriented, single-code base for all countries, and a three-tier client/server environment
- Epicor: Platinum for Windows and Platinum ERA
  (http://www.epicor.com/solutions/accounting.asp)
  Integration between front-office and back-office applications, customization options
- Great Plains Software: Great Plains Accounting
  (http://www.greatplains.com/accounting/)
  Twenty modules and tools for automating labor-intensive processes
- Infinium: Infinium Financial Management
  (http://www.infinium.com/html/fm.html)
  Freestyle reporting capabilities; multinational, multicurrency processing of payments, invoices, and receivables; Web-enabled accounts receivable function
- Macola Software: Progression Series
  (http://www.macola.com/macola/product/solutions/default.asp)
  Allows multiple budgets and prior year's data to be maintained
- Navision Software U.S.: Navision Financials
  (http://www.navision.com/)
  Integrated development environment; provides customization tools for customer-specific solutions
- Peachtree Software: Peachtree 2000
  (http://www.peachtree.com/peachtree2000/)
  Designed for small to medium-size businesses; features multiuser capabilities
- Sage Software: Acuity Financials
  (http://www.us.sage.com/acuity/)
  Designed for larger businesses or company divisions (100 to 1,000 employees); integrates Microsoft Office and BackOffice suites

- Solomon Software: Solomon IV
  (http://www.solomon.com/product/series/series_fin.htm)
  Full suite of financial management tools, including accounts payable/receivable, cash manager, and general ledger
- Tecsys: ControlSeries Project Financial Management
  (http://www.tecsys.com/)
  Client/server, activity-based management software package

MIDLEVEL PACKAGES

Buyers of midrange programs are tough to define by revenue, but they usually include four or five accounting users and have needs that are technically sophisticated. These buyers generally require more robust, multiuser features and management reporting while still retaining tools that are required for a small business. Essential features of a package include client/server architectures, custom report design, and Internet/Intranet-enabled functions.

- AccountMate Software: Visual AccountMate
  (http://www.accountmate.com/EN/products/)
  Client/server software available to almost any size business
- CheckMark Software: MultiLedger
  (http://www.checkmark.com/ML_Win.html)
  Integrated, cross-platform accounting program combining general ledger, accounts receivable/payable, and inventory
- Cyma Systems: Cyma IV Accounting for Windows
  (http://www.cyma.com/products/fms.asp)
  Full suite of accounting modules, including system manager, general ledger, accounts receivable/payable, and payroll; available in workstation, peer-to-peer, and client/server configurations
- PC Accountant: ProBooks
  (http://www.pcaccountant.com/).
  Features integrated point-and-click accounting
- Sage Software: BusinessWorks
  (http://www.us.sage.com/businessworks/).
  Features 10 fully integrated modules; can support up to 48 concurrent users
- SBT Accounting Systems: VisionPoint
  (http://www.sbt.com/products/vp.html).
  Designed for small to midsize enterprises; based on open architecture
- Syspro Impact Software: Impact Encore
  (http://www.syspro.com/).

Features a relational database; integrates with other desktop productivity tools such as Microsoft Word, Outlook, and Excel

- Windsoft International: Bottomline Accounting (http://www.windsoft.com/index2.htm)
  Designed for small and midsize companies that want to automate accounting data

LOW-END PACKAGES

Products in the low-end category are not short on capabilities or features. Rather, they are made for sole proprietorships, partnerships, and corporations that are closely held with only a few employees. These users need a package that will help them balance checkbooks, prepare payroll reports and deposits, and keep track of bills and customer invoices. They want features including single points of entry for data, on-the-fly updating, tight integration with the Internet, sophisticated customized reporting, built-in job costing, and electronic payroll and bill-paying services.

- Aatrix Software: Mac P&L Accounting (http://www.aatrix.com/1.800.426.0854/macpandl/index.html).
  Full suite of applications at low cost, including general ledger, payroll, and inventory management
- ACCPAC International: Simply Accounting (http://www.accpac.com/products/finance/simply/default.asp).
  Entry-level package for the small office/home office user
- Intuit: QuickBooks (http://www.intuit.com/products_services/small_business.shtml).
  Features include time tracking, job costing, and estimations; integrated with Microsoft Excel, Word, Outlook, and Symantec ACT!
- MYOB: Accounting Plus (http://www.myob.com/us/products/plus/index.htm).
  Features more than 100 accounting and financial management reports; supports multiple-currency accounting
- Peachtree Complete: One-Write Plus (http://www.onewrite.com/).
  Designed for small businesses converting from manual accounting systems
- SBT Accounting System: VisionPoint (http://www.sbt.com/products/vp.html).
  Designed for small to midsize enterprises; based on open architecture

Checklist for Selecting Accounting Software

When you make calls to vendors or perhaps meet with the most promising ones, here is a checklist of questions and key features you want to address. Does the package offer:

- Ability to drill down from summary general ledger data to individual transactions?
- Ability to import and export data to and from spreadsheets and word processing programs?
- Ability to generate custom reports?
- Fast posting of large batches of transactions?
- Strong security?
- Adequate technical support?
- Retention of historical data and ability to compare current results to past results?
- Ability to match direct expenses with specific clients and projects?
- Ability to allocate indirect costs to individual projects?
- Ability to integrate customer management and e-commerce functions?
- Preparation of 941s, W-2s, 1099s, and 940s?
- Ability to flow data from the program into your tax software?
- Ability to add more users at a later date with minimal cost increases?

Also, here is a wish list of functions the package should include:

- Offers ease of use, especially the ability to directly query the data and perform ad hoc reporting
- Enables fast and easy user training
- Requires a minimum of effort from the IT staff to keep it running at optimum efficiency
- Provides all-in-one accounts payable/receivable and general ledger functions
- Includes import and export features and a report writer
- Offers access to live people for technical support
- Requires a minimum of process modifications

For more in-depth analysis of various accounting packages, you may want to consult these professional organizations and manuals, some of which offer advice on purchasing software:

- Institute of Management Accountants (http://www.imanet.org).
- Family Firm Institute (http://www.ffi.org/).
- National Society of Accountants (http://www.nsa.org).

- American Institute of Certified Public Accountants (http://www.aicpa.org/).
- Accounting Technology (http://www.electronicaccountant.com), a great site for industry news, special reports, and product reviews.
- CPA Software News (http://www.softwarenews.net).
- CPA Technology Report (http://cpatech.hbpp.com).
- SoftWorld's Accounting and Finance Expo (http://www.softworld.com). These frequent trade shows are the best place for buyers to get hands-on demos of the latest accounting and finance products both in North America and Europe.

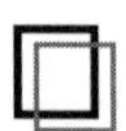

WRITE-UP SOFTWARE

With the development of easy-to-use and inexpensive accounting software, many companies that previously relied on CPAs to keep their books are doing it themselves. CPA firms can counter this trend with dedicated Write-up software that is easy to use and provides more features so as to add value to their write-up services.

Write-up software should allow you to do more than just record transactions. One of the biggest features to look for is the ability to easily create an array of printouts and reports that a client might need. This includes being able to link and transfer data from other software packages and applications.

Another important feature is the ability to customize the input screen so that it is consistent with the layout of the client's source documents, thereby reducing unneeded keystrokes. Easy setup is another means to reduce the cost of write-up service. The package should contain sample company data and the ability to copy common information and make changes to default information included in the setup on the fly.

Major Players

There is a large number of products in the Write-up area. Exhibit 10.1 lists five products.

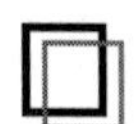

TAX PREPARATION SOFTWARE

Computer technology has had a significant impact on the way tax returns are prepared. Computerized tax return preparation lets the user prepare a return quickly and accurately, and allows the user to quickly analyze different tax planning strategies. Some software packages have built-in tools for tax research and permit for the electronic filing of tax returns. This software also lets the user easily do what-if planning, then quickly makes all the necessary changes.

e Enterprise
Microsoft Business Solutions
888-477-7789

Peachtree Client Write-Up
Peachtree Software
900-228-0068

ACCPAC Advantage Series
ACCPAC International
707-284-7500

Xpert Write-Up
Micronetics International
561-995-1477

Write-Up Solutions
Creative Solutions
800-968-0600

Exhibit 10.1 WRITE-UP SOFTWARE

Furthermore, data can be imported directly from accounting packages or electronic spreadsheets into tax preparation software.

While tax preparation software can help with tax planning, you should consider a dedicated tax research package for serious tax research. Most compact disk (CD)–based tax services can effectively replace the printed version of tax services. A major advantage of using CD-based tax services is having the ability to do electronic keyword searches. This can greatly facilitate the tax research process and make it much more efficient. In addition, it is easier to maintain and store all this information on a CD, thereby saving a good deal of library storage space.

The tax software industry is fiercely competitive and continues to go through consolidations and shakeouts. Thus it makes sense to deal with the larger, better-known vendors whose products are more likely to be supported in the future.

Market Leaders

Tax software can be categorized into segments:

- *Lower-cost alternatives:* The price for this category is generally under $1,000. In spite of their low price, their features compare favorably with the higher-priced products. The products included in this category are listed in Exhibit 10.2.
- *Mainstream:* These packages are suitable for mainstream tax practices. They are generally easy to use and learn, but they are not intended to handle every situation that may arise. The packages in this category are generally more powerful than those in the lower-cost category.

- *High-end alternatives:* This group is marketed for use by multistate regional and national firms. These packages are able to handle the most complex returns and track their progress through large offices.

Lower-Cost Alternatives

ProSeries
Intuit
800-374-7317

Tax/Pack Professional
Alpine Data Inc.
800-525-1040

Tax Relief
Micro Vision Software
800-829-7354

TAX$IMPLE
TAX$IMPLE
800-989-8955

Mainstream

CPA Software
CPA Software
800-272-7123

Lacerte Tax Planner
Lacerte Software Corporation
800-765-4065

Professional Tax System
Tax and Accounting Software Corp. (TAASC)
800-998-9990

TaxWorks
Laser Systems
800-343-1139

Ultra Tax
Creative Solutions Inc.
800-968-8900

High-End

Turbo Tax ProSeries
Intuit
800-934-1040

Go System
R/A
800-865-5257

ProSystem fx
CCH Inc.
800-457-7639

Exhibit 10.2 TAX SOFTWARE

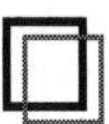

AUDIT SOFTWARE

Audit software is used by accountants to perform audits efficiently and effectively. Software audit tools include automated work papers, data extraction software, and trial balance software.

Products such as APG (Audit Program Generator) by the American Institute of Certified Public Accountants (AICPA) and the optional add-on modules allow you to prepare customized audit programs. They eliminate the photocopying, cutting, and pasting usually required when creating the audit program and guide users through the engagement.

Data extraction software, such as IDEA (Interactive Data Extraction and Analysis), also by the AICPA, allows auditors to access clients' files for audit testing. The auditor can either access the client's live data or obtain a copy of the company's data files on tape or disk. Data extraction software allows the auditor to audit through the computer. The auditor can, for example, select a sample of accounts receivables for confirmations, or perform analytical reviews and do ratio analysis. Transactions may be compared to predetermined criteria. Linton Shafer's Audit Sampling Software packages select random numbers and dates. They handle multiple ranges and evaluate results. They perform compliance and substantive testing.

Trial Balance software, such as the AICPA's ATB (Accountant's Trial Balance), helps the auditor organize client's general ledger balances into a working trial balance. The auditor can then perform adjustments and update account balances. The calculation of financial ratios is extremely simple with trial balance software. This type of software aids in the preparation of financial statements. While trial balance software is designed primarily for audits, it can be used instead of write-up software for compilation and review services.

Price Waterhouse Researcher is an accounting, auditing, and reporting research system on a single CD-ROM disk. Equivalent to a 100,000-page library, PW Researcher includes generally accepted accounting principles (GAAP), generally accepted auditing standards (GAAS), Securities and Exchange Commission (SEC) regulations, and U.S. cost accounting standards. The information on the CD includes American Institute of CPAs (AICPA), Financial Accounting Standards Board (FASB), SEC, and Emerging Issues Task Force (EITF) publications, along with Price Waterhouse guidance, analysis, and interpretations. The CD is updated quarterly and also includes international accounting and auditing standards. The easy-to-use database may be searched using a key word or phrase. Users may make personal notes and markers. We highly recommend this excellent product.

Price Waterhouse TeamMate is an electronic working paper system that helps automate the working paper preparation, review, reporting, and storage process. It includes standard and free-form schedule templates, an automatic tick mark system, and a powerful cross-referencing capability. PW TeamMate also integrates popular spreadsheet, word processing, and imaging software. There are hypertext links between documents and applications enabling the auditor to jump backward through related numbers in reports or spreadsheets to the original data. The search, cross-referencing, and retrieval capabilities allow the auditor to automatically correct errors in all affected documents. The working paper review features include automatic exception reporting, a working paper navigation system, and text and voice annotation. For example, the auditor can obtain a directory of all review notes pertaining to a document. The reporting features include key audit point summarization, report drafting, audit status reports, and time summaries. Financial data is quickly accessed by the sorting and filtering tools. A standard index provides a branch and node system for all papers. There is a simultaneous multiuser feature so that auditors/reviewers can work with the same document set even if they are working in various locations. PW TeamMate improves the quality, productivity, and effectiveness of the auditor's work.

Price Waterhouse Controls facilitates the documentation, evaluation, and testing of internal controls. The software expedites the collection and summarization of controls in place, appraises their effectiveness, and identifies areas of risk exposure. PW Controls can be used by auditors to document particular business processes. Control weaknesses are identified with resultant recommendations for improvement. The auditor can view control effectiveness at different levels within the company (e.g., by activity, by business unit). A comparison and analysis may be made of the relative control performance of different operating units.

Price Waterhouse Chekhov is a software package that automates the completion of checklists.

Exhibit 10.3 lists a number of audit software packages. They contain one or more features previously discussed.

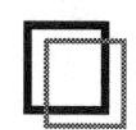

SPREADSHEETS

More than any other product, the electronic spreadsheet has done more to make the capabilities of microcomputers evident to the business community. An electronic spreadsheet allows the user to work with data in a huge number of rows and columns. The user works with this data in a columnar spreadsheet, a format familiar to accountants. A big advantage of the spreadsheet is that it eliminates the need

ACL
ACL Software
604-669-4225

CA-PanAudit Plus/PC
Computer Associates
800-225-5224

Case Ware Working Papers
Case Ware International
416-867-9504

Digital Analysis Tests Statistics
Richland
888-453-1231

ProSystem fx Audit
CCH
800-PFX-9998

Exhibit 10.3 AUDIT SOFTWARE

to perform manual calculations and can perform powerful computer-aided operations.

The spreadsheet has become a valuable tool in business planning, since it permits the user to perform what-if scenarios. Inputs can be continuously changed, and the results will automatically be recalculated throughout the spreadsheet. Thus, the effect of alternative decisions is easily determined and planning is greatly facilitated.

The use of templates is another important feature of spreadsheets. Templates provide the format and contain the formulas that are used to repeatedly solve various business applications. Since you do not have to be a programmer to construct a template, all firms can more easily use the vast power of the computer to help make better decisions in the management of a firm.

Major Players and Selection Considerations

The chief players in the spreadsheet field have been reduced to three:

- Lotus 1-2-3
  Lotus Development Corp.
  800-343-5414
- Microsoft's Excel
  Microsoft Corp.
  800-426-9400
- Quattro Pro
  Novell
  800-453-1267

In actuality, all the players have the same basic features. Although a particular feature may currently be lacking in a specific spreadsheet, it may very well be included in the next upgrade of that product. Therefore, the decision of which product to buy should not be based primarily on features. More importantly, be certain the planned spreadsheet supports and is compatible with the major applications of your business. Thus, make sure that the spreadsheet can directly access your databases and that any macros or templates that have already been developed are compatible with the proposed acquisition.

Managing Risk Using Fuzzy Analysis

A unique spreadsheet, FuziCalc, takes the computational complexity out of fuzzy arithmetic. This spreadsheet allows you to easily incorporate ranges or intervals in your analysis and to assign the ranges different weights.

Implicit in any type of decision analysis is the assumption that judgmental inputs can be accurately represented by a single precise number. However, it generally is not possible to quantify judgment with such precision. Most of the traditional tools for decision analysis are "crisp." By crisp we mean that the tools require precise inputs. In contrast, most of the problems facing managers are "fuzzy," vague, or imprecise. Traditionally, managers have incorporated imprecision in their analysis through probability theory. An alternate framework, based on the fuzzy set theory, allows imprecision in data analysis. It allows the decision maker to benefit from the structure of quantitative decision analysis without forcing the user to provide very precise numerical inputs.

From a practical perspective, fuzzy analysis is easy to do using the FuziCalc spreadsheet. There are no new techniques to learn. Anyone familiar with a conventional spreadsheet can quickly adapt to the FuziCalc spreadsheet. All fuzzy data can be represented by "belief graphs." Belief graphs are the heart of the FuziCalc spreadsheet. Fuzzy data inputs are made using belief graphs. The simplest way to represent a fuzzy number is to use a triangular shape. You need a minimum of three points to represent any fuzzy number. A triangular fuzzy number has many practical applications. To construct a triangular fuzzy number of sales price, we need to determine the highest, the most likely, and the lowest sales price. Let's assume our estimates for the highest, the most likely, and the lowest sales price are $35, $25, and $20, respectively. A belief graph of this fuzzy triangular number can then be constructed as shown in Exhibit 10.4.

Let's contrast the fuzzy number in Exhibit 10.4 with the crisp number 25 in Exhibit 10.5. A crisp number does not have a range of values; its belief graph is a straight line.

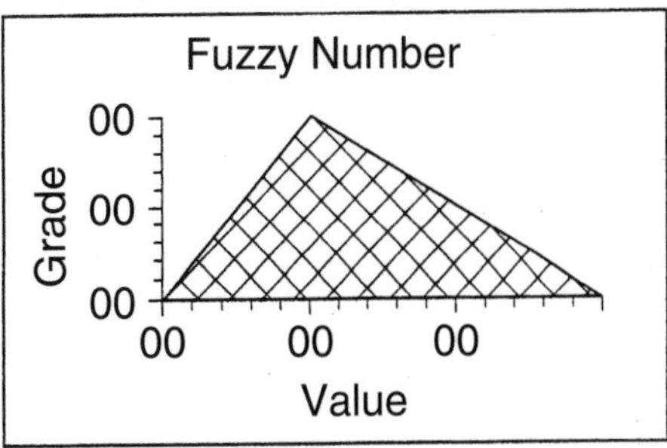

Exhibit 10.4 BELIEF GRAPH OF FUZZY TRIANGULAR NUMBER

FuziCalc provides five common shapes to represent fuzzy data. The five shapes from FuziCalc's *Gallery* are shown in Exhibit 10.6.

The triangular shape was discussed earlier; its use is appropriate when the user has a single best estimate of the most likely value and can specify the endpoints of the range. Sometimes it is not possible for the user to give one best estimate of the *most likely* value. A *trapezoidal* fuzzy number would be most appropriate when only a *range* of *most likely* values can be given. The user may select the multipeaked shape to represent fuzzy numbers where the low and high values are more likely than the middle values. The *tent* shape is most appropriate where all of the values in the range have a high possibility of occurring. The *rocket* shape might be used when the user believes a wide range exists, but a narrow range within it has a much better possibility. The five shapes will be sufficient for the needs of most users. However, FuziCalc allows users to easily alter the shape to represent any fuzzy number.

It is possible to add, subtract, multiply, and divide fuzzy numbers just like regular or crisp numbers. The advantage

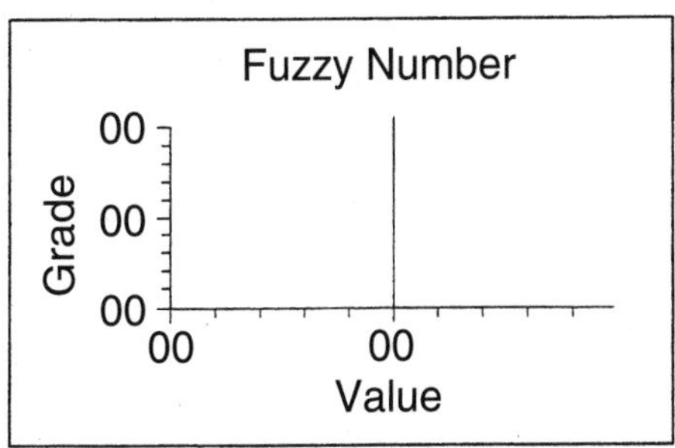

Exhibit 10.5 BELIEF GRAPH OF CRISP NUMBER

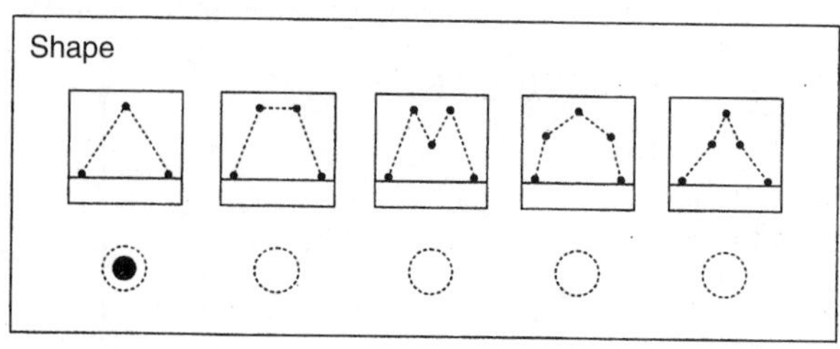

Exhibit 10.6 COMMON SHAPES OF FUZZY DATA

of using the FuziCalc spreadsheet is that users do not need to concern themselves with the complex underlying computations.

FuziCalc's primary strength is in modeling under uncertainty. Beyond that, FuziCalc offers little to spreadsheet users. As a spreadsheet, FuziCalc offers only the very basic features. Users of conventional spreadsheets might even find working in FuziCalc a little frustrating. Many of the features that you are accustomed to in conventional spreadsheets are missing in FuziCalc. Thus, it would be used to supplement rather than to replace a conventional spreadsheet.

FuziCalc is sold by:
FuziWare, Inc.
800-472-6183

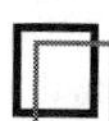

ABC SOFTWARE

An activity-based costing (ABC) system accumulates costs on the basis of production or service activities at a firm. Basically it assigns costs by activity and links them to specific products. It is argued that the resulting cost data is much more realistic and precise as compared to the data obtained from a traditional costing system.

Aided by computer software designed for ABC, the management accountant can more easily and accurately accumulate cost information and perform what-if testing. With this data, management is in a better position to evaluate and make decisions regarding its operations and products.

There is a good deal of software that the management accountant can use to aid in accumulating cost data. Some software products are actually spreadsheet applications; others are modules of mainframe packages. All these packages are for use on a personal computer and most are designed for activity-based costing or activity-based management. Exhibit 10.7 separates these packages into two categories: Those developed by independent vendors, and those supported or developed by a big-four CPA firm. It should be noted that some products include consulting support as part of the overall package.

Independent Vendors
Acorn Systems Cost Analyzer Acorn Systems 800-98-ACORN
ABM Tools Decimal Technologies, Inc 877-abm-tool
Activity Analyzer Lead Software 630-351-5155
QUOTE-A-PROFIT Manufacturing Management Systems, Inc. 916-428-4068
People Soft Activity-Based Management PeopleSoft, Inc 800-386-7638
Big-Four CPA Firms
TR/ACM Deloitte & Touche 617-261-8615
ACTIVA Price Waterhouse 314-425-0500
The Profit Manager Series KPMG Peat Marwick 313-983-0321
ABCost Manager Coopers & Lybrand 312-701-5783

EXHIBIT 10.7 ABC SOFTWARE

Price Waterhouse's ACTIVA is a comprehensive ABC, profitability, and performance management software tool. Its features and capabilities include budgeting and planning, product costing and pricing, cost management and analysis, decision support, process improvement, activity-based management, and variance determination and evaluation. Developed using state-of-the-art client/server technology, its additional features include capital investment analysis, production sourcing, distribution logistics, and foreign currency appraisal. ACTIVA aids in measuring the profitability by customer, product, service, market, process, and distribution channel. ACTIVA can support many users conducting diverse applications in multiple locations worldwide. The software contains sophisticated security features.

Lead Software's Activity Analyzer assigns activities to cost objects and calculates by activity costs and profitability. Profitability may be determined by product, service, customer, and territory.

ABC helps in determining what a product or process should cost, areas of possible cost reduction, and value-added versus nonvalue-added aspects. Activity-based costing is beneficial in appraising value-chain functions. Further, costs are a function of their consumption factors such as number of employees, units produced, labor hours, and so on.

- Online advisors are very helpful sources of information, such as the CPA Software Review Web site (www.cpasoftwarenews.com) and Accounting Software Advisor (www.accountingsoftwareadvisor.com) for reviews of various accounting-related software.
- Software vendors come and go. Software titles, vendor names, and telephone numbers are subject to change. Always check for up-to-date information using search engines such as MSN Search and Google.

EXTENSIBLE BUSINESS REPORTING LANGUAGE (XBRL)

There are too many data formats on the Internet, so users are prevented from analyzing financial information without many labor-intensive conversions. Excessive time is devoted to extracting useful information from available accounting and financial data. Further, time is wasted rekeying the same information into a spreadsheet. For example, data in the Securities and Exchange Commission's (SEC) database referred to as the Electronic Data Gathering, Analysis, and Retrieval System (EDGAR) cannot be imported directly into spreadsheets. EDGAR performs automated collection, validation, indexing, acceptance, and forwarding of submissions by companies and others who are required by law to file forms with the SEC. The comparison of numbers and ratios requires significant effort and very time-consuming rekeying.

Extensible Business Reporting Language (XBRL) makes financial information available in an easy-to-use format on the Internet. Formerly code named XFRML, a freely available electronic language for financial reporting, it is an XML-based framework that provides the financial community with a standards-based method to prepare, publish in a variety of formats, reliably extract, and automatically exchange financial statements of publicly held companies and the information they contain. XBRL is not about establishing new accounting standards but enhancing the usability of the ones that we have through the digital language of business. XBRL does not require additional disclosure from companies to outside audiences. This new language allows the financial community to communicate in a universal language.

How Companies Create XBRL Statements

Accounting software vendors put XBRL tags in their accounting systems to allow users to cross-reference their accounts to this framework, enabling a more efficient reporting process and a more meaningful experience for the users of financial information. Some of the most popular accounting software companies have already announced their plans to provide XBRL output in financial statements. The list includes SAP, Oracle, Great Plains, and ACCPAC. There are more than 50 companies in the United States and about 150 companies globally involved in the development and adoption of XBRL. On March 5, 2002, Microsoft became the first major corporation to publish its financial statements on the Internet using the XBRL framework.

Applications of XBRL

There are many accounting, financial, and business applications of XBRL including:

- Automating business reporting.
- Financial statement preparation and analysis. For example, XBRL financial statements on a company's Web site can go directly into Microsoft Excel so that rekeying is not required.
- Auditing of financial statements.
- Managing and distributing accounting data.
- Consolidating and reporting data to regulatory bodies.
- Collecting and updating financial data on borrowers such as by accessing the borrower's Web page.
- Assessing credit risk.
- Integrating investment information.
- Communicating financial performance to users of financial statements.
- Internal management reporting such as cost control and analysis.

There are several very useful XBRL products for accountants such as *Pricewaterhouse Cooper's Edgar Scan,* which is an interface to SEC EDGAR filings. Edgar Scan takes filings from the SEC's servers and breaks them down automatically to find key financial tables and standardizes financials to a common format for all companies. Using hyperlinks, users of financial reports can access specific sections of the filing including the financial statements, footnotes, extracted financial information, and relevant financial ratios. Tables of financial information and comparisons can be downloaded as Excel charts. Edgar Scan's XBRL Query Service converts extracted SEC filing information into XBRL instances. This HTTP service makes XBRL data available for in excess of 500 of the largest U.S. businesses. Financial statement preparers and users can request the XBRL data on these companies or other information about this product from Pricewaterhouse Coopers at http://edgarscan.pwcglobal.com/XBRL or e-mail edgar@uspwcglobal.com.

XBRL-enabled applications include the following:

- Federal Deposit Insurance Corporation's (FDIC) new *Call Report System*, XBRL based.
- One Source Information Services (www.onesource.com) is the first provider to deliver a fully NET-enabled Web service for XBRL information on U.S. companies.
- The Tokyo Stock Exchange accepts company financial summary filings in XBRL.

XBRL vendors include Decision Soft (http://xbrl.decisionsoft.com), Semansys Technologies (www.semansys.com), Universal Business's Matrix (http://www.ubmatrix.com), Navision (www.navision.com), Hyperion Solutions (www.hyperion.com), Corel (www.corel.com), Oracle (www.oracle.com), SAP (www.sap.com), CaseWare International (www.caseware.com), People Soft (www.peoplesoft.com), SYSPRO (www.syspro.com), Creative Solutions (www.creativesolutions.com), ACCPAC (www.accpac.com), and XBI Software (www.xbisoftware.com).

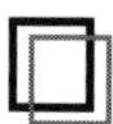

VALUE-CHAIN MANAGEMENT SOFTWARE

Firms employ a wide variety of software systems to process information and improve the operation of the value chain. They are enterprise resource planning (ERP) systems, supply-chain management (SCM) systems, and customer relationship management (CRM) systems.

Enterprise Resource Planning (ERP) Systems

Enterprise resource planning (ERP) systems grew out of material requirements planning (MRP) systems that have been used for more than 20 years. MRP systems computerize inventory control and production planning. Key features include an ability to prepare a master production schedule, a bill of materials, and purchase orders. ERP systems update MRP systems with better integration, relational databases, and graphical user interfaces. Features now encompass supporting accounting and finance, human resources, and various e-commerce applications including SCM and CRM.

Are you faced with the challenge of selecting an ERP application? It's a time-consuming process for IT/IS managers to assess application vendors, then compare what they are offering to what the organization needs. We've designed these lists to expedite the process and to help ensure that you touch all the bases as you investigate each vendor.

DATABASE AND NETWORK

- How many user licenses are required?
- Is the ERP designed to work with different RDBMSs (relational database management systems) such as Oracle, Sybase, and Informix?
- Does the vendor have any built-in programs to handle integration?
- How will the data warehousing aspects be addressed?
- What is the maximum time it takes for uploading the remote data?
- What is the minimum time it takes for uploading the remote data?
- Does the software support distributed data processing?
- Does the software support a parallel processing option?
- Has the vendor had any problems in the past regarding concurrency?
- Does the software have an audit trail on key transactions?
- How many security layers have been incorporated into the software?
- What kind of networking protocols does the software support?
- Does the software support various data types such as BLOB (*B*inary *l*arge *ob*ject)?
- What is the largest database the vendor has handled so far for the modules you're interested in?
- What is the smallest database handled by the vendor so far for the modules you're interested in?

IMPLEMENTATION

- Has the vendor implemented sites in this region?
- Has the vendor implemented ERP in your industry segment?
- Has the vendor implemented the same modules that your organization needs?
- Will there be immediate delivery of the product?
- Does the vendor have a specific implementation plan?
- How long did it take for the vendor to implement the same modules elsewhere?
- How many years of experience does the vendor have with implementation?
- Does the vendor have good project plan initiatives?
- Does the vendor have a good implementation team with the required skills?

- Does the vendor have the certification of excellence given by other customers?
- What is the minimum implementation time for the modules you've chosen?
- What is the maximum implementation time for the modules you've chosen?

BUSINESS PROCESSES

- Does the vendor promise any reduction in lead times of those business processes in which you have some interest?
- What is the minimum processing time for MRP (material requirement planning)?
- What is the maximum processing time for MRP?
- What is the minimum processing time for MPS (master production schedule)?
- What is the maximum processing time for MPS?
- Does the software optimize the business processes after implementation?
- Does the software use a built-in business process modeler?

HARDWARE AND SOFTWARE

- What kind of hardware support does the vendor offer?
- How many years of experience does the vendor have with the hardware/software that will be used for your project?
- Who are the alliance partners for the hardware support?
- What is the upgrade support for the software?
- Does the software have any interface to support the latest technology?
- How is the vendor maintaining the documentation for the software?
- Is the software Web enabled?
- Will the software be implemented in modules?
- Will the software be purchased in modules?
- Will the software accounting adhere to international standards and to each country's standards?
- How many operating systems does the software support?
- Does the software allow posting of transactions both in batch mode and online?
- Does the software support multilingual operation?

SUPPORT

- What support will the vendor provide after implementation?
- If the vendor is not in your country, how is support provided?

- How much time will the vendor devote to ERP training for end users?
- Describe the UI (user interface)/GUI (graphical user interface) package support and how each will give end users ease of operation.
- Did the vendor complete any customization at any previously implemented sites? (Describe by percentage and modules.)
- How will the vendor complete report customization?
- Does the software have any built-in programs to handle data conversions?
- Is the front-end application developed using proprietary software?
- Is the customization cost included in the ERP cost?
- Can the vendor give approval for accessing other customers' data?
- Does the vendor have any test data built into the software for proper training?
- If any bugs are found in the software during or after implementation, what is the replacement support?
- Is the vendor ready to work with third-party tools and software?

Supply-Chain Management (SCM) Systems

Supply-chain management (SCM) is the organization of activities between a company and its suppliers in an effort to provide for the profitable development, production, and delivery of goods to customers. By sharing information, production lead times and inventory holding costs have been reduced, while on-time deliveries to customers have been improved. SCM software systems support the planning of the best way to fill orders and help tracking of products and components among companies in the supply chain. Wal-Mart and Procter & Gamble (P&G) are two companies that have become well known for their cooperation in the use of SCM. When P&G products are scanned at a Wal-Mart store, P&G receives information on the sale via satellite and thus knows when to make more product and the specific Wal-Mart stores to which the product should be shipped. Related cost savings are passed on, at least in part, to Wal-Mart customers.

Customer Relationship Management Systems (CRM)

Customer relationship management (CRM) systems automate customer service and support. They also provide for customer data analysis and support e-commerce storefronts. While CRM is constantly evolving, it has already led to some remarkable changes in the way companies interact with customers. For example, Federal Express allows customers to track their packages on the Web. This service is becoming commonplace, but it did not exist 10 years ago. Amazon.com uses CRM technology to make suggestions to customers based on their personal purchase histories. The ultimate development of CRM remains to be seen, but undoubtedly mobile communication will play a significant role. Many companies are already experimenting with systems to send messages to cell phone users that offer them special discounts and buying opportunities.

CRM systems are designed to manage all the data related to customers such as marketing, field service, and contact management data. Over the course of the past year, CRM has become the primary focus of IS managers and CIOs responsible for prioritizing new systems acquisitions. CRM has also become the focus of ERP vendors who realize the need to tap into this growing market and to integrate CRM data with the other data already residing within the ERP system's database.

The concept behind CRM is that better customer service means happier customers and greater sales, particularly repeat sales. Part of the service concept is field service support and contact management. Contact management facilitates the recording and storing of information related to each contact a salesperson has with a client and the context of the conversation or meeting. Additionally, each time the client makes contact regarding queries or service help, this information is also recorded. The result is that a salesperson can review all the historical information before calling on a customer and can be better prepared to provide that customer with targeted products and services. These systems also support the recording information about the customer contact such as spouse's name, children, hobbies, and so on, facilitating the salesperson in making quality contact with the customer.

At the same time, the software supports the organizing and retrieving of information on historical sales activities and promotions planning. This facilitates the matching of sales promotions with customers' buying trends. It is a particularly crucial area for integration with any existing ERP system because much of the information necessary to support sales analyses comes from the recording of sales event data in the ERP system.

A third area that is prevalent in CRMs is support for customer service, particularly for phone operators handling customer support call-in centers. For many organizations, phone operators who have not had previous contact with the customer handle the bulk of customer service activities. The CRM quickly provides the phone operator with the information on the customer's history and usually links the operator with a database of solutions for various problems that a customer may be inquiring about. These solutions may simply be warranty or contract information, or at a more complex level, solutions to operations or maintenance problems on machinery or equipment. All this information can be efficiently stored for quick retrieval by the system's user.

Note: In today's mobile environment, phones, PDAs, and other devices will be connected by a variety of wireless technologies and will become mandatory for corporate communications with customers and employees. Mobile applications provide opportunities to interact with customers in new ways, in new places, and at new times. Adding mobility and immediacy to an application can be powerful: It offers the potential for new products and services, business process improvements, cost savings, and improved response times. A list of CRM software providers can be found in Appendix B.

COMPLIANCE SOFTWARE

In July 2002, the U.S. Congress passed the *Sarbanes-Oxley Act,* the most significant change to U.S. business regulations in 70 years. The act creates tough new penalties for corporate fraud, prevents accounting firms from offering consulting services to audit clients, and places restrictions on financial analysts. Section 404 (Management Assessment of Internal Controls) requires each annual report of an issuer to contain an internal control report that shall:

1. State the responsibility of management for establishing and maintaining an adequate internal control structure and procedures for financial reporting; and
2. Contain an assessment, as of the end of the issuer's fiscal year, of the effectiveness of the internal control structure and procedures of the issuer for financial reporting.

Technologies That Can Assist with Compliance

Much of compliance is a matter of putting rules in place and ensuring that they are followed. Technology can provide the solutions to the corporate governance and compliance problem. It includes computer software for business intelligence, business process management, document management, e-mail management, financial and accounting software, and enterprise resource planning (ERP). Appendix A provides a guide to compliance software.

- *Business intelligence:* Regulatory requirements for real-time disclosure of factors that affect financial performance mean that executives need access to timely, relevant data from all areas of the business. By drilling down into financial and company data and providing sophisticated reporting and analysis tools, business intelligence software can help ensure the accessibility of information.

- *Business process management (BPM):* Businesses have traditionally been built around functional silos, making it difficult to share information and obtain a consistent, enterprise-wide view. By extracting business processes from the underlying application code into an independent management layer, BPM software can help improve visibility.
- *Document management:* New corporate governance standards mean that companies need an efficient system for storing and retrieving important records and documents. Software packages that maintain audit trails of documents and set controls over how, where, and for how long files are stored can help companies meet these obligations.
- *E-mail management:* As the volume of e-mail continues to soar, the logistics of storing essential e-mails and being able to retrieve them quickly becomes increasingly complex. And with new regulatory requirements around internal controls and disclosure obligations, the need for comprehensive e-mail management software becomes ever more compelling.
- *Financial and accounting software:* To help comply with new standards such as Sarbanes-Oxley, many vendors are giving their traditional financing and accounting software a boost with modules that help with risk management, more accurate budgeting and forecasting, financial analysis, and the establishment of internal financial controls.
- *Enterprise resource planning (ERP):* ERP software can give organizations a consistent financial view across all divisions, thereby helping to maintain the accuracy of financial information. Many ERP providers are adding modules to their software to assist with compliance with Sarbanes-Oxley and other corporate governance standards.

CHAPTER 11

FINANCIAL MANAGEMENT INFORMATION SYSTEMS AND PACKAGES

A FINANCIAL MANAGEMENT INFORMATION SYSTEM

Finance has been an important functional area for virtually all types of organizations. The finance area monitors cash flow and profitability. Well-conceived financial information systems are capable of providing financial managers with timely information, which is vital to success in today's competitive global economy. History has witnessed the results of poor financial decisions. Banks and savings institutions have gone into bankruptcy because of bad decisions and unfavorable economic conditions. Companies with too much debt and leverage have also gone bankrupt. On the contrary, good financial decisions have resulted in growing and prosperous organizations.

A financial management information system provides financial information to all financial information to all financial managers within an organization. Specifically, the financial MIS assists financial managers in performing their responsibilities, which include the following:

- *Financial analysis and planning:* Analyzing historical and current financial activity and determining the proper amount of funds to employ in the firm; that is, designating the size of the firm and its rate of growth.
- *Investment decisions:* Allocating funds to specific assets (things owned). The financial manager makes decisions regarding the mix and type of assets acquired, as well as modification or replacement of assets.
- *Financing and capital structure decisions:* Projecting future financial needs and raising funds on favorable terms; that is, determining the nature of the company's liabilities (obligations). For instance, should funds be obtained from short-term or long-term sources?

Inputs	Subsystems	Outputs
Strategic goals	Financial forecasting	Financial forecasts
Transaction processing system	Financial data from departments (profit/loss and costing)	Funds management
Internal accounting		Financial budget planning, and control
External sources	Financial intelligence	

Exhibit 11.1 OVERVIEW OF A FINANCIAL MIS

- *Management of financial resources:* Monitoring and controlling the use of funds over time and managing cash, receivables, and inventory to accomplish higher returns without undue risk.

Exhibit 11.1 shows the inputs, function-specific subsystems, and outputs of a financial MIS.

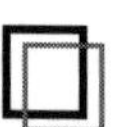

INPUTS TO THE FINANCIAL MANAGEMENT INFORMATION SYSTEM

Decisions supported by the financial MIS require diverse information needs (see Exhibit 11.1). The sources, both internal and external, are briefly discussed in the following sections.

Corporate Strategic Goals and Policies

The strategic plan covers major financial goals and targets. Earnings growth, loan ratios, and expected returns are some of the measures that can be incorporated in the strategic plan. The plan often projects financial needs three to five years down the road. More specific information needs, such as expected financing needs, the return on investment (ROI) for various projects, and desired debt-to-equity ratios, evolve directly from the strategic plan.

The Transaction Processing System

Important financial information is captured by a number of internal accounting systems. One is the order entry system, which enters the orders into the accounting system. Another is the billing system, which sends bills or invoices to customers. A third is the accounts receivable system, which collects the funds. Other key financial information is also collected from almost every transaction processing application—payroll, inventory control, accounts payable, and general ledger. Many financial reports are based on payroll costs, the investment in inventory, total sales over time, the amount of money paid to suppliers, the total amount owed to the company from customers, and detailed accounting data.

External Sources

Information from and about the competition can be critical to financial decision making. Annual reports and financial statements from competitors and general news items and reports can be incorporated into MIS reports to provide units of measure or as a basis of comparison.

Government agencies also provide important economic and financial information. Inflation, consumer price indexes, new housing starts, and leading economic indicators can help a company plan for future economic conditions. In addition, important tax laws and financial reporting requirements can also be reflected in the financial MIS.

FINANCIAL MIS SUBSYSTEMS AND OUTPUTS

Financial decisions are typically based on information generated from the accounting system. Depending on the organization and its needs, the financial MIS can include both internal and external systems that assist in acquiring, using, and controlling cash, funds, and other financial resources. The financial subsystems, discussed below, include financial forecasting, profit/loss and cost systems, and financial intelligence systems. Each subsystem interacts with the transaction processing system is a specialized, functionally oriented way and has informational outputs that assist financial managers in making better decisions. The outputs are financial forecasts, management of funds reports, financial budgets, and performance reports such as variance analysis used for control purposes.

Financial Forecasting

Financial forecasting, the process of making predictions on the future growth of products or the organization as a whole, is based on projected business activity. For example, expected sales of goods and services can be converted into expected revenues and costs. The sales price per unit and production cost factors can be multiplied by the number of units expected to be sold in order to arrive at a forecasted value for revenues and costs. Fixed costs, such as insurance, rent, and office overhead, are estimated and used to determine expected net profits on a monthly, quarterly, or yearly basis. These estimates are then incorporated into the financial MIS. The financial forecasting subsystem relies on input from another functional subsystem (namely, the marketing forecasting system) to determine projected revenues.

Having an estimate of future cash flows can be one of the first steps for sound financial management. Financial managers and executives use this valuable information to project future cash needs. For instance, an organization's managers will know in advance that in some months additional cash might be required, whereas in other months excess cash will have to be invested. Improperly managed cash flow is one of the major causes of business failure and bankruptcy. Financial forecasting can help financial executives avoid cash flow problems by predicting cash flow needs.

Profit/Loss and Cost Systems

Two specialized financial functional systems are profit/loss and cost systems. Revenue and expense data for various departments is captured by the transaction processing system (TPS) and becomes a primary internal source of financial information. Many departments within an organization are profit centers, which means they track total expenses, revenues, and net profits. An investment division of a large insurance or credit card company is an example of a profit center. Other departments may be revenue centers, which are divisions within the company that primarily track sales or revenues, such as marketing or sales departments. Still other departments may be cost centers, which are divisions within a company that do not directly generate revenue, such as manufacturing or research and development. These units incur costs with little or no revenues. Data on profit, revenue, and cost centers is gathered (mostly through the TPS but sometimes through other channels as well), summarized, and reported by the financial MIS.

Financial Intelligence

Financial intelligence is responsible for gathering data and information from stockholders, the financial community, and the government. Since the financial function controls the money flow through the firm, information is needed to expedite this flow. The day-to-day flow of money—from customers to vendors—is controlled by the internal accounting subsystem. The financial intelligence subsystem is concerned with flows other than those involved in daily operations. This system seeks to identify the best sources of additional capital and the best investments of surplus funds.

Most of the information flows from the firm to the stockholders in the form of annual and quarterly reports. Stockholders have an opportunity to communicate information (complaints, suggestions, ideas, etc.) to the firm through the stockholder relations department. Also, once a year an annual stockholders' meeting is held where stockholders can learn firsthand what the firm is doing. Very often, stockholders use these meetings as an opportunity to communicate directly with top management. Information gathered informally from stockholders is seldom entered into the computerized system, but it is disseminated by verbal communication and written memos to key executives in the firm.

The relationship between the firm and the financial community also receives attention from financial management.

There should be a balanced flow of money through the firm, but this equilibrium is not always achieved. At times additional funds are needed or investments of surplus funds are desired. It is the responsibility of the financial intelligence subsystem to compile information on sources of funds and investment opportunities. An important indirect environmental effect influences this money flow through the firm. The federal government controls the money market of the country through the Federal Reserve System. There are various means of releasing the controls to expedite the money flow and of tightening the controls to reduce the flow.

The firm therefore must gather information from both financial institutions and the Federal Reserve System. This information permits the firm to remain current on national monetary policies and trends and possibly to anticipate future changes. A variety of publications can be used for this purpose. They are prepared by both the financial institutions and the government. Two examples are the *Monthly Economic Letter* prepared by the City Bank of New York and the *Federal Reserve Bulletin* prepared by the Federal Reserve System.

In addition to the need to acquire funds, the firm frequently must invest surplus funds on either a short- or long-term basis. These funds can be invested in a number of different ways—in U.S. Treasury securities, commercial paper, or certificates of deposit (CDs). Since the terms and rates of return for some of these vary over time, it is necessary to monitor these rates continually so that the optimum investment can be made when needed.

Gathering information from the financial environment is the responsibility of the financial intelligence subsystem. As with the other two functional intelligence subsystems, the information is usually handled outside the computer system. This subsystem is one area where computer use could improve.

Two major financial dailies are worth mentioning as a great source of financial intelligence: The *Wall Street Journal (WSJ)* and *Investor's Business Daily (IBD)*. The *WSJ* contains news of happenings throughout the business community. It provides especially informative descriptions of the economic environment in which businesses operate. Simply by reading a periodical such as the *WSJ*, you can keep up with many of the important environmental influences that shape a manager's decision strategy.

Each day the front page contains a "What's News" section in columns 2 and 3. The "Business and Finance" column offers a distillation of the day's major corporate, industrial, and economic news. The "World-Wide" column captures the day's domestic and international news developments. "Special Reports" appears in column 5 each day. On Monday, "The Outlook" provides an economic overview, analyzing the economy from every conceivable angle. On Tuesday, the "Labor Letter" addresses work news of all kinds—government policy, management, unions, labor relations, and personnel. Wednesday brings the "Tax Report," which alerts readers to new tax trends. The "Business Bulletin" appears each Thursday and tries to spot emerging trends. The idea is to make information available while managers can still act on it. Finally, every Friday brings the "Washington Wire," providing an interpretation of government policy and its possible impacts on business.

Published by William O'Neil & Co., Inc., *Investor's Business Daily* reports daily coverage of (1) "The Top Story"—the most important news event of the day, (2) "The Economy"—a sophisticated analysis of current economic topics and government economic reports, (3) "National Issue/Business"—a major national and business issue of our time, (4) "Leaders & Success"—profiles of successful people and companies, (5) "Investor's Corner"—coverage of a wide variety of personal finance topics including investment ideas, and (6) "Today's News Digest"—35 to 40 brief but important news items of the day.

Funds Management

Funds management is another critical function of the financial MIS. Companies that do not manage and use funds effectively produce lower profits or face possible bankruptcy. Outputs from the funds management subsystem, when combined with other aspects of the financial MIS, can locate serious cash flow problems and help the company increase returns. Internal uses of funds include additional inventory, new plants and equipment, the acquisition of other companies, new computer systems, marketing and advertising, raw materials, and investments in new products. External uses of funds are typically investment related. On occasion, a company might have excess cash from sales that is placed into an external investment. Current profitability is only one important factor in predicting corporate success; current and future cash flows are also essential. In fact, it is possible for a profitable company to have a cash crisis; for example, a company with significant credit sales but a very long collection period may show a profit without actually having the cash from those sales.

Financial managers are responsible for planning how and when cash will be used and obtained. When planned expenditures require more cash than planned activities are likely to produce, financial managers must decide what to do. They may decide to obtain debt or equity funds or to dispose of some fixed assets or a whole business segment. Alternatively, they may decide to cut back on planned activities by modifying operational plans, such as ending a special advertising campaign or delaying new acquisitions, or to revise planned payments to financing sources, such as bondholders or stockholders. Whatever is decided, the financial manager's goal is to balance the cash available and the needs for cash over both the short and the long term.

Evaluating the statement of cash flows is essential if you are to appraise accurately an entity's cash flows from operating, investing, and financing activities and its liquidity and solvency positions. Inadequacy in cash flow has possible serious implications, including declining profitability, greater financial risk, and even possible bankruptcy.

Financial management also involves decisions relating to source of financing for, and use of financial resources within, an organization. Virtually all activities and decisions within an organization are reflected in financial information. One useful application of a real-time system to financial information involves inquiry processing. An online financial information system enables immediate response to inquiries concerning comparisons of current expenditure with budgeted expenditure, up-to-date calculations of profit center contribution, or information required for audit investigation.

The fund management subsystem can prepare a report showing cash flow for the next 12-month period. The report can be printed by a mathematical model that uses the sales forecast plus expense projections as the basis for the calculation.

Another application of real-time systems to financial management that has great potential is the area of computer models for financial planning, which is discussed later.

Financial Budgeting, Planning, and Control

More and more companies are developing computer-based models for financial planning and budgeting, using powerful yet easy-to-use financial modeling languages such as *Up Your Cash Flow* (discussed in Example 11.3, later in the chapter). The models help not only build a budget for profit planning but answer a variety of what-if scenarios. The resultant calculations provide a basis for choice among alternatives under conditions of uncertainty. Furthermore, budget modeling can also be accomplished using spreadsheet programs such as *Microsoft's Excel*.

In this section we will illustrate the use of spreadsheet software such as *Excel* and stand-alone packages such as *Up Your Cash Flow* to develop a financial model. For illustrative purposes, we will present:

- Three examples of projecting an income statement
- Forecasting financial distress with Z-score
- Forecasting external financing needs—the percent-of-sales method

EXAMPLE 11.1 PROJECTING AN INCOME STATEMENT

Given:

Sales for 1st month = $60,000
Cost of sales = 42% of sales, all variable
Operating expenses = $10,000 fixed plus 5% of sales
Taxes = 30% of net income
Sales increase by 5% each month

(a) Based on this information, Exhibit 11.2 presents a spreadsheet for the contribution income statement for the next 12 months and in total.
(b) Exhibit 11.3 shows the same in assuming that sales increase by 10% and operating expenses = $10,000 plus 10% of sales. This is an example of what-if scenarios.

EXAMPLE 11.2 THREE-YEAR INCOME PROJECTION

Delta Gamma Company wishes to prepare a three-year projection of net income using the following information:

1. 2005 base year amounts are as follows:

Sales revenues	$4,500,000
Cost of sales	2,900,000
Selling and administrative expenses	800,000
Net income before taxes	800,000

2. Use the following assumptions:

- Sales revenues increase by 6% in 2006, 7% in 2007, and 8% in 2008.
- Cost of sales increase by 5% each year.
- Selling and administrative expenses increase only 1% in 2006 and will remain at the 2006 level thereafter.
- The income tax rate = 46%.

Exhibit 11.4 presents a spreadsheet for the income statement for the next three years.

EXAMPLE 11.3 DEVELOPING A BUDGET

Based on specific assumptions (see Exhibit 11.5), develop a budget using *Up Your Cash Flow* (see Exhibit 11.6).

A budget is a tool for both planning and control. At the beginning of the period, the budget is a plan or standard; at the end of the period, it serves as a control device to help management measure its performance against the plan so that future performance may be improved. Each manager with

Projected Income Statement														
	1	2	3	4	5	6	7	8	9	10	11	12	Total	Percent
Sales	$60,000	$63,000	$66,150	$69,458	$72,930	$76,577	$80,406	$84,426	$88,647	$93,080	$97,734	$102,620	$955,028	100%
Less: VC														
Cost of sales	$25,200	$26,460	$27,783	$29,172	$30,631	$32,162	$33,770	$35,459	$37,232	$39,093	$41,048	$43,101	$401,112	42%
Operating expenses	$ 3,000	$ 3,150	$ 3,308	$ 3,473	$ 3,647	$ 3,829	$ 4,020	$ 4,221	$ 4,432	$ 4,654	$ 4,887	$ 5,131	$ 47,751	5%
CM	$31,800	$33,390	$35,060	$36,812	$38,653	$40,586	$42,615	$44,746	$46,983	$49,332	$51,799	$54,389	$506,165	53%
Less: FC														
Operating expenses	$10,000	$10,000	$10,000	$10,000	$10,000	$10,000	$10,000	$10,000	$10,000	$10,000	$10,000	$10,000	$120,000	13%
Net income	$21,800	$23,390	$25,060	$26,812	$28,653	$30,586	$32,615	$34,746	$36,983	$39,332	$41,799	$44,389	$386,165	40%
Less: Tax	$ 6,540	$ 7,017	$ 7,518	$ 8,044	$ 8,596	$ 9,176	$ 9,785	$10,424	$11,095	$11,800	$12,540	$13,317	$115,849	12%
NI after tax	$15,260	$16,373	$17,542	$18,769	$20,057	$21,410	$22,831	$24,322	$25,888	$27,533	$29,259	$31,072	$270,315	28%

Exhibit 11.2 PROJECTED INCOME STATEMENT

Projected Income Statement

Sales	$60,000	$66,000	$72,600	$79,860	$87,846	$96,631	$106,294	$116,923	$128,615	$141,477	$155,625	$171,187	$1,283,057	100%
Less: VC														
Cost of sales	$25,200	$27,720	$30,492	$33,541	$36,895	$40,585	$ 44,643	$4 9,108	$ 54,018	$ 59,420	$ 65,362	$ 71,899	$ 538,884	42%
Operating expenses	$ 6,000	$ 6,600	$ 7,260	$ 7,986	$ 8,785	$ 9,663	$ 10,629	$ 11,692	$ 12,862	$ 14,148	$ 15,562	$ 17,119	$ 64,153	5%
CM	$28,800	$31,680	$34,848	$38,333	$42,166	$46,383	$ 51,021	$ 56,123	$ 61,735	$ 67,909	$ 74,700	$ 82,170	$ 615,867	48%
Less: FC														
Operating expenses	$10,000	$10,000	$10,000	$10,000	$10,000	$10,000	$ 10,000	$ 10,000	$ 10,000	$ 10,000	$ 10,000	$ 10,000	$ 120,000	9%
Net income	$18,800	$21,680	$24,848	$28,333	$32,166	$36,383	$ 41,021	$ 46,123	$ 51,735	$ 57,909	$ 64,700	$ 72,170	$ 495,867	39%
Less: Tax	$ 5,640	$ 6,504	$ 7,454	$ 8,500	$ 9,650	$10,915	$ 12,306	$ 13,837	$ 15,521	$ 17,373	$ 19,410	$ 21,651	$ 148,760	12%
NI after tax	$13,160	$15,176	$17,394	$19,833	$22,516	$25,468	$ 28,715	$ 32,286	$ 36,215	$ 40,536	$ 45,290	$ 50,519	$ 347,107	27%

Exhibit 11.3 PROJECTED INCOME STATEMENT

DELTA GAMMA COMPANY THREE-YEAR INCOME PROJECTIONS (2005–2008)				
	2005	**2006**	**2007**	**2008**
Sales	$4,500,000	$4,770,000	$5,103,900	$5,512,212
Cost of sales	$2,900,000	$3,045,000	$3,197,250	$3,357,113
Gross profit	$1,600,000	$1,725,000	$1,906,650	$2,155,100
Selling & adm. exp.	$ 800,000	$ 808,000	$ 808,000	$ 808,000
Earnings before tax	$ 800,000	$ 917,000	$1,098,650	$1,347,100
Tax	$ 368,000	$ 421,820	$ 505,379	$ 619,666
Earnings after tax	$ 432,000	$ 495,180	$ 593,271	$ 727,434

Exhibit 11.4 PROJECTED INCOME STATEMENT

Category	**Assumptions**
Sales:	alternative 1 from Book up your cash flow
Cost of goods sold:	Use 45% of sales
Advertising:	59% of sales
Automobile:	Company has 4 autos @ 1,500 each 4 × 1,500 = –6,000 ÷ 12 = 1,500 per month
Bad debts:	Maintain @ 29% of sales – I hope
Business promotion:	Prior year was $65,000. 10% increase equals $71,500 ÷ 12
Collection costs:	Use 1,000 per month
Continuing education:	$10,000 for year = ÷ 12
Depreciation:	$84,000 for year - use 7,000 per month
Donations:	$10,000 for year = ÷ 12
Insurance-general:	agent said $24,000, use 2,000 per month
Insurance-group:	15 employees @ 1,500 ea. = 22,500 ÷ 12 = month
Insurance-life:	600 per month
Interest:	expect to borrow 250 m @ 15% = 37,500 ÷ 12 = 3,125 per month + other borrowings
Office supplies:	2% of sales - and keep it there please!
Rent:	4,000 per month
Repairs and maintenance:	Use 400 per month
Salaries:	Schedule the payroll per month
Taxes and license:	Prior year was 1.5% of sales, use same this year.
Taxes, payroll:	20% of monthly payroll
Telephone-utilities:	$29,000 last year. Use 33,000 ÷ 12 Travel - use $1,000 per month.

Exhibit 11.5 BUDGET ASSUMPTION

	Jan.	Feb.	Mar.	Apr.	May	June	July	Aug.	Sept.	Oct.	Nov.	Dec.	Total
Sales	$129,030	$129,030	$129,030	$129,030	$192,610	$192,610	$162,690	$129,030	$192,610	$129,030	$162,690	$192,610	$1,870,000
Cost of sales @ 45%	58,063	58,063	58,063	58,063	86,675	86,675	73,211	58,063	86,675	58,063	73,211	86,675	841,500
Gross profit	70,967	70,967	70,967	70,967	105,935	105,935	89,479	70,967	105,935	70,967	89,479	105,935	1,028,500
Advertising @ 5%	6,450	6,450	6,450	6,450	9,600	9,600	8,100	6,450	9,600	6,450	8,100	10,050	93,750
Automobile	500	500	500	500	500	500	500	500	500	500	500	500	6,000
Bad debts @ 2%	2,580	2,580	2,580	2,580	3,840	3,840	3,240	2,580	3,840	2,580	3,240	3,920	37,400
Business promotions	5,958	5,958	5,958	5,958	5,958	5,958	5,958	5,958	5,958	5,958	5,958	5,962	71,500
Collection costs	1,000	1,000	1,000	1,000	1,000	1,000	1,000	1,000	1,000	1,000	1,000	1,000	12,000
Continuing education	1,000	1,000	1,000	1,000	1,000	1,000	1,000	1,000	1,000	1,000	1,000	1,000	12,000
Depreciation	7,000	7,000	7,000	7,000	7,000	7,000	7,000	7,000	7,000	7,000	7,000	7,000	84,000
Donations		833	833	833	833	833	833	833	833	833	833	837	10,000
Dues & subscriptions	833	833	833	833	833	833	833	833	833	833	833	837	10,000
Insurance—general	2,000	2,000	2,000	2,000	2,000	2,000	2,000	2,000	2,000	2,000	2,000	2,000	24,000

Exhibit 11.6 BUDGETED PROFIT AND LOSS

	Jan.	Feb.	Mar.	Apr.	May	June	July	Aug.	Sept.	Oct.	Nov.	Dec.	Total
Insurance—group	1,875	1,875	1,875	1,875	1,875	1,875	1,875	1,875	1,875	1,875	1,875	1,875	22,500
Insurance—life	600	600	600	600	600	600	600	600	600	600	600	600	7,200
Interest	3,125	3,125	3,125	3,125	4,375	4,375	4,375	4,450	4,450	4,450	4,450	4,450	47,875
Legal & accounting	1,000	1,000	1,000	1,000	1,000	1,000	1,000	1,000	1,000	1,000	1,000	1,000	12,000
Office supplies @ 2%	2,580	2,580	2,580	2,580	3,840	3,840	3,240	2,580	3,840	2,580	3,240	3,920	37,400
Rent	4,000	4,000	4,000	4,000	4,000	4,000	4,000	4,000	4,000	4,000	4,000	4,000	48,000
Repairs	400	400	400	400	400	400	400	400	400	400	400	400	4,800
Salaries	21,000	21,000	21,000	21,000	21,000	21,000	24,833	24,833	24,833	24,833	24,833	24,835	275,000
Taxes & license @ 1.5%	1,935	1,935	1,935	1,935	2,880	2,880	2,430	1,935	2,880	1,935	2,430	2,890	28,000
Taxes, payroll	4,200	4,200	4,200	4,200	4,200	4,200	4,966	4,966	4,966	4,966	4,966	4,970	55,000
Telephone—utilities	2,750	2,750	2,750	2,750	2,750	2,750	2,750	2,750	2,750	2,750	2,750	2,750	33,000
Travel	1,000	1,000	1,000	1,000	1,000	1,000	1,000	1,000	1,000	1,000	1,000	1,000	12,000
Profit	$(1,652)	$(1,652)	$(1,652)	$(1,652)	$25,451	$25,451	$7,546	$(7,576)	$20,777	$(7,576)	$7,471	$20,139	$85,075

Exhibit 11.6 BUDGETED PROFIT AND LOSS *(continued)*

budget responsibilities receives a monthly report showing actual expenditures compared with the budget and figures and appropriate variances so that unusual variances can be addressed and properly rewarded or penalized.

In addition to the budget, the financial control system generates a number of performance measures or ratios that enable managers on all levels to compare their performance with benchmarks such as standards or targets. There are quite a few financial or operational ratios. A couple of ratios are given as an example. One popular ratio is the current ratio, which measures a firm's ability to pay short-term bills.

$$\text{Current} = \left(\frac{\text{Current assets}}{\text{Current liabilities}}\right)$$

Another popular ratio is the debt ratio, which reveals the amount of money a company owes to its creditors. Excessive debt means greater risk to the company. The debt ratio is:

$$\text{Debt ratio} = \frac{\text{Total liabilities}}{\text{Total assets}}$$

FORECASTING FINANCIAL DISTRESS WITH Z-SCORE

There has recently been an increasing number of bankruptcies. Will your company go bankrupt? Will your major customers or suppliers go bankrupt? What warning signs exist and what can be done to avoid corporate failure?

How to Use Prediction Models

Prediction models can help in a number of ways: In merger analysis, they can help to identify potential problems with a merger candidate. Bankers and other business concerns can use them to determine whether to give a new loan (credit) or extend the old one. Investors can use them to screen out stocks of companies that are potentially risky. Internal auditors can use prediction models to assess the financial health of the company. Those investing in or extending credit to a company may sue for losses incurred. The model can help as evidence in a lawsuit.

Financial managers, investment bankers, financial analysts, security analysts, and auditors have been using early warning systems to detect the likelihood of bankruptcy. But their system is primarily based on financial ratios of one type or the other as an indication of financial strength of a company. Each ratio (or set of ratios) is examined independent of others. Plus, it is up to the professional judgment of a financial analyst to decide what the ratios are really telling.

To overcome the shortcomings of financial ratio analysis, it is necessary to combine mutually exclusive ratios into a group to develop a meaningful predictive model. Regression analysis and multiple discriminant analysis (MDA) are two statistical techniques that have been used thus far.

Z-Score Model

This section describes the Z-score predictive model, which uses a combination of several financial ratios to predict the likelihood of future bankruptcy. If business failure is predicted, management may take corrective steps to prevent it. Edward Altman developed a bankruptcy prediction model that produces a Z-score as follows:

$$Z = 1.2*X1 + 1.4*X2 + 3.3*X3 + 0.6*X4 + 0.999*X5$$

where

X1 = Working capital/Total assets
X2 = Retained earnings/Total assets
X3 = Earnings before interest and taxes (EBIT)/Total assets
X4 = Market value of equity/Book value of debt (Net worth for privately held firms)
X5 = Sales/Total assets

Altman established the following guideline for classifying firms:

Z-score	Probability of failure
1.8 or less	Very high
3.0 or higher	Unlikely
1.81–2.99	Not sure

The Z-score is known to be about 90% accurate in forecasting business failure one year in the future and about 80% accurate in forecasting it two years in the future. There are more updated versions of Edward Altman's model such as the ZETA model.

Example 11.4 Altman's Bankruptcy Prediction Model

Navistar International (formerly International Harvester), the maker of heavy-duty trucks, diesel engines, and school buses, continues to struggle. Exhibit 11.7 shows the 23-year financial history and the Z-scores of Navistar. Exhibit 11.8 presents the corresponding graph.

The graph shows that Navistar International performed at the edge of the ignorance zone ("unsure area") for the year 1981. Since 1982, though, the company started signaling a sign of failure. However, by selling stock and assets, the firm managed to survive. Since 1985, the company showed an improvement in its

EXAMPLE 11.4 ALTMAN'S BANKRUPTCY PREDICTION MODEL *(continued)*

Z-scores, although the firm continually scored in the danger zone. Note that the 1991–2003 Z-scores are in the high-probability range of <1.81, except the year 1999. In late 2004, the company was in talks with truck component makers in India about sourcing components in a bid to cut manufacturing costs.

More Applications of the Z-Score

Various groups of business people can take advantage of this tool for their own purposes. For example,

- *Merger analysis:* The Z-score can help identify potential problems with a merger candidate.
- *Loan credit analysis:* Bankers and lenders can use it to determine if they should extend a loan. Other creditors such as vendors have used it to determine whether to extend credit.
- *Investment analysis:* The Z-score model can help an investor in selecting stocks of potentially troubled companies.
- *Auditing analysis:* Internal auditors are able to use this technique to assess whether the company will continue as a going concern.
- *Legal analysis:* Those investing or giving credit to your company may sue for losses incurred. The Z-score can help in your company's defense.

Words of Caution

The Z-score offers an excellent measure for predicting a firm's insolvency. But, like any other tool, you must use it with care and skill. The Z-score of a firm should be looked upon not for just one or two years but for a number of years. Also, it should not be used as a sole basis of evaluation.

The Z-score can also be used to compare the economic health of different firms. Here again, extreme care should be exercised. Firms to be compared must belong to the same market. Also, Z-scores of the same periods are to be compared. For further reference, see Kyd, Charles W., "Forecasting Bankruptcy with Z Scores." *Lotus,* September 1985, pp. 43–47; and Shim, Jae K., "Bankruptcy Prediction: Do It Yourself," *Journal of Business Forecasting,* Winter 1992.

Balance Sheet						Income Statement			Stock Data	Calculations						Misc. Graph Values	
Year	Current Assets (CA)	Total Assets (TA)	Current Liability (CL)	Total Liability (TL)	Retained Earnings (RE)	Working Capital (WC)	Sales	EBIT	Market Value or Net Worth (MKT-NW)	WC/TA (X1)	RE/TA (X2)	EBIT/TA (X3)	MKT-NW/TL (X4)	SALES /TA (X5)	Z-Score	Top GRAY	BOTTOM GRAY
1981	2672	5346	1808	3864	600	864	7018	-16	376	0.1616	0.1122	-0.0030	0.0973	1.3128	1.71	2.99	1.81
1982	1656	3699	1135	3665	-1078	521	4322	-1274	151	0.1408	-0.2914	-0.3444	0.0412	1.1684	-0.18	2.99	1.81
1983	1388	3362	1367	3119	-1487	21	3600	-231	835	0.0062	-0.4423	-0.0687	0.2677	1.0708	0.39	2.99	1.81
1984	1412	3249	1257	2947	-1537	155	4861	120	575	0.0477	-0.4731	0.0369	0.1951	1.4962	1.13	2.99	1.81
1985	1101	2406	988	2364	-1894	113	3508	247	570	0.0470	-0.7872	0.1027	0.2411	1.4580	0.89	2.99	1.81
1986	698	1925	797	1809	-1889	-99	3357	163	441	-0.0514	-0.9813	0.0847	0.2438	1.7439	0.73	2.99	1.81
1987	785	1902	836	1259	-1743	-51	3530	219	1011	-0.0268	-0.9164	0.1151	0.8030	1.8559	1.40	2.99	1.81
1988	1280	4037	1126	1580	150	154	4082	451	1016	0.0381	0.0372	0.1117	0.6430	1.0111	1.86	2.99	1.81
1989	986	3609	761	1257	175	225	4241	303	1269	0.0623	0.0485	0.0840	1.0095	1.1751	2.20	2.99	1.81
1990	2663	3795	1579	2980	81	1084	3854	111	563	0.2856	0.0213	0.0292	0.1889	1.0155	1.60	2.99	1.81
1991	2286	3443	1145	2866	332	1141	3259	232	667	0.3314	0.0964	0.0674	0.2326	0.9466	1.84	2.99	1.81
1992	2472	3627	1152	3289	93	1320	3875	-145	572	0.3639	0.0256	-0.0400	0.1738	1.0684	1.51	2.99	1.81

Exhibit 11.7 NAVISTAR INTERNATIONAL—NAV (NYSE) Z-SCORE—PREDICTION OF FINANCIAL DISTRESS

Balance Sheet						Income Statement			Stock Data	Calculations						Misc. Graph Values	
Year	Current Assets (CA)	Total Assets (TA)	Current Liability (CL)	Total Liability (TL)	Retained Earnings (RE)	Working Capital (WC)	Sales	EBIT	Market Value or Net Worth (MKT-NW)	WC/TA (X1)	RE/TA (X2)	EBIT/TA (X3)	MKT-NW/TL (X4)	SALES /TA (X5)	Z-Score	Top GRAY	BOTTOM GRAY
1993	2672	5060	1338	4285	-1588	1334	4696	-441	1765	0.2636	-0.3138	-0.0872	0.4119	0.9281	0.76	2.99	1.81
1994	2870	5056	1810	4239	-1538	1060	5337	233	1469	0.2097	-0.3042	0.0461	0.3466	1.0556	1.24	2.99	1.81
1995	3310	5566	1111	4696	-1478	2199	6342	349	966	0.3951	-0.2655	0.0627	0.2057	1.1394	1.57	2.99	1.81
1996	2999	5326	820	4410	-1431	2179	5754	188	738	0.4091	-0.2687	0.0353	0.1673	1.0804	1.41	2.99	1.81
1997	3203	5516	2416	4496	-1301	787	6371	316	1374	0.1427	-0.2359	0.0573	0.3055	1.1550	1.37	2.99	1.81
1998	3715	6178	3395	5409	-1160	320	7885	515	1995	0.0518	-0.1878	0.0834	0.3688	1.2763	1.57	2.99	1.81
1999	3203	5516	2416	4496	-1301	787	8642	726	2494	0.1427	-0.2359	0.1316	0.5547	1.5667	2.17	2.99	1.81
2000	2374	6851	2315	5409	-143	59	8451	370	2257	0.0086	-0.0209	0.0540	0.4173	1.2335	1.64	2.99	1.81
2001	2778	7164	2273	6037	-170	505	6739	162	2139	0.0705	-0.0237	0.0226	0.3543	0.9407	1.28	2.99	1.81
2002	2607	6957	2407	6706	-721	200	6784	-89	2146	0.0287	-0.1036	-0.0128	0.3200	0.9751	1.01	2.99	1.81
2003	2210	6900	2204	6590	-824	6	7340	149	2118	0.0009	-0.1194	0.0216	0.3214	1.0638	1.16	2.99	1.81

(1) To calculate Z-score for private firms, enter Net Worth in the MKT-NW column. (For public-held companies, enter Markey Value of Equity.)

(2) EBIT = Earnings before Interest and Taxes.

Exhibit 11.7 NAVISTAR INTERNATIONAL—NAV (NYSE) Z-SCORE—PREDICTION OF FINANCIAL DISTRESS *(continued)*

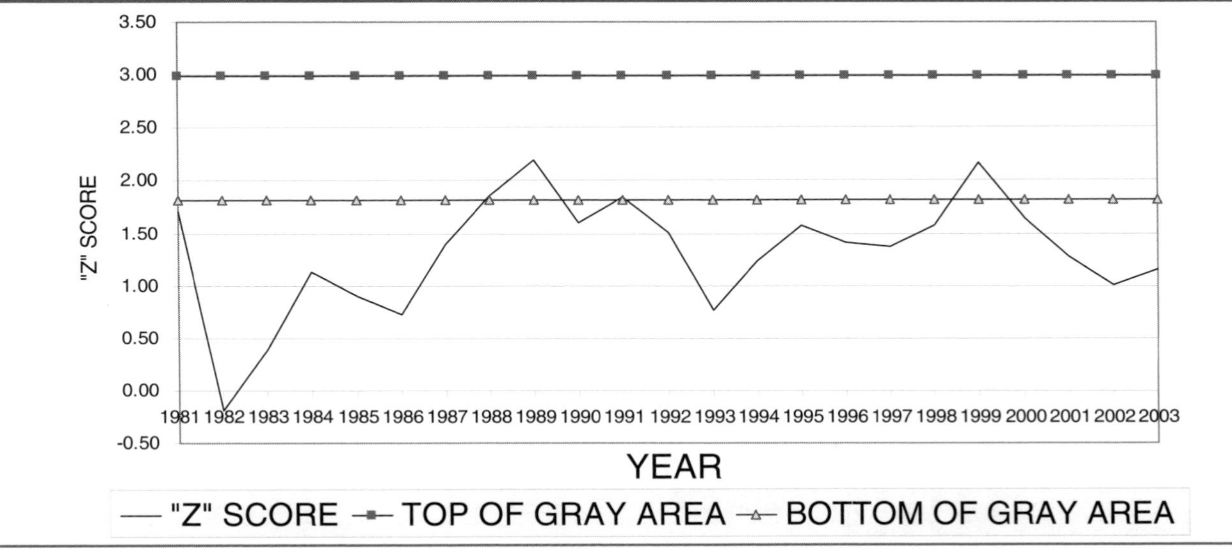

Exhibit 11.8 "Z" Score Graph (Navistar)

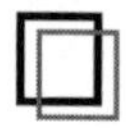

FORECASTING EXTERNAL FINANCING NEEDS—THE PERCENT-OF-SALES METHOD

Percentage of sales is the most widely used method for projecting the company's financing needs. Financial officers need to determine the next year's fund requirements, the portion of which has to be raised externally. This way they can have a head start for arranging a least-cost financing plan.

This method involves estimating the various expenses, assets, and liabilities for a future period as a percent of the sales forecast, then using these percentages, together with the projected sales, to construct pro forma balance sheets.

Basically, forecasts of future sales and their related expenses provide the firm with the information needed to project its future needs for financing. The basic steps in projecting financing needs are:

1. Project the firm's sales. The sales forecast is the initial most important step. Most other forecasts (budgets) follow the sales forecast.
2. Project additional variables such as expenses.
3. Estimate the level of investment in current and fixed assets that are required to support the projected sales.
4. Calculate the firm's financing needs.

Example 11.5 illustrates how to develop a pro forma balance sheet and determine the amount of external financing needed. Exhibit 11.9 presents the projected balance sheet.

	Present (20x1)	% of Sales (20x1 Sales = $20)	Projected (20x2 Sales = $24)
ASSETS			
Current assets	2	10	2.4
Fixed assets	4	20	4.8
Total assets	6		7.2
LIABILITIES AND STOCKHOLDERS' EQUITY			
Current liabilities	2	10	2.4
Long-term debt	2.5	n.a.	2.5
Total liabilities	4.5		4.9
Common stock	0.1	n.a.	0.1
Paid-in-Capital	0.2	n.a.	0.2
Retained earnings	1.2		1.92 a
Total equity	1.5		2.22

Exhibit 11.9 PROJECTED BALANCE SHEET (IN MILLIONS OF DOLLARS)

	Present (20x1)	% of Sales (20x1 Sales = $20)	Projected (20x2 Sales = $24)
Total liabilities and stockholders' equity	6	Total financing provided	7.12
		External financing needed	0.08 b
		Total	7.2

a. 20x2 retained earnings = 20x1 retained earnings + projected net income - cash dividends paid
= $1.2 + 5% ($24) - 40% [5% ($24)]
= $1.2 + $1.2 - $0.48 = $2.4 - $0.48 = $1.92

b. External financing needed = projected total assets - (projected total liabilities + projected equity)
= $7.2 - ($4.9 + $2.22) = $7.2 - $7.12 = $0.08

The major advantage of the percent-of-sales method of financial forecasting is that it is simple and inexpensive to use. To obtain a more precise projection of the firm's future financing needs, however, the preparation of a cash budget is required. One important assumption behind the use of the method is that the firm is operating at full capacity—that is, the company has no sufficient productive capacity to absorb a projected increase in sales and thus requires additional investment in assets.

Exhibit 11.9 PROJECTED BALANCE SHEET (IN MILLIONS OF DOLLARS) *(continued)*

EXAMPLE 11.5
PROJECTING FINANCING NEEDS

Assume that sales for 20X1 = $20, projected sales for 20X2 = $24, net income = 5% of sales, and the dividend payout ratio = 40%.

The steps for the computations are outlined as follows:

1. Express those balance sheet items that vary directly with sales as a percentage of sales. Any item such as long-term debt that does not vary directly with sales is designated "n.a.," or "not applicable."
2. Multiply these percentages by the 20X2 projected sales = $2.4 to obtain the projected amounts as shown in the last column.
3. Simply insert figures for long-term debt, common stock, and paid-in-capital from the 20X1 balance sheet.
4. Compute 20X2 retained earnings as shown in (b).

EXAMPLE 11.5
PROJECTING FINANCING NEEDS *(continued)*

5. Sum the asset accounts, obtaining total projected assets of $7.2, and also add the projected liabilities and equity to obtain $7.12, the total financing provided. Since liabilities and equity must total $7.2 but only $7.12 is projected, we have a shortfall of $0.08 external financing needed.

FINANCIAL MODELING LANGUAGES

Remember that financial models are essentially used to generate pro forma financial statements and financial ratios. These are the basic tools for budgeting and profit planning. Also, the financial model is a technique for risk analysis and what-if experiments. The financial model is needed for day-to-day operational and tactical decisions for immediate planning problems. For these purposes, the use of computers is essential. Spreadsheet software and computer-based financial modeling software have been developed and utilized for budgeting and planning in an effort to speed up the budgeting process and allow CFOs to investigate the effects of changes in budget assumptions and scenarios.

FINANCIAL ANALYSIS WITH SPREADSHEETS

Companies large or small, whether profit-oriented or nonprofit, employing 100 or 10,000, live or die by the extent of their powers in financial planning. There are other important contributing factors to success in business, but nothing can send a company into the abyss of Chapter 11 bankruptcy faster than a few major ill-fated financial decisions. Financial analysis is employed in an effort to be a bit more scientific about coming to a good financial decision. Questions must be asked about the company—and accurate answers found—to gain insight that will assist in determining the most prudent use of precious resources for some period in the future. The questions stem from numerous aspects of the business. Some are straightforward and easily answered: Are profits greater this year than last? Other questions are not as easily answered: Will an increase in advertising expenditures lead to increased profits? Would a price cut be more appropriate? Would some combination of the two be best?

Spreadsheet programs are ideally suited for performing financial analyses because they possess the capacity to hold and process complex formulas and functions while making modification and manipulation of one or more variables or functions an easy operation. With a micro, software, and some training and practice, you can master rather complex financial analysis techniques.

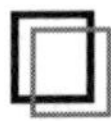

FINANCIAL RATIO ANALYSIS

Financial ratio analysis is a means of determining how well the business is performing. Problem spots can be identified, and groundwork can be established for predictions and projections of future performance. The types of questions include:

- How well is the business doing?
- What are its strengths?
- What are its weaknesses?
- How does the firm rate vis-à-vis other similar firms in the industry?

Relevant factors for consideration in critiquing the performance of the firm are:

- Profitability ratios
- Liquidity ratios
- Valuation ratios
- Efficiency of asset use
- Growth ratios
- Use of debt capital

These ratios are not necessarily useful in and of themselves. To give them relevance, the financial manager should calculate these same ratios for several different periods so that they can be compared and trends can be identified. They can also be compared to industry norms to see how the firm measures up.

The numbers with which these ratios are calculated come from the balance sheet and income statement for a given period. Simple formulas are entered onto the spreadsheet, which accesses the two financial statements (assuming that they, too, are on the spreadsheet) to obtain the pertinent figures, perform the necessary computations, and come up with the appropriate ratios. If the financial statements of the period for which ratios are being prepared are not contained on the spreadsheet, the pertinent figures can be manually entered to the appropriate spreadsheet cells with relative ease. If ratios are desired for a number of past periods for which only hard copies of their financial statements exist, the financial manager enters the figures for a period in the aforementioned manner, has the spreadsheet calculate the results, then prints the results to obtain a hard copy for later comparison. You then move on to the financial statements of the next period to be analyzed, entering those figures to the spreadsheet for computation.

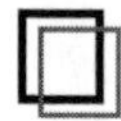

MAXIMUM VERSUS MINIMUM PROFITS

Accounting systems are human creations, and although they are usually thought of as cold and objective, they can be manipulated to arrive at different results for different purposes based on different philosophies. The most obvious example is the two ways in which accounting can be used—on the one hand to increase and maximize profits in order to look good to outsiders, while on the other hand to minimize profits for tax purposes. It is not uncommon for a company to maintain two (sometimes even more) sets of accounting records—one for each purpose.

Spreadsheets can perform many functions to assist in determination of the two different bottom lines. This includes the actual production of the two opposing income statements. Basically, any calculation you might perform on paper in arriving at the two figures can be set up and performed on the spreadsheet. Also, certain calculation routines on the spreadsheet can use figures from cells on the spreadsheet that contain the results of other calculations, thus avoiding repetitive entries. All of these numbers and computations should interact and funnel down to their appropriate final position in the different income statements.

CHOICE OF DEPRECIATION METHOD

Whenever a company purchases a depreciable asset, it must decide which depreciation method will be used to write off the value of the asset over its useful life. The chosen method depends on the objective of management: Is it the greatest possible tax relief in the current period or the largest bottom line profit possible? The lowest possible tax liability in the near term is the most common objective when choosing a depreciation method for tax purposes. Depreciation methods are as follows:

- Straight-line depreciation
- Accelerated depreciation
- Modified accelerated cost recovery system (MACRS)
- Production basis depreciation

It is up to the firm to determine its motives and establish objectives in deciding on a depreciation method. Whatever they are, the spreadsheet can play an important and useful role in the decision process—a role that will not be altered by the motives. The idea is to determine which method best produces the results. The following are required:

- Cost of the asset
- Estimation of the asset's postuseful life salvage value
- IRS guidelines on the asset's useful life (found in IRS publication number 534)
- IRS guidelines on MACRS

The spreadsheet is used to compute projections for certain elements of the income statement and income tax return. Based on these projections, the appropriate depreciation method can be determined. The projections should include:

- Depreciation expense
- Income before taxes
- Income tax
- Net income

PLANNING AND FORECASTING

Once you enter the realm of the future for the business through forecasting and planning, the power of a spreadsheet or integrated program can really pay off. Performing repeated what-if calculations is the essence of forecasting—and the electronic worksheet's specialty. Possible planning and forecasting questions include:

- What will the projected profit and cash flows be, based on current operational plans?
- If the financial manager proceeds with present plans, how will it affect the company's current and fixed assets?
- What levels of expenditures are needed to increase current and fixed assets?
- What will be the additional cash requirements of the business if present plans are followed?
- What is the break-even point?
- In what areas is the firm strong and how can such strengths be maximized?
- Where is the company weak and what can be done to improve?
- What are what-if scenarios and their impact on profit, break-even point, cash flow, assets required, return on assets, funding required, working capital, etc.?

In performing ratio analysis, you scrutinize historical data to gain insight on things that have already occurred. In forecasting and planning, however, you are creating a picture of future events if present plans are followed; you predict how future financial statements will appear.

Before embarking on this process, work with the staff to develop the best guesses possible about future market conditions, market share, net sales, and so forth. These predictions are combined with present conditions to create a model on the spreadsheet for future company performance. The methods are rather straightforward and easy to master. For example, one part of the spreadsheet would multiply current net sales by the estimated percentage of market sales increase (or decrease) to arrive at next year's projected net sales. Running the program again at this point would yield projected net sales for year 2 of the forecast (or perhaps the formula could be set up to automatically provide projected net sales in year 5 immediately, etc.); changes in the firm's market share would also be programmed in if they were anticipated.

SHORT-TERM DECISIONS

The short-term decisions that businesses make are usually more or less involved with working capital. The types of issues addressed include:

- What is a safe minimum cash balance for the firm?
- How much does the cash flow fluctuate seasonally?
- When do these seasonal fluctuations occur?
- What are the temporary seasonal working capital borrowing requirements versus borrowing for more permanent items?
- How much should your company borrow to increase inventory?
- When is the best time for this borrowing to occur?
- When is the best time to pay it back?
- What is the cost of capital?
- What would be the effect on revenues and profit of a change in the firm's credit terms?
- What is the amount lost if the company does not avail itself of all discounts offered by suppliers for expeditious payment?

The following financial ratios are useful in determining the status of the firm and in rating the financial manager's working capital decisions:

- Current ratio
- Quick ratio
- Net working capital
- Accounts receivable turnover
- Inventory turnover
- Sales to working capital
- Sales to fixed assets

The computations of these ratios are easily set up and performed on a spreadsheet program. A spreadsheet can also be used to generate a cash budget for determining the requirements, timing, and character of cash sought; and for analyzing the effects of credit terms as a component of the marketing mix through analysis of the following factors:

- Present sales
- Change in sales attributable to changes in credit terms
- Gross margin
- Potential effect on bad debts
- Credit terms on increase in sales
- Cost of short-term borrowing

Spreadsheets are also ideal for calculating interest received or extended in any of various credit situations, such as past due accounts receivable and missed discounts.

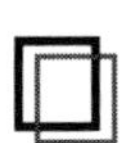

LONG-TERM ASSET DECISIONS

Long-term asset decisions by their very nature are encountered less frequently than the types of working capital decisions previously discussed. Issues include:

- Does this particular fixed-asset purchase decision make sense and seem appropriate?
- Which of several proposals seem the most advantageous?
- Should the firm buy this item at all, or would it be better to make it?
- Based on several proposals, which should be the priority purchase if funds are limited?

Spreadsheet programs can be very helpful in answering these types of questions. One of their most useful abilities in this particular area is that of calculating present values (or the time value of money). They all have the net present value (NPV) function built in for convenience and efficiency. By calculating the NPV of two or more long-term fixed-asset options, the more advantageous option becomes evident: the highest NPV is the most profitable. Thus, use of a spreadsheet program for calculating NPV can make fixed-asset decision making a more straightforward and less difficult process.

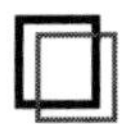

LONG-TERM FINANCING DECISIONS

The third major financial decision type is that of long-term financing. The types of issues addressed include:

- The lease or buy decision

- Debt versus equity as a means of raising capital
- Safe debt limitations and sources of financing

The lease-or-buy decision can involve production equipment, motor vehicles, buildings, office equipment, computers, and tools.

A spreadsheet can be used to determine the net cash outflow associated with leasing versus buying a given item. This can help in making the best decision, since the lower present value of net cash outflow of the two given options is the cheaper one. When deciding on the use of debt versus equity financing, the financial manager can set up formulas in the spreadsheet to show the effects of each option on the following:

- Cash flow
- Net income
- Degree of company solvency
- Company value
- Debt capacity

This is accomplished by projecting certain elements of the balance sheet and income statement, as well as certain financial ratios for each alternative. By analyzing the results and determining which alternative yields the highest earnings per share—and considering other factors such as if the debt ratio is acceptable—you arrive at the optimum alternative.

POPULAR BUDGETING AND PLANNING SOFTWARE

In recent years, the focus has been on moving away from spreadsheets to enterprise budgeting applications in order to make the planning and budgeting process more efficient and the data more reliable. However the underlying process remains fundamentally unchanged; it is still about capturing and consolidating line item expenses. Some popular programs are described briefly:

Adaytum Planning

Adaytum Planning by Adaytum Software (www.adaytum.com; 800-262-4445) is a multiuser budgeting, planning, and forecasting system. It gives you the flexibility to:

- Update hierarchies directly from the general ledger (GL)
- Combine top-down planning with bottom-up budgeting
- Make last-minute changes to model structure
- Empower end users to do ad hoc modeling without information system (IS) support

Budget Maestro Version 5.8

Centage's Budget Maestro (www.centage.com) is probably the best answer to distributed budgeting, strategic planning, and financial control. Budget Maestro shortens your budgeting cycle and puts you in control of the process. Its information-driven environment guides you through budgeting, planning, modeling, forecasting, resource management, consolidation, analysis, and reporting. CFOs and budget managers can plan, analyze, and manage in ways never before possible. Look at a user's screen and make changes directly without ever being there. Deliver budget models and deploy reconfigured software updates to many users at once. Plus manage budgetary information, even enterprise-wide information systems, with a single consistent interface.

Budget Maestro is designed to put CFOs and financial managers in control of all aspects of managing budgets, creating financial models, and building and deploying financial plans. It allows business managers unparalleled flexibility in analyzing cash flow and business performance throughout the enterprise. Budget Maestro significantly shortens your budgeting and planning cycles. It eliminates rekeying and formatting of data. It increases your data accuracy and integrity. It allows time for managing and analyzing your business. It is an excellent tool that provides you the ability to perform:

- Budgeting
- Forecasting; rolling forecasts
- Planning
- What-if scenario building
- Payroll and benefits management
- Headcount planning
- Capital asset planning
- Debt management
- Automatic data consolidation
- Management reports
- Extensive drill-down reporting
- Income statement, balance sheet, and statement of cash flows

As an alternative to spreadsheets, Budget Maestro automates many of the complex and repetitive tasks in the budgeting process while eliminating the need for creating complicated formulas and manual consolidation of multiple worksheets. Budget Maestro offers three editions:

1. *Desktop Edition:* A single user license that is ideal for the CEO, CFO, or controller of small to midsize organizations that have a centralized budgeting and planning process

2. *Small Business Edition:* Supports up to three users operating in a collaborative environment to generate budgets, forecasts, and financial reports
3. *Enterprise Edition:* An enterprise-wide application for use by finance executives and departmental/line managers to foster a more collaborative and participatory planning environment

Microsoft Business Solutions for Analytics—Forecaster

This is a Web-based budgeting and planning solution from FRx Software (www.frxsoftware.com/). Many organizations find it difficult to perform the ongoing budgeting and planning processes necessary to keep business performance on target. Financial surprises are met with panic, and more often than not, companies are forced to make sacrifices in places they cannot afford. The result is a direct, negative impact on their strategic objectives. But it is not for lack of trying. Finance departments simply do not have the time it takes to combine multiple spreadsheets submitted from across the company (let alone the resources to make sure all line managers understand the importance of the budgeting and planning process, and of submitting well-planned information on time!). Forecaster puts the systems and processes in place to help you immediately realize the benefits of an effective budgeting and planning process, and to make it an ongoing part of your business strategy.

Host Budget Version 3.2

Host Budget (www.hostanalytics.com) is an integrated budgeting and planning software program that provides streamlined budgeting, forecasting, reporting, and analysis. Modules are used to automatically manage, consolidate, and change information for planning and replanning. These budgeting, forecasting, and planning modules include:

- Integration with Host's Performance Measurement Scorecard
- Selling and General & Administrative (SG&A) Budget module
- Human Resources Budget module
- Sales and Operation Planning (S&OP) module
- Sales Forecasting module
- Capital Expenditure Budget module and others

Host Budget is architected for the Web so that the individuals involved in budgeting and planning can use all of the features. All that is needed by the user is a Web browser to access and update the application. Microsoft Excel spreadsheets can be used online or live to the database for queries and updates. Or if users prefer to work disconnected from the central database, they can work off-line and easily upload the Excel file later or submit it via e-mail.

Because of the streamlined effects of Host Budget on an organization's budgeting process, budgets and forecasts can be refined on an ongoing basis. Managers can consider what has happened so far and can regularly look into the future aided by actual versus budgeted information along with current forecast projections in their effort to meet financial goals. Executive managers can create top-down budgets and push down the budget to lower levels of the organization. Line managers and department heads can create budgets from the bottom up and submit budgets for approval.

Continuous rolling forecasts can easily be created with Host Forecaster, and bidirectional data integration allows the detailed budgets to be loaded to or from other applications. Based on best practices, Host Forecaster provides a rich set of tools to facilitate sales forecasting using standard methods including:

- Statistical forecasting
- Top-down forecasting allocated to the stock-keeping unit (SKU) level based on prior year history, current estimate, average sales for last two years, and other factors
- Bottom-up forecasting for product introductions and discontinued products
- Ability to smooth forecasts to eliminate the impact of infrequent sales events

SRC Systems

SRC Budgeting

Balancing flexibility and control, sophistication and ease of use, SRC Budgeting (www.srcsoftware.com) provides the tools you need to create and execute detailed budgets, transforming strategic goals into operational plans. SRC Budgeting not only simplifies the budgeting process but also streamlines the sharing of data with key managers. The results are greater accuracy, enhanced accountability, and increased ownership by business units—all while dramatically reducing the time required for the planning process. The benefits are:

- Increasing collaboration while streamlining the budget process
- Modeling budgets to fit your business
- Aligning budgets with strategic plans and forecasts
- Creating flexible and sophisticated budgets

SRC Sales Planning

With SRC Sales Planning, all deals can be tracked—not just the hot ones—and sales managers can adjust focus, training, and incentives to increase sales. Greater visibility into how leads play out at various points in the sales pipeline improves management decision-making ability. Understand which leads are working and which ones are not. Understand which products and services are in demand, identify and investigate changes and fluctuations, and take appropriate action—whether it means realigning the sales force or adjusting production and distribution.

The benefits are:

- Creating a robust sales forecast
- Making more accurate and timely planning decisions
- Aligning sales, supply chain, and operations

SRC FORECASTING

This system allows you to create timely, high-level, dimensionally independent rolling forecasts driven by the strategic plan and translated into operational targets. SRC Forecasting streamlines and speeds the forecasting cycle, leverages a sophisticated and customizable modeling process, and helps ensure organizational alignment. The benefits are:

- Streamlining financial forecasting
- Customizing and modeling forecasts for accurate planning
- Aligning forecasts with detailed budgets

ProPlans

ProPlans creates your financial plan automatically and accurately—and slices months from your annual planning and reporting process. You just enter your forecast data and assumptions into easy-to-follow, comprehensive data entry screens, and ProPlans automatically creates the detailed financials you need to run your business for the next year—your income statement, balance sheet, cash flow statement, receipts and disbursements cash flow statements, and ratio reports. (Template)

Profit Planner

Profit Planner provides titles and amounts for revenues, cost of sales, expenses, assets, liabilities, and equity in a ready-to-use Lotus 1-2-3 template. Financial tables are automatically generated on screen. It presents results in 13 different table formats, including a pro forma earnings statement, balance sheet, and cash flow statements. Profit Planner even compares your earnings statement, balance sheet, and ratios against industry averages so that you're not working in a vacuum. (Template)

Up Your Cash Flow

The program generates cash flow and profit and loss forecasts; detailed sales by product/product line and payroll by employee forecasts; monthly balance sheets; bar graphs; ratio and break-even analyses; and more. (Stand-alone)

Cash Collector

Cash Collector assists you in reviewing and aging receivables. You always know who owes what; nothing falls through the cracks. What happens when collection action is required? Simply click through menu-driven screens to automatically generate letters and other professionally written collection documents (all included) that are proven to pull in the payments. (Stand-alone)

Cash Flow Analysis

This software provides projections of cash inflow and cash outflow. You input data into eight categories: sales, cost of sales, general and administrative expense, long-term debt, other cash receipts, inventory build-up/reduction, capital expenditures (acquisition of long-term assets such as store furniture), and income tax. The program allows changes in assumptions and scenarios and provides a complete array of reports. (Stand-alone)

CapPLANS

CapPLANS evaluates profitability based on net preset value (NPV), internal rate of return (IRR), and payout period. Choose among five depreciation methods, including the modified accelerated cost recovery system (MACRS). Run up to four sensitivity analyses. Project profitability over a 15-year horizon. In addition to a complete report of your analysis, CapPLANS generates a concise four-page executive summary—great for expediting approval. Add ready-made graphs to illustrate profitability clearly, at a glance. (Template)

Project Evaluation Toolkit

This program calculates the dollar value of your project based on six valuation methods, including discounted cash flow and impact on the corporate balance sheet. Assess intangibles such as impact on corporate strategy, investors, or labor relations. Use scenario planning to show the effects of changing start dates, sales forecasts, and other critical variables. (Template)

@Risk

How will a new competitor affect your market share? @Risk calculates the likelihood of changes and events that affect your bottom line. First use @Risk's familiar @functions to define the risk in your worksheet. Then let @Risk run thousands of what-if tests using one of two proven statistical sampling techniques—Monte Carlo or Latin Hypercube. You get a clear, colorful graph that tells you the likelihood of every possible bottom-line value. At a glance you'll know if your risk is acceptable or if you need to make a contingency plan. (Add-in)

What's Best!

If you have limited resources—for example, people, inventory, materials, time, or cash—then What's Best! can tell you how to allocate these resources in order to maximize or minimize a given objective, such as profit or cost. What's Best! uses a proven method—linear programming (LP)— to help you achieve your goals. This product can solve a variety of business problems that cut across every industry at every level of decision making. (Stand-alone)

Inventory Analyst

Inventory Analyst tells precisely how much inventory to order and when to order it. Choose from four carefully explained ordering methods: economic order quantity (EOQ), fixed-order quantity, fixed-month requirements, and level load by workdays. Inventory Analyst ensures that you'll always have enough stock to get you through your ordering period.

Just load up to 48 months worth of inventory history, and Inventory Analyst makes the forecast based on one of three forecasting methods: time series, exponential smoothing, or moving averages. It explains which method is best for you. Inventory Analyst will adjust your forecast for seasonality. (Template)

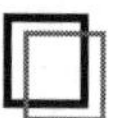

THE LATEST GENERATION OF BUDGETING AND PLANNING (B&P) SOFTWARE

The new budgeting and planning (B&P) software represents a giant step forward for accountants. Finance managers can use these robust, Web-enabled programs to scan a wide range of data, radically speed up the planning process, and identify managers who have failed to submit budgets. More often known as active financial planning software, this software includes applications and the new level of functionality that combine budgeting, forecasting analytics, business intelligence, and collaboration. Exhibit 11.10 lists popular B&P software.

Budget Express

Budget Express "understands" the structure of financial worksheets and concepts such as months, quarters, years, totals, and subtotals, speeding up budget and forecast preparation. The program creates column headers for months, automatically totals columns and rows, and calculates quarterly and yearly summaries. And for sophisticated what-if analyses, just specify your goal and Budget Express displays your current and target values as you make changes. (Add-in)

Companies	Web Sites	Software
ABC Technologies	www.abctech.com	Oros
ActiveStrategy	www.activestrategy.com	ActiveStrategy Enterprise
Actuate	www.actuate.com	e.Reporting Suite
Adaytum Software	www.adaytum.com	e.Planning
Applix	www.applix.com	iPlanning, iTM1
Brio Technology	www.brio.com	Brio.ONE, Brio.Impact, Brio.Inform
Business Objects	www.businessobjects.com	e-BI, BusinessObjects Auditor, BusinessObjects BW Connect, WebIntelligence
Cartesis	www.cartesis.com	Cartesis Budget Planning, Cartesis Carat, Cartesis Magnitude
Closedloop Solutions	www.closedloopsolutions.com	CBizPlan Manager, SpendCapManager, TopLine Manager
Cognos	www.cognos.com	Cognos Finance, Cognos Visualizer, Cognos Enterprise, Business Intelligence
Comshare	www.comshare.com	Management Planning and Control (MPC) Application, Comshare Decision
CorVu	www.corvu.com	CorManage, CorVu Rapid Scorecard, CorBusiness, CorPortfolio
E.Intelligence	www.eintelligence-inc.com	e.Intelligence Suite
Epicor	www.epicor.com	Epicor eIntelligence Suite
Geac	www.geac.com	Geac Smartstream Financials, Enterprise Solutions Expert Series, FRx
Great Plains Software	www.greatplains.com	eEnterprise, FRx Budget Controller, Dynamics
Hyperion	www.hyperion.com	Hyperion Financial Management, Hyperion Planning, Hyperion Essbase

Exhibit 11.10 ACTIVE FINANCIAL PLANNING SOFTWARE—NEXT-GENERATION BUDGETING AND PLANNING (B&P) SOFTWARE

Companies	Web Sites	Software
J.D. Edwards	www.jdedwards.com	J.D. Edwards Financial Planning and Budgeting, Business Intelligence, OneWorld Xe
Lawson Software	www.lawson.com	Enterprise Budgeting SEA Applications — including E-Scorecard; Analytic Extensions
Longview Solutions	www.longview.com	Khalix
MIS-AG	www.misag.com	MIS Alea Decisionware, MIS DelaMiner, Collaborative Analytic Processing
NextStrat	www.nextstrat.com	NextStrat Strategic Implementation Portal (NextSIP)
Oracle	www.oracle.com	Oracle Strategic Enterprise Management (SEM)
OutlookSoft	www.outlooksoft.com	OutlookSoft Financial Planning and Analysis (FPA), OutlookSoft Enterprise Analytic Portal
PeopleSoft	www.peoplesoft.com	Enterprise Performance Management (EPM), PeopleSoft Balanced Scorecard, PeopleSoft Enterprise Warehouse, PeopleSoft eBusiness Analytics, PeopleSoft Activity-Based Management
SAP	www.sap.com	SAP Strategic Enterprise Management (SEM), SAP Financial Analyzer Business Intelligence with mySAP.com
SAS Institute	www.sas.com	SAS Total Financial Management, Strategic Vision, SAS/Warehouse Administrator, SAS Enabling Technology (OLAP)
Slivon	www.silvon.com	Stratum
SRC Software	www.srcsoftware.com	Budget Advisor, Payroll Planner, Information Advisor

Exhibit 11.10 ACTIVE FINANCIAL PLANNING SOFTWARE—NEXT-GENERATION BUDGETING AND PLANNING (B&P) SOFTWARE *(continued)*

CHAPTER 12

MANUFACTURING INFORMATION SYSTEMS AND PACKAGES

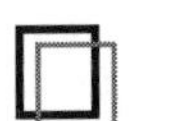

MODELS OF THE MANUFACTURING INFORMATION SYSTEM

Manufacturing is a broad and complicated subject. With different products manufactured, the processes and operations may be totally different. The mission of a manufacturing information system is to apply computer technology to improve the process and the efficiency of a manufacturing system so that the quality of products is better and the costs to manufacture them are lower. In other words, a manufacturing system takes material, equipment, data, management, and information systems technology as the input, and uses manufacturing and information processes to generate better final products as output (see Exhibit 12.1).

Manufacturing consists of many different disciplinary areas, including product engineering, facility design and scheduling, fabrication, and quality control management. Each of them can be dramatically improved by using information systems.

Product Engineering

Product engineering is the starting point of the manufacturing process. It is the step in which the design and technical specifications for the product are finalized. Product design

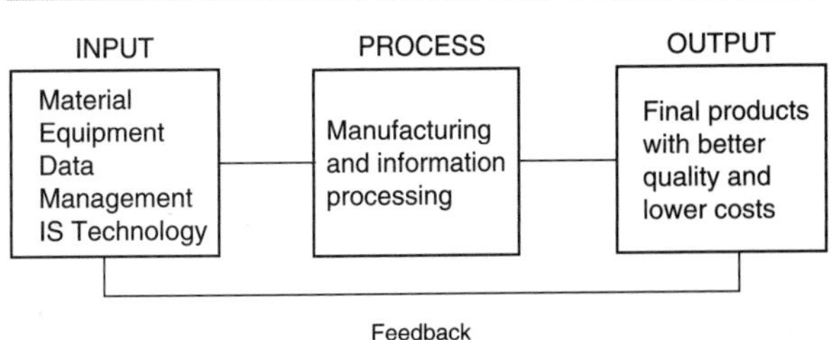

Exhibit 12.1 MANUFACTURING INFORMATION SYSTEM MODEL

and engineering are becoming more computerized through computer software packages such as computer-aided design (CAD) and computer-aided manufacturing (CAM). With CAD, product designers use technologies to design a prototype of the product, test this product, and modify the design on the computer before it goes into production.

The initial design can be input to the CAD system in various ways, including drawing sketches on a digital tablet, or using a digital camera or a scanner to digitize photographs or graphics into the system. After the product is digitized, the design can be simulated and tested under real-world conditions predefined by the designer. As changes are suggested, the original design can be modified—similar to editing a letter on a word processing package. In addition, artificial intelligence (AI) has been used in CAD systems. Artificial intelligence agents can help human designers make changes, formulate suggestions, or do tests based on different circumstances.

After the product has been designed, another important issue is how to produce the product efficiently and effectively. The design of products for easy and cheap assembly is critical, since assembly often accounts for over half of the total manufacturing costs. For example, by reducing the number of components by 30%, a manufacturer can drastically cut manual assembly times and manufacturing costs. Large corporations such as IBM, GM, Ford, HP, and GE have sophisticated product designs that reflect how a product should be functioning as well as how it can be manufactured efficiently and economically.

Facility Design and Scheduling

After the product is designed, the facility or equipment used to produce the product should be arranged. This decision may be as simple as changing several tools or as complex as redesigning the entire plant. Some computer software packages can arrange the plant layout based on the production information of the designed product. Many of the proposed layout algorithms use an improvement approach, a construction approach, or a simulation approach.

Improvement Approach

This approach requires users to specify initial conditions and parameters. A combinatorial-based approach will then be applied to improve the initial layout. This process is usually done by intelligent search techniques to try numerous alternatives in order to find the best possible solution. For example, machine A can switch with machine B to see the effects on the manufacturing process.

Construction Approach

This approach builds one or more layout solutions from scratch with or without a user's initial suggestions. The best one will then be selected.

SIMULATION APPROACH

Monte Carlo simulation has been used to solve facility layout problems. This approach simulates the real production environment based on the assumptions provided by the designer. This process requires a lot of computer resources and time to generate good results.

Fabrication

Fabrication or manufacturing is the process of making new products from raw materials. There are two types of production methods: job-shop production and process production.

JOB-SHOP PRODUCTION

Each work order is considered a job. Raw materials required to process the work order are routed to work centers according to the production steps required. The job shop is more flexible in terms of the products that can be produced. Therefore, a variety of products can be produced at the same time. Today, many computer software packages are able to generate a job-shop schedule using mathematical programming or artificial intelligence technologies.

PROCESS (FLOW-SHOP) PRODUCTION

One or a few products travel through a set of fabrication activities specially arranged for the particular products. In this approach, we have repetitive manufacturing (e.g., an automobile assembly line) and process industries such as oil refineries in which no significant stoppage in the flow of materials is evidenced, and flow rate becomes the critical decision. The layout of the assembly line and the flow rate can be determined by expert systems with the rule base retrieved from many manufacturing experts.

Quality Control Management

Quality control relates to activities that ensure the final product is of satisfactory quality. The quality control function is concerned with detecting existing quality deficiencies and preventing future product quality problems. If the quantity produced is small and the final product is expensive, all products are inspected for quality control. However, if a large quantity of the units is produced and they are inexpensive (such as pencils and diskettes), a statistical sample will be used to determine if the quality of this lot of products is acceptable. Total quality management (TQM) is a quality revolution taking place in recent years. It consists of these principles:

- *Customer focused:* All efforts should be based on customers, including external customers and internal customers such as an accounting department within the company.

- *Continuous improvement:* TQM does not believe quality can be attained completely. Quality can always be improved.
- *Everything TQM:* TQM includes everything the company produces—a product, a service, or how a customer service call is answered.
- *Accurate measurement:* TQM uses statistical techniques to measure every critical variable available and compares against benchmarks to identify problems.
- *Empowerment of employee:* TQM involves everyone in the company to improve quality. Teamwork is heavily emphasized in the TQM process.

TQM represents a counterpoint to the traditional management theories that emphasize cost reduction more than anything else. The American auto industry represents a classic case of what can go wrong when attention is focused on trying to keep the cost down to improve productivity without good quality management. As a matter of fact, productivity goes down when defects, recalls, and expensive repairs of defective products are factored in.

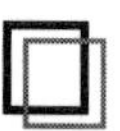

MANUFACTURING INTELLIGENCE

Expert Systems in Manufacturing

Expert systems identify, analyze, and solve (including explanations) manufacturing problems, and they help implement the solutions. Expert systems (see Exhibit 12.2) use a rule base to generate decision suggestions. Users can input facts and preconditions so that the rules will be triggered to provide results. Expert systems have been applied in many aspects of manufacturing. Much factory work has shifted to knowledge work such as planning, designing, and quality assurance. Previously, the emphasis was on labor work such as machining, assembling, and handling. As a matter of fact, knowledge work accounts for about two-thirds of total manufacturing costs.

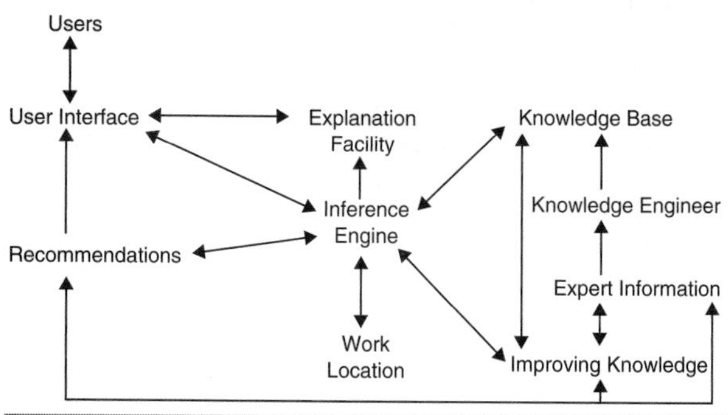

Exhibit 12.2 EXPERT SYSTEM FRAMEWORK

Robotics, expert systems, and other information systems can improve the productivity of labor work. For example, an expert system implemented at Northrop Corporation, a major producer of jet fighter planes, is responsible for the planning of manufacture and assembly of up to 20,000 parts that go into an aircraft. A parts designer is able to enter a description of the engineering drawing of a part, and the expert system will tell him or her what materials and processes are required to manufacture it. This particular system actually improves the productivity of part designing by a factor of 12 to 18 times. Without the help of an expert system, the same task would require several days instead of several hours.

An expert system is a computer system including computer hardware and software, which can perform reasoning using a knowledge base. Expert systems are made up of a user's interface, a knowledge base, and an inference engine. The user's interface has the function of providing end users with proper interactive channels so that users can interact with the system. A knowledge base contains a set of rules or cases to provide an expert system with necessary information to conduct reasoning. An inference engine (processing system) is the brain of an expert system. It receives the request from the user interface and conducts reasoning in the knowledge base. The inference engine asks for additional information and makes assumptions. Different rules or cases can be triggered to conclude a solution. After several questioning/answering sessions, a conclusion or suggestion can be generated and provided to the end user through the user interface. The inference engine may also determine the degree to which a recommendation is qualified, or for multiple solutions, the ranking of those solutions.

Expert System Knowledge Bases

An expert system contains the subject knowledge of the human experts, called the knowledge base. The knowledge base consists of two types of knowledge representations: inductive knowledge (case based) and deductive knowledge (rule based). Expert systems are discussed in detail in Chapter 15.

Benefits and Limitations of Expert Systems

The technology of expert systems has been successfully applied in thousands of organizations worldwide to problems ranging from cancer research to the analysis of computer configurations. Some reasons that expert systems have become so popular are discussed below:

- *Improved quality:* Expert systems (ESs) provide advice or suggestions based on preprogrammed logistics that are consistent and accurate. This reduces possible mistakes caused by human errors.

- *Obtaining of scarce expertise:* The scarcity of experience becomes evident in situations where there are not enough experts for a task, where the expert is about to retire or leave the job, or where expertise is required over a broad geographic location.
- *Operation in hazardous environment:* An ES, such as a robot with AI, can reduce human interaction with hazardous materials.
- *Provision of training:* An ES can be a very good training tool.

Robotics in Manufacturing

A robot with AI capability is an electromechanical manipulator able to respond to a change in its environment based on its perception of that environment. The sensory subsystem is programmed to "see" or "feel" its environment and respond to it. For example, an industrial robot can manufacture one of many parts in its repertoire and manipulate it to inspect it for defects, recognizing very small departures from established standards. Robots have been used extensively in Japan to improve the quality and reduce the cost of their products. They are reliable, consistent, accurate, and insensitive to hazardous environments.

A robot is a device that mimics human actions and appears to function with some degree of intelligence. Robots are commonly used in manufacturing and in other situations where it would be unsafe or unhealthy for a human to perform the same task.

Neural Networks in Manufacturing

The human brain's powerful thinking, reasoning, creating, remembering, and problem-solving capabilities have inspired many scientists to attempt computer modeling of its operation. Some researchers have sought to create a computer model that matches the functionality of the brain in a very fundamental manner; the result has been neural computing.

The neuron is the fundamental cellular unit of the nervous system and the brain. Each neuron functions as a simple microprocessing unit that receives and combines signals from many other neurons through input processes called dendrites. If the combined signal is strong enough, it activates the firing of the neuron, which produces an output signal; the path of the output signal is along a component of a cell called the axon. This simple transfer of information is chemical in nature but has electrical side effects that we can measure. The brain consists of hundreds of billions of neurons loosely interconnected. The axon (output path) of a neuron splits up and connects to dendrites (input path) of other neurons through a junction referred to as a synapse. The transmission across this junction is chemical in nature and the amount of signal transferred depends on the amount of chemical (neurotransmitters) released by the axon and received by the dendrites. This synaptic efficiency is what is modified when the brain learns. The synapse, combined with the processing of information in the neuron, forms the basic memory mechanism of the brain.

In an artificial neural network, the unit analogous to the biological neuron is referred to as a processing element. A processing element has many input paths and combines—usually by a simple summation—the values of these input paths. The result is an internal activity level for the processing element. The combined input is then modified by a transfer function, which can be a threshold function. This threshold function only passes information along if the combined activity level reaches a certain point, or it can be a continuous function of the combined input. The output path of a processing element can be connected to input paths of other processing elements through connection weights that correspond to the synaptic strength of neural connections. Since each connection has a corresponding weight, the signals on the input lines to a processing element are modified by these weights prior to being summed. Thus, the summation function is a weighted summation.

A neural network consists of many processing elements joined together in the manner just described. Processing elements are usually organized into groups called layers or slabs. A typical network consists of a sequence of layers or slabs with full or random connections between successive layers. There are typically two layers with connections to the outside world: an input buffer where data is presented to the network and an output buffer that holds the response of the network to a given input. Layers distinct from the input and output buffers are called hidden layers. Applications of neural networks are language processing (text and speech), image processing, character recognition (handwriting recognition and pattern recognition), and financial and economic modeling.

PRODUCTION PLANNING AND CONTROL

Production Planning

Planning encompasses defining the organization's objectives or goals and establishing an overall strategy for achieving these goals. Planning can be classified into several categories:

- *Strategic versus operational:* Plans that apply to the entire organization to establish the organizational overall objectives are called strategic plans. Plans that specify the detailed process of how the strategic plan can be achieved are called operational plans.

- *Short term versus long term:* Plans that cover more than one year are called long term. Long-term plans tend to be strategic and short-term plans tend to be operational.
- *Specific versus directional:* Specific plans have clearly defined objectives while directional plans identify general guidelines. They provide focus but do not lock management into following specific objectives or specific courses of action.

Production planning consists of four key decisions: capacity, location, process, and layout.

Capacity Planning

Capacity planning deals with determining the proper size of your plant to satisfy the demand of the market. Capacity planning begins with taking a forecast of sales demand, then estimating production to determine capacity requirements. This model can be easily entered into a spreadsheet to generate results (see Exhibit 12.3).

Location Planning

When you determine the need for a new facility, you must determine where this facility should be installed. The location of the facility depends on which factors have the greatest impact on total production and distribution costs. These include availability of labor skills, labor costs, energy costs, and proximity to suppliers or customers.

Process Planning

In process planning, management determines how a product or service will be produced. Process planning encompasses evaluating the available production methods and selecting the set that will best achieve the operating objectives.

Layout Planning

Layout planning deals with the access and selection among alternative layout options for equipment and work stations. The objective of layout planning is to find the best physical

Product	Units/Demand	Machine-Hours/ Unit	Total Machine-Hours
A	200	3	600
B	400	2	800
C	100	7	700
		Total machine-hours =	2100

Each machine is on for 24 hours a day with a break-down rate of 5%

24 hours × number of machines needed × 95% >= 2100 machine hours

Number of machines needed = 93

Exhibit 12.3 CAPACITY PLANNING

arrangement to facilitate production efficiency. There are three types of work flow layouts:

- *Process layout:* Arrange manufacturing components together according to similarity of function.
- *Product layout:* Arrange manufacturing components according to the progressive steps by which a product is made.
- *Fixed-position layout:* A manufacturing layout in which the product stays in place while tools, equipment, and human skills are brought to it.

Production Control

Control can be defined as the process of monitoring activities to ensure that they are being accomplished as planned and of correcting any significant deviations. The control process consists of three steps: measuring actual performance, comparing actual performance against a standard, and taking managerial action to correct deviations or inadequate standards. There are three types of controls: feedforward control, concurrent control, and feedback control. Feedforward control prevents anticipated problems. Concurrent control occurs when an activity is in progress. Feedback control is imposed after an action has occurred. All three types of controls can be implemented by information systems.

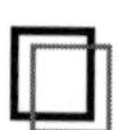

INVENTORY PLANNING AND CONTROL

A manufacturing company has three types of inventory: raw material, work in process, and finished goods. To reach the goals of inventory control, two objectives must be achieved: minimizing costs due to an out-of-stock situation and minimizing inventory carrying costs.

At the finished products level, out-of-stock can result in loss of sales, and too much inventory increases the carrying cost. At the raw material and work-in-process level, out-of stock means that the production line must be stopped, and too much inventory means a higher cost in final products. A mathematical model used to determine the optimal ordering point is called the EOQ model.

Economic Order Quantity (EOQ) Model

The objective of the EOQ model is to minimize the total carrying costs and ordering costs. As the amount gets larger and larger, average inventory increases and so do carrying costs. But placing larger orders means fewer orders and thus lower ordering costs. To compute the optimal order quantity, the information can be entered into a spreadsheet for calculation (see Exhibit 12.4).

D: forecasted demand for the item during the period

OC: the cost of placing each order

V: the value or purchase price of the item

CC: the carrying cost of maintaining the total inventory expressed as a percentage

$EOQ = (2*D*OC)/(V*CC)^{1/2}$

EOQ Model Spreadsheet

D: forecasted demand for the item during the period

OC: the cost of placing each order

V: the value or purchase price of the item

CC: the carrying cost of maintaining the total inventory expressed as a percentage

$EOQ = (2*D*OC)/(V*CC)^{1/2}$

D =	2000
OC =	500
V =	100
CC =	0.5
EOQ =	40

Exhibit 12.4 EOQ MODEL

Linear Programming Model

Another model uses linear programming to determine the optimal solution. This model requires an objective function, determinable variables, and constraints. For example, ABC company manufactures type A and type B chairs. Each type A chair requires 3 pounds of steel and 7 pounds of plastic. Each type B chair requires 6 pounds of steel and 2 pounds of plastic. Total steel available is 200 pounds and total plastic available is 700 pounds. The profit by selling chair A is $54 per chair and chair B is $19 per chair. Use this information to figure out how many of each type should be produced to reach the maximum profit. This linear programming model can be solved by a spreadsheet package with an LP solver (see Exhibit 12.5).

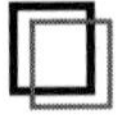

MATERIAL REQUIREMENTS PLANNING (MRP) AND MANUFACTURING RESOURCES PLANNING (MRPII)

Material requirements planning (MRP) differs from manufacturing resources planning (MRPII). MRPII satisfies the requirements of supplying materials to shop operations. In MRPII, the MIS is used to sequence material inputs in accordance with chronological need. The evolution of MRPII from MRP is the logical outgrowth of the maturing of the use of computer applications in manufacturing.

X1 = number of Chair A produced

X2 = number of Chair B produced

Objective Function

Max Z = 54X1 + 19X2

Constraints

3X1 + 6X2 <= 200

7X1 + 2X2 <= 700

X1 >= 0

X2 >= 0

LINEAR PROGRAMMING SOLVER

Product	A	B	Equation	Total Material Available
Steel required per chair	3	6	<=	200
Plastic required per chair	7	2	<=	700
Profit per unit	$54	$19		

The optimal solution is to have the largest profit within the material limitation.

Exhibit 12.5 LINEAR PROGRAMMING SOLVER

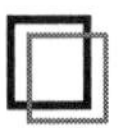

COMPUTER-AIDED DESIGN (CAD) AND COMPUTER-AIDED MANUFACTURING (CAM)

CAD programs are software programs for the design of products. CAD programs can be found in all types of computers from mainframe systems to microcomputers. They were developed to help engineers design products from airplanes to pens. The advantages of CAD software are that the design can be drawn in three dimensions, the design can be simulated in the computer, and design changes can be made very efficiently. Good CAD packages are AutoCAD, TurboCAD, and EasyCAD2. Some CAD programs are developed for nonprogrammers. For example, a relatively unskilled person can use this type of software to design an office or a home interior. The programs include libraries of options such as cabinetry, furniture, trees, and even shadows. Once the design is completed, users can "walk into the design" and view this structure from different points of view. This is similar to a virtual reality system.

CAM is an umbrella term that includes almost any use of computers in manufacturing operations. It consists of the following functions:

- *Monitoring:* Computers can be used to control and monitor manufacturing operations in a dangerous environment. For example, an oil refinery facility uses CAM to open and shut valves when a certain temperature is reached in a tank.

- *Numeric control:* Using computer technology to control the manufacturing operations. For example, CAM can help production workers produce parts that require a high degree of precision because computers are used to improve the accuracy of manufacturing.
- *Optimization:* Many manufacturing operations involve finding the best solution among many options. For example, an oil refinery is looking for the cheapest way to mix crude oils to achieve a finished gasoline that meets certain restrictions. Auto assembly plants try to arrange the best schedule so that operating costs can be minimized. By using CAM techniques, optimization can be improved and the operation can be more economical and efficient.
- *Robotics:* Robotics is the use of computer-controlled machines to perform motor activities previously done by humans, including welding joints, painting, and fitting parts together. The automobile industry uses robotics to improve the productivity and quality of its products.

JUST-IN-TIME (JIT)

Just-in-time is fast becoming as familiar and identifiable in the lexicon of manufacturing terminology as "mass production." Although the term is familiar to many people, the true meaning and definition remains clouded and unclear. The most common misunderstanding of just-in-time is that it is a system used to deliver inventory when it is needed. That means to reduce inventory while the operation is maintained. However, this is not the true meaning of just-in-time. The true definition of just-in-time is an awareness that true optimum manufacturing performance revolves around the dictate to eliminate waste in all of its many manifestations. The goal of JIT is to eliminate all manufacturing waste by following the objectives listed below:

- Produce the product the customer wants.
- Produce the product when the customer wants it.
- Produce a good-quality product.
- Produce instantly—with no lead time.
- Produce with no waste of labor, material, or equipment.

QUALITY CONTROL AND TOTAL QUALITY MANAGEMENT (TQM)

Quality control relates to activities that ensure the final products are satisfactory. Major functions of quality control are detecting existing quality deficiencies and preventing future product quality problems. Due to the large quantity of units produced, quality control is usually conducted by statistical sampling of final products. The whole lot of final products can be either rejected or accepted based on a small sample. However, if statistically the manufacturer passes a lot that is supposed to be rejected, the consequence would be that customers will purchase defective merchandise, ruining the reputation of this manufacturer. If the manufacturer rejects a lot that is supposed to be accepted, good products can be discarded and manufacturing resources wasted. Quality control is both an important area of expense and an important area of opportunities. Regarding expense, a typical factory spends about a quarter of its production budget just fixing and finding mistakes. And this cost does not reflect the true cost associated with this problem.

Total quality management (TQM) has been touted as one of the few management practices that will make companies competitive, particularly against the onslaught of Japanese competition. TQM has come to mean powerful solutions to all that ails modern North American industry. It implies that if we pay supreme attention to the needs and desires of our customers, we deliver on those aspirations. Then we are bound to be successful. TQM focuses on awareness techniques for making products to the best of the organization's abilities. TQM theory can be described as a triangle:

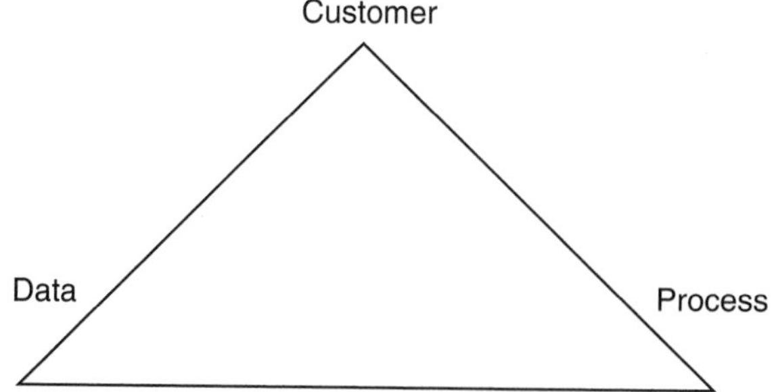

The focus is on the customer's requirements at the apex of the triangle. This in turn generates a process for achieving the requirements. The process is implemented and data is generated from which the effectiveness of the plan is evaluated. The results are then compared with the customer's requirements and the process is modified to improve results. TQM emphasizes a continuous improvement at all times. The modifications are implemented and the results are analyzed to see if they are in compliance with the customer's needs. In other words, TQM is continuous improvement until perfection is achieved.

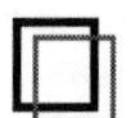

FLEXIBLE MANUFACTURING SYSTEMS (FMSs)

Flexible manufacturing systems (FMS) were introduced to provide a shorter life cycle for the manufacturing process and to have more responsive manufacturing facilities. For example, a VCR factory can use FMS to produce different models using a similar facility that can be rescheduled and rearranged to fit into different manufacturing patterns.

CHAPTER 13

MARKETING MANAGEMENT INFORMATION SYSTEMS AND PACKAGES

The internal accounting information system is the primary source of marketing information in most business organizations and provides two basic types of information to management: information generated from processing of sales orders, and cost report and analyses. Profitability analysis is generated from sales data records together with product cost data. Sales data processing also includes analysis of sales trends. In addition to the accounting and marketing departments, other departments within the company may contribute to the flow of information to marketing personnel. For example, the production or engineering department may provide information relating to product quality or design that is useful to product planning or to salespeople. The economics department may provide useful analysis of the economy or of the particular field within which the firm operates. The personnel department may provide information relating to potential marketing department employees. While information from all the sources may be important, it is generally not as regular or as voluminous as the information provided by the accounting department. The information needs for marketers, in the order of importance, are shown in the survey results in Exhibit 13.1.

Rank	Main Information Needs
1	Improving new product development
2	Improving the use of market information
3	Measuring and managing brand equity
4	Market orientation and bottom line
5	Market segmentation and implementation
6	Identifying, anticipating, and responding to competitors
7	Studying buyer behavior
8	Strategic new product issues
9	Integrating marketing mix
10	Service quality/performance links

Exhibit 13.1 INFORMATION NEEDS OF MARKETING MANAGERS

Source: J. Honomichi, "Time Is Ripe to Overhaul Traditional Marketing Research Departments," *Marketing News* 27, no. 12 (June 7, 1993), pp. H34–39.

Inputs	Subsystems	Outputs
Strategic plan	Product development	Product development reports
Transaction processing system	Marketing research	Marketing research reports
Internal sources	Promotion and advertising system	
External sources: Competition the market	Pricing system	Locational analysis Supply and demand analysis
	Place planning system	Sales by product Sales by salesperson Sales by customer

Exhibit 13.2 AN OVERVIEW OF A MARKETING MIS

A marketing MIS supports managerial activity in the areas of product development, marketing mix, distribution, pricing decisions, promotional effectiveness, and sales forecasting. Recall that an MIS is made up of three sets of activities: information collection, information analysis, and information dissemination. A marketing MIS is certainly no exception. Exhibit 13.2 shows the inputs, subsystems, and outputs of a typical marketing MIS.

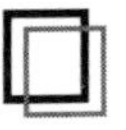

INPUTS TO THE MARKETING MIS

Among the other functional areas, the marketing MIS relies more heavily on external sources of data. These sources include commercial intelligence, competition, customers, trade shows, trade journals and magazines, and other publications. There are also important internal company information sources. An overview of these inputs is presented in the following sections.

The Corporate Strategic Plan or Policies

Marketing depends on the company's strategic plan for sales goals and projections. For instance, a strategic plan might show sales are expected to grow by a stable 5% for the next three years. A marketing MIS report for this company might detail current sales performance in terms of this strategic target. In addition to sales projections, the strategic plan can spell out detailed information about anticipated needs for the sales force, pricing, distribution channels, promotion, and new product features. The strategic plan can provide a framework in which to integrate marketing information and make appropriate marketing decisions.

The Transaction Processing System (TPS)

The TPS encompasses a huge amount of sales and marketing data on products or services, customers, and the sales force. Technology is revolutionizing the selling process. Most firms collect an abundance of information on a regular basis that can also be used in making marketing decisions. Sales data on products can expose which products are selling at high volumes, which ones are slow sellers, and how much they are contributing to profits. The marketing MIS might synthesize this information in such a way as to be useful in formulating promotional plans. It can also be used to activate product development decisions. Analysis of sales by customers may display which customers are contributing to profits. This data can also be disseminated to determine which products specific customers are buying to help the sales force with their promotional efforts. The performance of the sales force can also be monitored from data captured in the TPS, which can help develop bonus and incentive programs to reward high-performing salespeople.

Internal Company Information

Internal company information includes routinely collected accounting records, such as daily sales receipts, weekly expense records and profit statements, production and shipment schedules, inventory records, orders, monthly credit statements, and quarterly and biennial reports. Field salespeople are increasingly likely to have portable personal computers, pagers, and personal digital assistants (PDAs) to log in data for immediate transmission back to the company or to customers, and to receive information from the company and from customers. Technology is revolutionizing the selling process. Most companies collect an abundance of information on a regular basis that can also be used in making marketing decisions.

External Sources: The Competition and the Market

In most marketing decisions it is important to determine what is happening in the business's external environment, particularly anything that involves the competition, the economy, the market, and consumers. External information can be obtained from many sources. Some of the most commonly used sources are commercial intelligence, trade shows, trade journals, the government, private publications, commercial data suppliers, and the popular press. Many companies purchase their competition's products, then perform "autopsies" to find out what makes them tick so that they can improve on them. Marketing managers attend trade shows and read trade journals to keep an eye on the competition.

Exhibit 13.3 lists some trade journals and publications. Information can be purchased from information brokers–individuals and companies who help businesses by electronically

Air Conditioning, Heating & Refrigeration News
American Banker
American Druggist
American Gas Association Monthly
Automotive Industries
Aviation Week & Space Technology
The Banker
Best's Industry Report
Broadcasting
Brewers Digest
Chain Store Age
Chemical Week
Computer Decisions International
Credit and Financial Management
Drug & Cosmetic Industry
Electronic News
Fleet Owner
Flight International
Food Management
Food Processing
Forest Industries
Fuel Oil & Oil Heat and Solar Systems
Housing
Industry Week
Journal of Retailing
Labor Law Journal
Leather and Shoes
Merchandising
Modern Plastics
National Petroleum News
Oil and Gas Journal
Paper Trade Journal
PC World
Personnel
Pipeline & Gas Journal
Polk's National New Car Sales
Printer's Ink
Progressive Grocer
Public Utilities Fortnightly
Pulp & Paper
Quick Frozen Foods
Television Digest
Textile World
Transportation Journal
Ward's Auto World
World Oil

Exhibit 13.3 TRADE JOURNALS AND PUBLICATIONS

searching information bases for useful data. Valuable information can be obtained by training salespeople to listen to and observe customers, suppliers, members of the distribution system, and the competition, then contributing this intelligence to the MIS. The intent should be to obtain usable *marketing intelligence* (information that is available to the public) and not to conduct *industrial espionage* (stealing information not available to the public). The latter is unethical and illegal. Marketers should be savvy enough to realize that as they are collecting information about their competition, the competition is probably collecting information about them.

An additional external source of important information for the marketing MIS is the market for a company's products. A large amount of useful data can be obtained from the TPS for markets already being served by the company, but insights into buyer behaviors and preferences in new markets can only be obtained from sources outside the firm.

The Internet may become the ultimate information source for both the competition and the market. It already provides access to information provided by government (.gov), for-profit business (.com), nonprofits (.org), universities (.edu), and individuals.

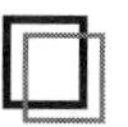

MARKETING MIS SUBSYSTEMS AND OUTPUTS

Subsystems for the marketing MIS include forecasting, marketing research, product development, place planning, promotion planning, and pricing. These subsystems and their outputs help marketing managers and executives increase sales, reduce marketing expenses, and develop plans for future products and services to meet the changing needs of customers.

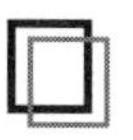

COMPREHENSIVE SALES PLANNING

The preceding chapter gave an overview of a comprehensive profit plan. The initiating management decisions in developing the plan were the statements of broad objectives, specific goals, basic strategies, and planning premises. The sales planning process is a necessary part of profit planning and control because (1) it provides for the basic management decisions about marketing, and (2) based on those decisions, it is an organized approach for developing a comprehensive sales plan. If the sales plan is not realistic, most if not all of the other parts of the overall profit plan also are not realistic. Therefore, if the management believes that a realistic sales plan cannot be developed, there is little justification for profit planning and control. Despite the views of a particular management, such a conclusion may be an implicit admission of incompetence. Simply, if it is really impossible to assess the future revenue potential of a business, there would be little incentive for investment in the business initially or for continuation of it except for purely speculative ventures that most managers and investors prefer to avoid.

The primary purposes of a sales plan are (1) to reduce uncertainty about the future revenues, (2) to incorporate management judgments and decisions into formation of the planning process (e.g., in the marketing plans), (3) to provide necessary information for developing other elements of a comprehensive profit plan, and (4) to facilitate management's control of sales activities.

Sales Planning Compared with Forecasting

Sales planning and forecasting are often confused. Although related, they have distinctly different purposes. A *forecast* is not a plan; rather it is a statement and/or a quantified assessment of future conditions about a particular subject (e.g., sales revenue) based on one or more explicit assumptions. A forecast should always state the assumptions upon which it is based. A forecast should be viewed as only one input into the development of a sales plan. The management of a company comprehensive may accept, modify, or reject the forecast. In contrast, a *sales plan* incorporates management decisions that are based on the forecast, other inputs, and management judgments about such related items as sales volume, prices, sales efforts, production, and financing,

Testing the Top Line

Most companies do not really manage top-line growth. They allocate resources to businesses they think will be most productive and hope the economy cooperates. But a growing number are taking a less passive approach and studying revenue growth more carefully. They argue that quantifying the sources of revenue can yield a wealth of information, which results in more targeted and more effective decision making. With the right discipline and analysis, they say, growing revenues can be as straightforward as cutting costs. Some companies go so far as to link the two efforts. The idea is to bring the same systematic analysis to growing revenue that we have brought to cost cutting.

A sources-of-revenue statement (SRS) is useful in this effort. The information on revenue captured by traditional financial statements is woefully inadequate. Sorting revenues by geographic market, business unit, or product line tells you the source of sales. But it does not explain the underlying reason for those sales. The SRS model breaks revenue into five categories:

1. Continuing sales to established customers (known as base retention)
2. Sales won from the competition (share gain)
3. New sales from expanding markets
4. Moves into adjacent markets where core capabilities can be leveraged
5. Entirely new lines of business unrelated to the core

To produce a sources-of-revenue statement, five steps are required in addition to establishing total revenues for comparable periods, as is commonly done for purposes of completing an income statement:

1. Determine revenue from the core business by establishing the revenue gain or loss from entry to or exit from adjacent markets and the revenue gain from new lines of business, and subtracting this from total revenue.
2. Determine growth attributable to market positioning by estimating the market growth rate for the current period and multiplying this by the prior period's core revenue.
3. Determine the revenue not attributable to market growth by subtracting the amount determined in step 2 from that determined in step 1.
4. To calculate base retention revenue, estimate the customer churn rate, multiply it by the prior period's core revenue, and deduct this from the prior period's core revenue.
5. To determine revenue from market share gain, subtract retention revenue, growth attributable to market positioning, and growth from new lines of business and from adjacent markets from core revenue.

Forecasting

Forecasts are needed for marketing, production, purchasing, manpower, and financial planning. Further, top management needs forecasts for planning and implementing long-term strategic objectives and planning for capital expenditures. Based on the firm's projected sales, the production function determines the machine, personnel, and material resources needed to produce its products or services. Marketing managers use sales forecasts to (1) determine optimal sales force allocations, (2) set sales goals, and (3) plan promotions and advertising. Other things such as market share, prices, and trends in new product development are required.

As soon as the company makes sure that it has enough capacity, the production plan is developed. If the company does not have enough capacity, it will require planning and budgeting decisions for capital spending for capacity expansion. Production planners need forecasts in order to schedule production activities, order materials, establish inventory levels, and plan shipments. Some other areas that need forecasts include material requirements (purchasing and procurement), labor scheduling, equipment purchases, maintenance requirements, and plant capacity planning.

The personnel department requires a number of forecasts in planning for human resources in the business. Workers must be hired and trained, and for these personnel there must be benefits that are competitive with those available in the firm's labor market. Also, trends that affect such variables as labor turnover, retirement age, absenteeism, and tardiness need to be forecast as input for planning and decision making in this function. On this basis, the financial manager must estimate the future cash inflow and outflow. He or she must plan cash and borrowing needs for the company's future operations. Forecasts of cash flows and the rates of expenses and revenues are needed to maintain corporate liquidity and operating efficiency. In planning for capital investments, predictions about future economic activity are required so that returns or cash inflows accruing from the investment may be estimated. There are many forecasting methods in use, one of which is regression analysis. It is illustrated below, using Excel.

Using Regression on Excel

To utilize Excel for regression analysis, the following procedure needs to be followed:

1. Click the Tools menu.

EXAMPLE 13.1 EXCEL REGRESSION

A firm wishes to develop a sales forecasting model by relating sales to price and advertising.

Month	Sales (Y)	Advertising (X1)	Price (X2)
1	25	4	75
2	26	5	82
3	32	6	94
4	30	6	95
5	32	7	98
6	37	7	110
7	38	8	110
8	41	8	99
9	46	9	95
10	48	10	97

EXAMPLE 13.1 EXCEL REGRESSION *(continued)*

Summary Output

Regression Statistics

Multiple R	0.97366474
R Square	0.94802302
Adjusted R Square	0.93317246
Standard Error	2.0400664
Observations	10

Anova

	df	SS	MS	F	Significance F
Regression	2	531.3669036	265.6835	63.838	3.20139E-05
Residual	7	29.13309639	4.161871		
Total	9	560.5			

	Coefficients	Standard Error	t Stat
Intercept	10.1734656	6.251683507	1.627316
X Variable 1	4.41923505	0.480669674	9.193913
X Variable 2	–0.0587237	0.081383757	–0.72157

2. Click Add-Ins.
3. Click Analysis ToolPak. (If Analysis ToolPak is not listed among your available add-ins, exit Excel, double-click the MS Excel Setup icon, click Add/Remove, double-click Add-Ins, and select Analysis ToolPak. Then restart Excel and repeat the above instruction.)

After ensuring that the Analysis ToolPak is available, you can access the regression tool by completing the following steps:

1. Click the Tools menu.
2. Click Data Analysis.
3. Click Regression.

Marketing Research

Marketing research is essentially a twofold activity. It involves (1) collecting current data describing all phases of the marketing operations and (2) presenting the findings to marketing managers in a form suitable for decision making. The focus is on the timeliness of the information. The goal of marketing research is to conduct a systematic, objective, bias-free inquiry of the market and customer preferences. A variety of tools such as surveys, questionnaires, pilot studies, and in-depth interviews are used for marketing research. Marketing research can identify the features that customers really want in a product or from a service. Important attributes of products or services—style, color, size, appearance, and general fit—can be investigated through the use of marketing research.

Marketing research broadly encompasses advertising research and consumer behavior research. *Advertising research* is research on such advertising issues as ad and copy effectiveness, recall, and media choice. *Consumer behavior research* answers questions about consumers and their brand selection behaviors and preferences in the market-place. Research results are used to make marketing mix decisions and for pricing, distribution channels, guarantees and warranties, and customer service. Statistical analysis software is used to analyze the data collected from marketing research endeavors. These software packages can determine trends, test hypotheses, compute statistical values, and more. This data is then often input into the marketing MIS so that marketing managers can be better informed and can better make their planning and resource allocation decisions.

Product Development

Product development is one of the four Ps in the marketing mix—product, place, promotion, and price—each of which is explained later. Product development involves the transformation of raw materials into finished goods and services, and primarily focuses on the physical attributes of the product. Many factors, including materials, labor skills, plant capacity, and technical factors, are important in product development decisions. In many cases, a computer program for mathematical programming and simulations can be utilized to analyze these various factors and to select the appropriate mix of labor, materials, plant and equipment, and engineering designs. Make-or-outsource decisions can also be made with the assistance of computer software. A framework, called the product life cycle, guides the manager in making product development decisions. It takes into account four stages in the life cycle: introduction, growth, maturity, and decline.

Place Planning

Place planning involves planning on the means of physically distributing the product to the customer. It includes production, transportation, storage, and distribution on both the wholesale and retail levels. Where to deliver the product to the customer and how to get the product to this location are the principal concerns of place analysis subsystems. Typically, a distribution chain starts at the manufacturing plant and ends at the final consumer. In the middle is a network of wholesale and retail outlets employed to efficiently and effectively bring goods and services to the final consumer. But where are the best places to locate manufacturing facilities, wholesale outlets, and retail distribution points? Factors such as manufacturing costs, transportation costs, labor costs, and localized demand levels become critical to answering this issue. Today, marketing MIS subsystems can analyze these factors and determine the least-cost placement of manufacturing facilities, wholesale operations, and retail outlets. The purpose of these locational analysis programs is to minimize total costs while satisfying product demand. Digital maps combined with customer database information in computer mapping software can be used to pinpoint locations for new retail outlets. For example, Yamaha Motor Corporation, USA has made decisions as to where to locate their dealerships by blending computer graphics with behavioral demographics. Behavioral demographics link psychological, lifestyle, and family expenditure data to geographic locations, often by zip code.

Promotion Planning

One of the most important functions of any marketing effort is promotion. Promotion is concerned with all the means of marketing the sale of the product, including advertising and personal selling. Product success is a direct function of the effectiveness of advertising and sales promotion. The size of the promotion budget and the allocation of this budget to various promotional mixes are important factors in deciding which type of campaign will be launched. Television coverage, newspaper ads and coverage, promotional brochures and literature, and training programs for salespeople are all components of these promotional and advertising mixes. Because of the time and scheduling savings they offer, computer software is widely used to establish the original budget and to monitor expenditures and the overall effectiveness of various promotional campaigns.

Promotional effectiveness can be monitored through the TPS, or it may be monitored through a specialized functional system focusing exclusively on sales activity. For example, a significant proportion of many marketing managers' compensation is determined by the results of their promotional campaigns through specialized sales activity subsystems. Such systems often use data from retail outlet bar-code scanners to compile information on how effective certain promotions were within the promotional period. Without such sales activity, the time delay between wholesale shipments and retail sales would prevent the promotion's effectiveness from being accurately measured. The following example illustrates the use of linear programming to determine optimal media selection for sales promotion.

Example 13.2 Media Selection

The management of an electric products company decided to spend up to $1 million on the advertising of women's electric razors that it manufactures. The advertising budget is to be spent in 12 consumer magazines with full-page, full-color advertisements. Let Xi be the number of dollars spent on advertising in magazine i.

EXAMPLE 13.2 MEDIA SELECTION *(continued)*

Management is advised by an advertising agency that an appropriate goal is to *maximize* the number of effective exposures given the advertising budget. Management wants to assure that no more than 12 insertions are made in any one magazine and that it wishes the number of insertions in *Mademoiselle* and *Ladies Home Journal* to be less than or equal to 7 and 2, respectively. Suppose also that management wishes to specify minimum expenditures in certain of the magazines, say, X2 ≥ 17,810, X3 ≥ 67,200, X5 ≥ 42,840, and X10 32,550. Finally, management desires an expenditure of no more than $320,000 in four of the magazines, say, 3, 9, 10, and 12. The following table presents the number of exposures and cost for each advertising medium:

Media	Effective Readings per Dollar Spent	Cost of One Full-Page, Full-Color Advertisement
1. *Cosmopolitan*	158	$5,500
2. *Mademoiselle*	263	5,950
3. *Family Circle*	106	33,600
4. *Good Housekeeping*	108	27,400
5. *McCall's*	65	42,840
6. *Modern Romance*	176	3,275
7. *Film Quarterly*	285	3,415
8. *Soap Opera Digest*	86	2,248
9. *TV Guide*	120	25,253
10. *Woman's Day*	51	32,550
11. *Seventeen*	190	8,850
12. *Ladies Home Journal*	101	35,000

The LP model is:

Maximize 158 X1 + 263 X2 + 106 X3 + 108 X4 + 65 X5 + 176 X6 + 285 X7 + 86 X8 + 120 X9 + 51 X10 + 190 X11 + 101 X12

Subject to
(1) 0 ≤ Xi ≤ 12 (i = 1,2,3,. . ., 12)
(2) X2 ≤ 7, X12 ≤ 2
(3) 5950 X2 ≥ 17,810, 33600 X3 ≥ 67,200, 42840 X5 ≥ 42,840, 32550 X10 ≥ 32,550
(4) 33600 X3 + 25253 X9 + 32550 X10 + 35000 X12 ≤ 320,000

The LINDO input and output are summarized below.

```
MAX 158 X1 + 263 X2 + 106 X3 + 108 X4 + 65 X5 + 176 X6
+ 285 X7 + 86 X8 + 120 X9 + 51 X10 + 190 X11 + 101 X12

Subject to
 2)  X1 <= 12
 3)  X2 <= 12
 4)  X3 <= 12
 5)  X4 <= 12
 6)  X5 <= 12
 7)  X6 <= 12
```

EXAMPLE 13.3 MEDIA SELECTION *(continued)*

8) X7 <= 12
9) X8 <= 12
10) X9 <= 12
11) X10 <= 12
12) X11 <= 12
13) X12 <= 12
14) X2 <= 7
15) X12 <= 2
16) 5950 X2 >= 17810
17) 33600 X3 >= 67200
18) 42480 X5 >= 42480
19) 32550 X10 >= 32550
20) 33600 X3 + 25253 X9 + 32550 X10 + 35000 X12
<= t 320000

END

LP Optimum found at Step 14.

Objective Function Value

1) 15966.6100

Variable	Value	Reduced Cost
X1	12.000000	.000000
X2	7.000000	.000000
X3	2.000000	.000000
X4	12.000000	.000000
X5	12.000000	.000000
X6	12.000000	.000000
X7	12.000000	.000000
X8	12.000000	.000000
X9	8.721736	.000000
X10	1.000000	.000000
X11	12.000000	.000000
X12	.000000	65.316860

Pricing

Pricing is an important managerial decision that has a long-term effect on the sales and profitability of the firm. In most instances, especially in the field of durable consumer goods, notably audio-video equipment, automobiles, and so on, the scope for product differentiation allows competing firms to have considerable leeway in setting the prices of their products. Three popular pricing approaches are a cost-based pricing policy, a return on investment (ROI)–based pricing policy, and a demand-based pricing policy. The MIS can support the manager in all three pricing policies. With the cost-based approach, the accounting system can provide accurate product cost data on which to base a decision. With the other approaches, the MIS enables the manager to engage in what-if modeling to determine the price level that maximizes contribution to profits yet retards competitive activity.

A major factor in determining pricing policy is an analysis of the demand curve, which attempts to determine the relationship between price and sales. Most companies try

Price	$e_p > 1$	$e_p = 1$	$e_p < 1$
Price rises	S falls	No change	S rises
Price falls	S rises	No change	S falls

Exhibit 13.4 RELATIONSHIP BETWEEN PRICE AND ELASTICITY

to develop pricing policies that will maximize total sales revenues. This is usually a function of price elasticity. If the product is highly price sensitive, a reduction in price can generate a substantial increase in sales, which can result in higher revenues. A product that is relatively insensitive to price can have its price substantially increased without a large reduction in demand. Exhibit 13.4 shows the relationships between price elasticity (e_p) and sales revenue (S), which can aid a firm in setting its price.

Computer programs exist that help determine price elasticity and various pricing policies. With the aid of computer software for spreadsheets and statistical packages, the marketing managers can typically develop what-if scenarios in which they can alter factors to see price changes on future demand and total revenues.

EXAMPLE 13.3 ROI PRICING

One of the widely used pricing methods, especially in large corporations, is pricing to achieve a targeted rate of return on investment (ROI). Furthermore, there is an increasing tendency among firms to adopt some form of target ROI pricing. This is mainly due to a growing awareness of the need to integrate pricing policy with the objective of achieving a satisfactory rate of return on capital invested. ROI pricing is certainly the most widely used pricing method today. The use of spreadsheet software and what-if analysis can be readily applied to the area of product pricing.

The conventional ROI pricing technique is generally along the following lines: a standard volume of production is estimated; the variable cost per unit is calculated for this level of production; and fixed factory overhead, selling, and administrative expenses are allocated over the number of units at standard volume of production. Depreciation on assets is included in the fixed costs. The rate of depreciation is either an estimated rate, which in the opinion of the management reflects the fall in the value of assets, or more likely, the depreciation rate allowed under the tax law is generally adopted. The markup per unit is arrived at by calculating the desired dollar return (on the total capital invested—i.e., debt as well as equity) and dividing by the number of units at standard volume. The return on investment rate expected is determined by management according to its

EXAMPLE 13.3 ROI PRICING *(continued)*

expectations of what constitutes a fair return. Tax aspects are generally ignored. The outline of an ROI pricing model (with assumed figures) is presented below:

X = Estimated Sales (units)		100,000
OI = Opening Inventory value $45,000		10,000
CI = Closing Inventory (units) value $100,000		20,000
(valuation at variable cost & FIFO)		
Production (units)		110,000
VC = Variable Cost (@ $5)		550,000
FC = Fixed Cost (manufacturing, selling, administrative)		200,000
RR = Recoveries Required:		
Interest (INT)	50,000	
Dividends	60,000	
Debt Recovery	100,000	
Equity Recovery	90,000	300,000
T = Tax Rate		40%
D = Depreciation allowable under tax laws		30,000

The selling price can then be calculated by the following formula:

$$SP = \frac{RR + FC - (t)[FC + D + INT + OI - CI] + VC/unit}{(1 - t) \times X}$$

Substituting the assumed figures in the above formula:

$$SP = \frac{30000 + 20000 - (.40)[20000 + 3000 + 5000 + 45000 - 100000] + 5}{(1 - .40)(100000)}$$

$$= \$11.83 \text{ per unit}$$

The spreadsheet contains parameters for what-if (sensitivity) analysis on three levels: normal, optimistic, and pessimistic. Consequently, the template generates product prices under optimistic, pessimistic, and normal expectations of the person making the pricing decision. A printout of the worksheet with assumed figures is shown in Exhibit 13.5.

Sales Analysis

Sales analysis assists managers in identifying products, sales personnel, and customers who are contributing to profits and those who are not. Several reports can be generated to help marketing managers make good sales decisions. The *sales-by-product* report lists all major products and their sales for a period of time, such as a month. This report shows which products are doing well and which ones need improvement or should be discarded altogether. The *sales-by-salesperson* report lists total sales for each salesperson for each week or month. This report can also be subdivided by product to show which products are being sold by each salesperson. The *sales-by-customer* report is a useful way to identify high- and low-volume customers.

Variation Type	Normal	Pessimistic	Optimistic		Normal	Pessimistic	Optimistic
(%)	100%	96%	102%	Sales (Units)	100,000	96,000	102,000
				Beginning inventory	10,000	10,000	10,000
				Value @ $4.5	$ 45,000	$ 45,000	$ 45,000
Desired level % of sales			20	Ending inventory	20,000	19,200	20,400
				Value	$ 100,000	$ 107,520	$ 91,800
				Production (Units)	110,000	105,200	112,400
				Costs			
Unit cost	$ 5.00	$ 5.60	$ 4.50	Variable costs	$ 550,000	$ 589,120	$ 505,800
(%)	100%	101%	99%	Fixed costs (Manufacturing, selling & adm.)	$ 200,000	$ 202,000	$ 198,000
				Total costs	$ 750,000	$ 791,120	$ 703,800
				Recoveries			
				Interest	$ 50,000	$ 50,000	$ 50,000
				Dividends	$ 60,000	$ 60,000	$ 60,000
				Debt recovery	$ 100,000	$ 100,000	$ 100,000
				Equity recovery	$ 90,000	$ 90,000	$ 90,000
					$ 300,000	$ 300,000	$ 300,000
Tax rate			40%				
Depreciation (allowable under tax laws)			$ 30,000	Selling price	$ 11.83	$ 12.79	$11.13

Exhibit 13.5 PRODUCT PRICING WORKSHEET (WHAT-IF) PARAMETERS

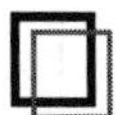

POPULAR FORECASTING AND STATISTICAL SOFTWARE

There are numerous computer software packages that are used for forecasting purposes. They are broadly divided into two major categories: forecasting software and general-purpose statistical software. Some programs are stand-alone, while others are spreadsheet add-ins. Still others are templates. A brief summary of some popular programs follows.

Sales & Market Forecasting Toolkit

It is a Lotus 1-2-3 template that produces sales and market forecasts, even for new products with limited historical data.

- Eight powerful methods for more accurate forecasts
- Spreadsheet models, complete with graph, ready-to-use with your numbers

The Sales & Market Forecasting Toolkit offers a variety of forecasting methods to help you generate accurate business forecasts even in new or changing markets with limited historical data. The forecasting methods include:

- Customer poll
- Whole-market penetration
- Chain method
- Strategic modeling
- Moving averages, exponential smoothing, and linear regressions

The customer poll method helps build a forecast from the ground up by summing the individual components such as products, stores, or customers. Whole-market penetration, market share, and the chain method are top-down forecasting methods used to predict sales for new products and markets lacking sales data. The strategic modeling method develops a forecast by projecting the impact of changes to pricing and advertising expenditures. Statistical forecasting methods include exponential smoothing, moving averages, and linear regression.

You can use the built-in macros to enter data into your forecast automatically. For example, enter values for the first and last months of a 12-month forecast. The compounded-growth-rate macro will automatically compute and enter values for the other 10 months.

Forecast! GFX

Forecast! GFX is a stand-alone forecasting system that can perform five types of time-series analysis: seasonal adjustment, linear and nonlinear trend analysis, moving-average analysis, exponential smoothing, and decomposition. Trend analysis supports linear, exponential, hyperbolic, S-curve, and polynomial trends. Hyperbolic trend models are used to analyze data that indicates a decline toward a limit, such as the output of an oil well or the price of a particular model of personal computer. Forecast! GFX can perform multiple-regression analysis with up to 10 independent variables.

ForeCalc

ForeCalc, a Lotus add-in, uses nine forecasting techniques and includes both automatic and manual modes, and eliminates the need to export or reenter data. In automatic mode, just highlight the historical data in your spreadsheet, such as sales, expenses, or net income; then ForeCalc tests several exponential-smoothing models and picks the one that best fits your data.

Forecast results can be transferred to your spreadsheet with upper and lower confidence limits. ForeCalc generates a line graph showing the original data, the forecasted values, and confidence limits.

ForeCalc can automatically choose the most accurate forecasting technique:

- Simple one-parameter smoothing
- Holt's two-parameter smoothing
- Winters's three-parameter smoothing
- Trendless seasonal models
- Dampened versions of Holt and Winters's smoothing

ForeCalc's manual mode lets you select the type of trend and seasonality, yielding nine possible model combinations. You can vary the type of trend (constant, linear, or dampened), as well as the seasonality (nonseasonal, additive, or multiplicative).

StatPlan IV

StatPlan IV is a stand-alone program for those who understand how to apply statistics to business analysis. You can use it for market analysis, trend forecasting, and statistical modeling.

StatPlan IV lets you analyze data by range, mean, median, standard deviation, skewdness, kurtosis, correlation analysis, one- or two-way analysis of variance (ANOVA), cross-tabulations, and t-test.

The forecasting methods include multiple regression, stepwise multiple regression, polynomial regression, bivariate curve fitting, autocorrelation analysis, trend and cycle analysis, and exponential smoothing.

The data can be displayed in X-Y plots, histograms, time-series graphs, autocorrelation plots, actual versus forecast plots, or frequency and percentile tables.

Geneva Statistical Forecasting

Geneva Statistical Forecasting, stand-alone software, can batch-process forecasts for thousands of data series, provided the series are all measured in the same time units (days, weeks, months, and so on). The software automatically tries out as many as nine different forecasting methods, including six linear and nonlinear regressions and three exponential-smoothing techniques, before picking the one that best fits your historical data.

The program incorporates provisions that simplify and accelerate the process of reforecasting data items. Once you complete the initial forecast, you can save a data file that records the forecasting method assigned to each line item. When it is time to update the data, simply retrieve the file and reforecast, using the same methods as before.

SmartForecasts

SmartForecasts, a stand-alone forecasting software program, features the following:

- Automatically chooses the right statistical method
- Lets you manually adjust forecasts to reflect your business judgment
- Produces forecast results

SmartForecasts combines the benefits of statistical and judgmental forecasting. It can determine which statistical method will give you the most accurate forecast and handles all the math. Forecasts can be modified using the program's Eyeball utility. You may need to adjust a sales forecast to reflect an anticipated increase in advertising or a decrease in price. SmartForecasts summarizes data with descriptive statistics, plots the distribution of data values with histograms, plots variables in a scattergram, and identifies leading indicators.

You can forecast using single- and double-exponential smoothing, and simple- and linear-moving averages. It even builds seasonality into your forecasts using Winters's exponential smoothing, or you can eliminate seasonality by using time-series decomposition and seasonal adjustment.

In addition, SmartForecasts features simultaneous multi-series forecasting of up to 60 variables and 150 data points per variable, offers multivariate regression to let you relate business variables, and has an Undo command for mistakes.

Tomorrow

Tomorrow, a stand-alone forecasting package, uses an optimized combination of linear regression, single exponential smoothing, adaptive rate response single exponential smoothing, Brown's one-parameter double exponential smoothing, Holt's two-parameter exponential smoothing, Brown's one-parameter triple exponential smoothing, and Gardner's three-parameter damped trend. Some of the main features include:

- There is no need to reformat your existing spreadsheets. Tomorrow recognizes and forecasts formula cells (containing totals and subtotals, for example). It handles both horizontally and vertically oriented spreadsheets. It accepts historical data in up to 30 separate ranges.

- Allows you to specify seasonality manually or calculates seasonality automatically.
- Allows you to do several forecasts of different time series (for example, sales data from different regions) at once.
- Recognizes and forecasts time-series headings (names of months, etc.).
- Forecast optionally becomes a normal part of your spreadsheet.
- Undo command restores original spreadsheet.
- Browse feature allows you to look at any part of the spreadsheet (including the forecast) without leaving Tomorrow.
- Checks for and prevents accidental overlaying of nonempty or protected cells.
- Optional annotation mode labels forecast cells, calculates MAPE, and, when seasonality is automatically determined, describes the seasonality.
- Comprehensive context-sensitive online help.

Forecast Pro

Forecast Pro, a stand-alone forecasting program, is the business software that uses artificial intelligence. A built-in expert system examines your data. Then it guides you to exponential smoothing, Box-Jenkins, or regression—whichever method suits the data best.

MicroTSP

MicroTSP is a stand-alone software package that provides the tools most frequently used in practical econometric and forecasting work. It covers the following:

1. Descriptive statistics
2. A wide range of single-equation estimation techniques including ordinary least squares (multiple regression), two-stage least squares, nonlinear least squares, and probit and logit.

Forecasting tools include exponential smoothing (including single exponential, double exponential, and Winters's smoothing) and Box-Jenkins methodology.

Sibyl/Runner

Sibyl/Runner is an interactive, stand-alone forecasting system. In addition to allowing the usage of all major forecasting methods, the package permits analysis of the data, suggests available forecasting methods, compares results, and provides several accuracy measures in such a way that it is easier for the user to select an appropriate method and forecast needed data under different economic and environmental conditions. For details, see Makridakis, S., Hodgsdon, and S. Wheelwright, "An Interactive Forecasting System," *American Statistician,* November 1974.

Other Forecasting Software

There are many other forecasting software programs such as Autocast II, 4 Cast, and Trendsetter Expert Version.

General-Purpose Statistical Software

There are numerous statistical software programs that can be utilized in order to build a forecasting model. Some of the more popular ones include:

- SAS Application System
- SPSS
- Minitab
- RATS
- BMD

Today's managers have some powerful tools at hand to simplify the forecasting process and increase its accuracy. Several forecasting models are available, and the automated versions of these should be considered by any manager who is regularly called upon to provide forecasts. A personal computer with a spreadsheet is a good beginning, but the stand-alone packages currently available provide the most accurate forecasts and are the easiest to use. In addition, they make several forecasting models available and can automatically select the best one for a particular data set.

CHAPTER 14

DECISION SUPPORT SYSTEMS

DISTINGUISHING AMONG TPS, MIS, EIS, DSS, AND ES

As discussed in Chapter 1, information systems are distinguished by the type of decisions they support, the operator who uses the system, the management control level of the system, the function of the system, and its attributes (see Exhibit 1.1). There are information systems to support structured decisions, unstructured decisions, and anything in between. At the strategic level of management, decisions are unstructured, and decision styles may differ significantly among managers. Furthermore, a specific decision problem may occur only once. Thus, information systems developed for this level often are decision specific. Once the decision is made, the information system used for it is no longer applicable in its current form. For subsequent decisions, the system must be modified or discarded—a development that has major implications for the design of information systems. Whereas executive information systems and decision support systems aid in decisions that are unstructured, transaction processing systems and expert systems aid in decisions that are structured.

The manager who uses the information system helps distinguish the system. Transaction processing systems (TPSs) are used at the operational level of an organization such as by clerks or secretaries. Executive information systems (EISs) are used specifically by personnel at the senior management level such as vice presidents or presidents of an organization. Decision support systems (DSSs) are used by middle management such as managers of the accounting department. Expert systems (ESs) are used by personnel at all levels of an organization.

Another factor that distinguishes information systems is the function of the systems. Transaction processing systems were established to computerize manual systems. Executive information systems (EISs) were designed to aid senior managers in decision making. Decision support systems were designed to aid middle managers in decision making, and expert systems (ESs) were designed to aid all personnel in decision making.

The final distinguishing factor of information systems is the attributes of the system. Transaction processing systems are used to handle day-to-day transactions such as the accounts payable system of an organization. Attributes of executive information systems include visual summaries of forecasts and budgets of an organization. Decision support system attributes include visual displays of the sales, income or interest estimates for the day, month, or year. Expert system attributes include systems that assess bad debts or authorize credit.

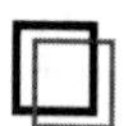

DECISION SUPPORT SYSTEMS (DSSs)

A DSS is a computer-based information system that assists managers in making many complex decisions, such as decisions needed to solve poorly defined or semistructured problems. Instead of replacing the manager in the decision process, the DSS supports the manager in his or her application of the decision process. In other words, it is an automated assistant that extends the mental capabilities of the manager. Most authorities view the DSS as an integral part of the MIS, in that its primary purpose is to provide decision-making information to managerial decision makers. A DSS allows the manager to change assumptions concerning expected future conditions and to observe the effects on the relevant criteria. As a result of these direct benefits, a DSS enables the manager to gain a better understanding of the key factors affecting the decision. It enables the manager to evaluate a large number of alternative courses of action within a reasonably short time frame.

A DSS summarizes or compares data from either or both internal and external sources (see Exhibit 14.1). Internal sources include data from an organization's database such as sales, manufacturing, or financial data. Data from external sources includes information on interest rates, population trends, new housing construction, or raw material pricing.

DSSs often include query languages, statistical analysis capabilities, spreadsheets, and graphics to help the user evaluate the decision data. More advanced decision support systems include capabilities that allow users to create a model of the variables affecting a decision. With a model, users can ask what-if questions by changing one or more of the variables and seeing what the projected results would be. A simple model for determining the best product price would include factors for the expected sales volume at each price level. Many people use electronic spreadsheets for

Graphical
Large database
Integrates many sources of data
Report and presentation flexibility
Geared toward individual decision-making styles
Modular format
Optimization and heuristic approach
What-if and simulation
Goal-seeking and impact analysis
Performs statistical and analytical analysis

Exhibit 14.1 CHARACTERISTICS OF A DECISION SUPPORT SYSTEM (DSS)

simple modeling tasks. A DSS is sometimes combined with executive information systems (EISs). DSS applications used in business include systems that estimate profitability, plan monthly operations, determine the source and application of funds, and schedule staff.

PALISADE'S DECISIONTOOLS SUITE

Palisade's DecisionTools Suite is a DSS tool in the area of risk and decision analysis. It includes such programs as @RISK, @RISK for Project, TopRank, PrecisionTree, BestFit, and RISKview. These programs analyze risk, run Monte Carlo simulations, perform sensitivity analyses, and fit data to distributions.

- *@RISK* is a risk analysis and simulation add-in for Microsoft Excel and Lotus 1-2-3. It is the risk analysis tool. Replace values in your spreadsheet with @RISK distributions to represent uncertainty, then simulate your model using powerful Monte Carlo simulation methods. @RISK recalculates your spreadsheet hundreds (or thousands) of times. The results: distributions of possible outcome values! Results are displayed graphically and through detailed statistical reports.
- *@RISK for Project* adds the same powerful Monte Carlo techniques to Microsoft Project models, allowing users to answer questions such as, What is the chance the project will be completed on schedule?
- *TopRank* is a what-if analysis add-in for either Microsoft Excel or Lotus 1-2-3 for Windows. Take any spreadsheet model, select the cells that hold your results, and TopRank automatically determines which spreadsheet values affect your results the most. TopRank then ranks the values in order of importance. Your results can be displayed in Tornado, Spider, and Sensitivity high-resolution graphs, allowing

you to easily understand the outcome at a glance. TopRank works easily and effectively with @RISK by identifying the critical cells that users should concentrate on when running Monte Carlo simulations.

- *PrecisionTree* is a powerful, innovative decision analysis tool. You can enter decision trees and influence diagrams directly in your spreadsheet models, and detail all available decision options to identify the optimal decision. Your decision analysis factors in your attitudes toward risk and the uncertainty present in your model. Sensitivity analysis identifies the critical factors that affect the decision you'll make. PrecisionTree is a real plus for outlining all available options for a decision or identifying and presenting the best course of action.
- *BestFit* is the distribution fitting solution for Windows. BestFit takes data sets (up to 30,000 data points or pairs) and finds the distribution that best fits the data. BestFit accepts three types of data from text files: direct entry, cut and paste, or direct link to data within Excel or Lotus 1-2-3 spreadsheets. BestFit tests up to 26 distribution types using advanced optimization algorithms. Results are displayed graphically and through an expanded report that includes goodness-of-fit statistics. BestFit distributions can be used directly in @RISK for Excel, Lotus 1-2-3, and Microsoft Project models.
- *RISKview* is the distribution viewing companion to @RISK, @RISK for Project, or BestFit. It is a powerful tool for viewing, assessing, and creating probability distributions.

DSS APPLICATIONS

Many DSS practical applications are described in the following sections:

1. Hewlett-Packard developed *Quality Decision Management* to perform production and quality-control functions. It can help with raw material inspection, product testing, and statistical analysis.
2. *Manufacturing Decision Support System (MDSS)*, developed at Purdue University to support decisions in automated manufacturing facilities, is especially useful for CAD/CAM operations.
3. RCA has developed a DSS to deal with personnel problems and issues. The system, called *Industrial Relations Information Systems (IRIS)*, can handle problems that may not be anticipated or that may occur once, and can assist in difficult labor negotiations.

4. The Great Eastern Bank Trust Division developed a DSS called *On-line Portfolio Management (OPM)* that can be used for portfolio and investment management. The DSS permits display and analysis of various investments and securities.
5. *ReolPlan,* a DSS to assist with commercial real estate decisions, is useful for various decision aspects of purchasing, renovating, and selling property.
6. *EPLAN (Energy Pion)* is a DSS being developed by the National Audubon Society to analyze the impact of U.S. energy policy on the environment.
7. The *Transportation Evacuation Decision Support System (TEDSS)* is a DSS used in nuclear plants in Virginia. It analyzes and develops evacuation plans to assist managers in crisis management decisions regarding evaluation times and routes and the allocation of shelter resources.
8. The U.S. Army has developed an enlisted manpower DSS to help with recruitment, training, education, reclassification, and promotion decisions. It encompasses simulation and optimization to model personnel needs and requirements. It interacts with an online database and other statistical analysis software packages.
9. *Voyage Profitability Estimator* is a DSS used by a shipping firm to compute the income from decisions affecting charter rates to be charged for particular trips. The system saves time and makes it possible to evaluate trade-offs between speed and fuel usage. The analysis involves ship and voyage characteristics such as tonnage, rate of fuel consumption, and port cost.
10. *Monthly Plan Calculations* serves as a corporate budgeting tool to measure the levels of manpower needed to perform various functions, to calculate costs, and in general to evaluate the adequacy of proposed operational plans. Using simple formulas, this system calculates the cost of materials and inventory, among other items, based on input that consists of monthly production and shipment plans. Typically, the system is used iteratively in an attempt to generate a plan that is sufficiently profitable and that meets the company's goal of maintaining reasonable-level production in spite of the seasonal nature of the product.
11. *Source and Application of Funds* is an online budget of source and applications of funds that has been used for operational decision making and financial planning in an insurance company to provide monthly cash flow figures. The DSS "output" is used at weekly meetings of an investment committee to help

in allocating funds across investment areas and to minimize the amount of cash that is left idle in banks.

12. *Interactive Audit Staff Scheduling Systems*, an integer programming model, was designed by Balachandran and Zoltners to assist public accounting firms in scheduling their audit staff in an optimal and effective manner. The computerized management support system for scheduling staff to an audit can include the basic model along with a judgmental scheduling system and a scheduling information database. Motivation, morale, turnover, and productivity of the audit staff can all be affected by scheduling. In the scheduling process, the audit firm needs to consider its audit philosophy, objectives, staff size, rotational plans, and auditor evaluation. Many feasible audit staff schedules may fill these needs, but the firm needs to select the schedule that best meets its own objectives.

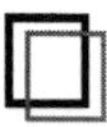

EXECUTIVE INFORMATION SYSTEMS (EISs)

An executive information system (EIS) is a DSS made specially for top managers and specifically supports strategic decision making. An EIS is also called an executive support system (ESS). It draws on data not only from systems internal to the organization but also from those outside, such as news services and market research databases. The EIS user interface often uses a mouse or a touch screen to help executives unfamiliar with using a keyboard. One leading system uses a remote-control device similar to those used to control a television set. An EIS might allow senior executives to call up predefined reports for their personal computers, whether desktops or laptops. They might, for instance, call up sales figures in many forms—by region, by week, by fiscal year, by projected increases. The EIS includes capabilities for analyzing data and doing what-if scenarios.

Another aspect of the EIS user interface is the graphic presentation of user information. The EIS relies heavily on graphic presentation of both the processing options and data. Again, this is designed to make the system easier to use.

Because executives focus on strategic issues, the EIS often has access to external databases such as the Dow Jones News/Retrieval service. Such external sources of information can provide current information on interest rates, commodity prices, and other leading economic indicators. Exhibit 14.2 presents the attributes of an executive information system.

A popular EIS software is Xecutive Pulse developed by Megatrend System, Inc. It is a Windows-based executive information system. The software interfaces with many

Graphical
Easy-to-use interface
Broad, aggregated, perspective
Different data sources
Optionally expand to detail level
Provide context
Timeliness crucial

Exhibit 14.2 CHARACTERISTICS OF EXECUTIVE INFORMATION SYSTEMS (EISS)

popular LAN-based accounting applications. It provides decision makers with easy access to financial and sales information including trend analysis using drill-down and drill-across technology. Hundreds of charts, graphs, and views are available with a mouse click. The system extracts data from accounting history files, builds a database, and stores up to three years of information for each accounting period. Users can drill down through five organizational levels, compare actual versus history and actual versus budget, and display report or graphic results. Xecutive Pulse features extensive sales, cash flow, and human resource analysis, plus daily trends for accounts receivable, accounts payable, margins, sales, and inventory.

Limitations of Current EISs

Although they offer great promise, many EISs have not been successfully implemented and many executives have stopped using them. A common reason cited in several failed attempts is the mistake of not modifying the system to the specific needs of the individual executives who will use the system. For example, many executives prefer to have information presented in a particular sequence with the option of seeing different levels of supporting detailed information such as cost data on a spreadsheet. The desired sequence and level of detail varies for each executive. It appears that an EIS must be tailored to the executives' requirements or the executives will continue to manage with information they have obtained through previously established methods. This limitation can be corrected by *tailoring* the software based on the particular needs of the managers within the specific company. After the software has been appropriately modified, it will have significant practical applications.

EIS Applications

There are many EIS applications for managers, including those described in the following sections.

EIS IN MEASURING PRODUCTIVITY

This application bears on management's concern over productivity. Management may use both internal and external information extracted from the EIS to show how productivity in an organization has declined in recent years. Financial data can be retrieved from the EIS database to demonstrate how increases in unit labor costs over time have been primarily responsible for significant increases in the product's unit cost and have been damaging to the company's competitiveness by forcing increases in the product's selling price. Executives can also compare company sales (internal data) to industry sales trends (external data) from the EIS to project market share changes in response to changes in selling price.

External information may also be extracted from the EIS database to indicate how competitors achieve greater efficiency by using less labor and more advanced technology to manufacture a quality product at a materially lower unit cost. As a result, management may demonstrate that the competition is able to sell greater quantities of their products at lower prices. This information may provide justification for closing the unprofitable plant and opening a modern facility that will enable a company to be more competitive in the industry.

EIS IN PRODUCT COSTING DECISIONS

Resolving the conflict between profitability in the short run and increasing market share in the long run requires a mix of both external and internal data for a rational decision. Executives need information on product demand and elasticity, competing products and strategies, the economy, and other factors such as the cost of manufacturing the product and trade-offs that exist relative to different product quality levels under different cost assumptions. Some questions executives may raise are:

- What is the current level of quality and how does the level differ from the desired level?
- What is the current full cost of producing a unit and how does the amount differ from the full cost at the desired level of quality?
- What costs are variable over different levels of product quality?
- What costs are controllable relative to producing and selling the products?

EIS can provide data for solutions to some of these questions by computation. Many internal decisions depend on assumptions and measurements that require judgment and may be subject to different interpretations. In product costing decisions, issues involving appropriate cost and product quality trade-offs are equally subjective and unlikely to have a unique interpretation.

CHAPTER 15

ARTIFICIAL INTELLIGENCE (AI) AND EXPERT SYSTEMS (ESs)

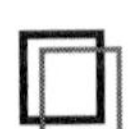

WHAT IS ARTIFICIAL INTELLIGENCE (AI)?

Artificial intelligence is the application of human reasoning techniques to machines. Artificial intelligence systems use sophisticated computer hardware and software to simulate the functions of the human mind. Expert systems are the most promising applications of artificial intelligence and have received the most attention.

Expert systems are computer programs exhibiting behavioral characteristics of experts. Expert systems involve the creation of computer software that emulates the way people solve problems. Like a human expert, an expert system gives advice by drawing upon its own store of knowledge and by requesting information specific to the problem at hand. Expert systems are not exactly the same thing as decision support systems. A DSS is computer-based software that assists decision makers by providing data and models. It performs primarily semistructured tasks, whereas an expert system is more appropriate for unstructured tasks. Decision support systems can be interactive just like an expert system. But, because of the way decision support systems process information, they typically cannot be used for unstructured decisions that involve nonquantitative data. Unlike expert systems, decision support systems do not make decisions but merely attempt to improve and enhance decisions by providing indirect support without automating the whole decision process.

Some general characteristics indicate whether a given business application is likely to be a good candidate for the development of an expert system. For example, the application must require the use of expert knowledge, judgment, and experience. The business problem must have a heuristic nature and must be defined clearly. The area of expertise required for the application must be well defined and recognized professionally, and the organization developing the expert system must be able to recruit an expert who is willing to cooperate with the expert system's development team. The size and complexity of the application must be manageable in the context of organizational resources, available technical skills, and management support.

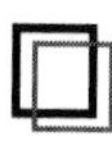

EXPERT SYSTEMS

An expert system (ES), sometimes called a knowledge system, is a set of computer programs that perform a task at the level of a human expert. Expert systems are created on the basis of knowledge collected on specific topics from human experts, and they imitate the reasoning process of a human being. Expert systems have emerged from the field of artificial intelligence, which is the branch of computer science that is attempting to create computer systems that simulate human reasoning and sensation. We describe artificial intelligence in more detail later in the chapter.

Expert systems are used by management and nonmanagement personnel to solve specific problems, such as how to reduce production costs, improve workers' productivity, or reduce environmental impact. Based on methodically using a narrowly defined domain of knowledge that is built into computer programs, the expert system comes up with a solution to a problem much the same way an expert would. The key to the definition is that the domain must be narrowly defined. An expert system cannot (at this point) be developed to give useful answers about all questions—it is limited, as a human expert is limited, to a particular field. For example, one expert system would not tell the controller both whether to lease or buy a piece of equipment based on the tax differences and also whether a pending business combination needs to be treated as a pooling or as a purchase.

How Expert Systems Work

Expert systems are usually considered to have six major components. The relationships of these components are illustrated in Exhibit 15.1. Based on the relationships illustrated in Exhibit 15.1, it is apparent that expert systems must work interactively with system users to help them make better decisions. The system interacts with the user by continuously asking for information until it is ready to make a decision. Once the system has sufficient information, an answer or result is returned to the user. It is essential to note that not only must the system assist in making

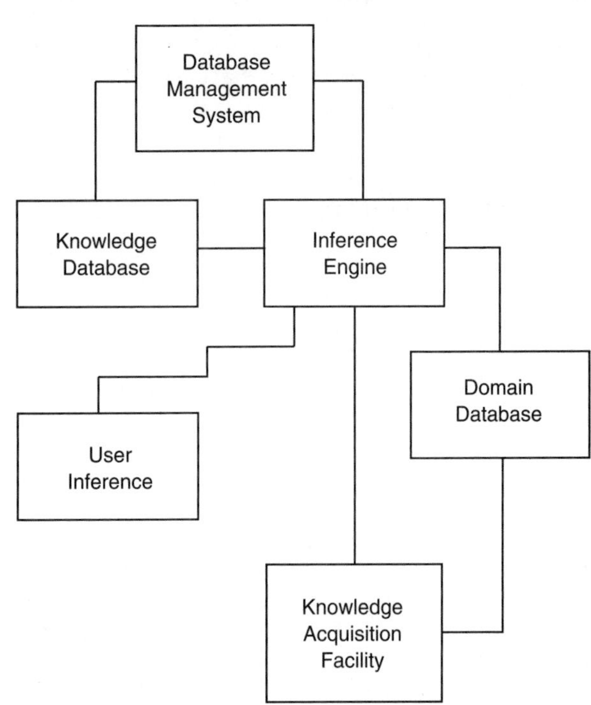

1. *Knowledge rule database:* Contains the rules, problem-solving knowledge, and cases used when making decisions.
2. *Domain database:* The set of facts and information relevant to the domain (area of interest).
3. *Database management system:* Controls input and management of both the knowledge and domain databases.
4. *Inference engine* (Processing System): Contains the inference strategies and controls used by experts to manipulate knowledge and domain databases. It is the brain of the expert system. It receives the request from the user interface and conducts analysis, reasoning, and searching in the knowledge base. The inference engine aids in problem solving such as by processing and scheduling rules. It asks for additional information from the user, makes assumptions about the information, and draws conclusions and recommendations. The inference engine may also determine the degree to which a recommendation is qualified and in the case of multiple solutions rank them.

EXHIBIT 15.1 EXPERT SYSTEM RELATIONSHIPS

5. *User interface:* The explanatory features, online help facilities, debugging tools, modification systems, and other tools designed to assist the user in effectively utilizing the system.
6. *Knowledge acquisition facility:* Allows for interactive processing between the system and the user; how the system acquires "knowledge" from human experts in the form of rules and facts. More advanced technology allows intelligent software to "learn" knowledge from different problem domains. The knowledge learned by computer software is more accurate and reliable than that of human experts.

EXHIBIT 15.1 EXPERT SYSTEM RELATIONSHIPS *(continued)*

the decision itself, it must also provide the user with the logic it employed to reach its decision.

The inference engine processes the data the user inputs to find matches with the knowledge base. The knowledge base is where the expert's information is stored. The user interface is what allows the user to communicate with the program. The explanation facility shows the user how each decision was derived. Expert systems are only as good as their programming. If the information in the knowledge base is incorrect or if the inference engine is not designed properly, the results will be useless. GIGO holds true: garbage in, garbage out.

The knowledge consists of two types of knowledge representations: inductive knowledge (case based) and deductive knowledge (rule based).

RULE-BASED EXPERT SYSTEMS

The rule base of an expert system contains a set of production rules. Each rule has a typical if-then clause. Expert system users provide facts or statements so that production rules can be triggered and the conclusion can be generated. Ford Motor Company uses an expert system to diagnose engine repair problems. Typically, Ford dealers will call the help line in Ford headquarters to receive a suggestion when a complicated engine problem cannot be diagnosed. Today, dealers can access the company's expert systems and receive correct engine diagnosis within seconds. Expert systems can be used at any type of business domain and at any level in an organization. Examples are diagnosing illness, searching for oil, making soup, and analyzing computer systems. More applications and more users are expected in the future.

CASE-BASED EXPERT SYSTEMS

A case-based expert system uses an inductive method to conduct expert system reasoning. In this type of expert system, a case base is employed. A case base consists of many *historical* cases, which have different results. Cases consist of information about a situation, the solution, results of using that solution, and key attributes. The expert inference engine will search through the case base and find the appropriate historical case, which matches the characteristics of the current problem to be solved. After a match has been allocated, the solution of a matched historical case will be modified and used as the new suggestion for this current problem. The *index library* is used to efficiently search and retrieve cases most similar and relevant to solving the current problem. There is an adaption module that creates a solution for the current problem by modifying a prior solution (structural adaptation) or creating a new solution based on similar processes used in previous cases (derivational adaptation).

Lockheed uses an expert system to help speed the purchase of materials ranging from industrial coolant to satellite and rocket parts. The old MISs requested a purchase order to include more than 100 different forms, which were seldom completed by the purchaser. Lots of time was spent to make corrections and changes to make a purchase order complete. By using an expert system, less information is asked and the time required to finish a purchasing order is reduced.

Expert System Shells and Products

An ES shell is a collection of software packages and tools used to design, develop, implement, and maintain expert systems. Expert system shells exist in many different forms. There are a number of off-the-shelf expert system shells that are complete and ready to run. The user enters the appropriate data or parameters, and the expert system provides output to the problem or situation. Some of the expert system shells include Level 5 and VP-Expert. Other shells are described in Exhibit 15.2.

Furthermore, a number of other expert system development tools make the development of expert systems easier and faster. These products help capture if-then rules for the rule base, assist in using tools such as spreadsheets and programming languages, interface with traditional database packages, and generate the inference engine.

Once developed, an expert system can be run by people with virtually no computer experience. The expert system asks the user a series of questions. Subsequent questions are often based on answers to previous questions. After the user answers the system-generated questions, the expert system generates conclusions. Many expert systems have

1st-Class Fusion offers a direct, easy-to-use link to the knowledge base. It also offers a visual rule tree, which graphically shows how rules are related.

Financial Advisor is an ES shell that can analyze capital investments in fixed assets such as equipment and facilities.

Knowledgepro is a high-level language that combines functions of expert systems and hypertext. It allows the setup of classic "if-then" rules, and can read database and spreadsheet files.

Leonardo is an ES shell that employs an object-oriented language used to develop an expert system called COMSTRAT, which can be used by marketing managers to help analyze the position of their companies and products relative to their competition.

Personal Consultant (PC) Easy is a shell used to route vehicles in warehouses and manufacturing plants.

Exhibit 15.2 POPULAR ES SHELLS

word processing capabilities that can generate letters asking users for additional information.

General Uses of Expert Systems

CASE 1

Cyc (short for encyclopedia) is an AI (artificial intelligence) application developed by Cycorp Inc. in Austin, Texas. The system is the brainchild of Douglas B. Lenat. Cyc uses a top-down system to organize knowledge within its knowledge base and to enable the storage of up to 2 million rules. A half-dozen companies including Glaxo Wellcome, Digital Equipment, IBM, and United Healthcare have snapped up the first commercial versions. The ability of Cyc to store mass quantities of data and rules helps United Healthcare manage huge online thesauruses of pharmaceutical and health care terms that have associations based on drug contents and/or interaction effects, thus limiting the need for employees to deal with the complexity of terms.

CASE 2

A newer product based on Cyc is a photo retrieval system. The knowledge base in Cyc is able to learn the relationships between different phrases and use these relationships to search related photographs stored in files along with searchable captions. Type "strong and daring person" and Cyc pulls up a picture captioned "man climbing mountain." Cyc knows that a man is a person, and that mountain climbing demands strength and is dangerous.

CASE 3

Firefly is a web-based Cyc derivative that allows viewers to identify music and artists they like. Based on the information that thousands of other users have entered, Firefly identifies additional music for viewers' consideration. Essentially, Firefly builds patterns in the data and uses the patterns to identify missing pieces in a new user profile. These missing pieces are music or artists who will likely appeal to the viewer.

CASE 4

Derivative products of Cog have also found their way into commercial applications. The principles underlying Cog were used to develop a crablike robot for the Navy that can locate and detonate mines on beaches. Another robot, Hermes, will be used by NASA to explore the surface of Mars. The plan is to literally launch hordes of Hermes to scour the landscape in search of interesting items before calling in the main experimental until to collect samples.

Applications of Expert Systems

The use of expert systems is on the rise. Sales of expert system shells are increasing at about 20% per year, with about 60% of the sales for use on IBM PCs or compatibles. One of the main challenges to the development and use of expert systems is to integrate expert system concepts and functions into existing applications, including transaction processing. The applications of expert systems are many and varied, including security, capacity planning for information systems, military analysis, the construction of maps, and law enforcement. A number of expert systems have been in existence for several years or more. Some of these systems are briefly described below:

- *CoverStory* is an expert system that extracts marketing information from a database and automatically writes marketing reports.
- Westinghouse Electric has an expert system, called *Intelligent Scheduling and Information System (ISIS-11),* for scheduling complex factory orders.
- *CARGEX—Cargo Expert System* is used by Lufthansa, a German airline, to help determine the best shipping routes.
- NCR Corporation has an expert system for communications. The system allows the collection and encoding of an expert's knowledge into a form that can be used by a personal computer. The overall emphasis of the product is to allow more efficient analysis of difficulties regarding data communications.
- *ACE* is an expert system used by AT&T to analyze the maintenance of telephone networks.
- General Electric has an expert system called *Delta* that assists in engine repair.

- *XCON (Expert VAX System Configuration)* is an expert system developed by Digital Equipment Corporation (DEC) to help in configuring and organizing minicomputer systems. The system uses thousands of rules and helps DEC get the correct minicomputer system to customers.
- *Authorizer's Assistant (AA)* is an ES developed by American Express for credit authorization. It is used to weed out bad credit risks and reduce losses.
- *Watchdog Investment Monitoring System* is an ES developed by Washington Square Advisors, the investment management subsidiary of Northwestern National Life Insurance Company. It is used to analyze potential and existing corporate bonds to enhance clients' revenue. The analysis includes a change in financial ratios as an indicator of past performance and predictor of future financial directions.
- *Escape* is an expert system by Ford Motor Company for claim authorization and processing.
- *Auditor,* developed by C. Duncan (University of Illinois), is an expert system to aid internal auditors in analyzing a company's allowance for bad debts.
- *TICOM,* developed by A. Baily and M. Gagle (University of Minnesota), is an expert system to evaluate internal control systems.
- *Financial Advisor,* developed by MIT's Sloan School of Management, provides expert advice on projects, products, and mergers and acquisitions.
- *Plan Power,* developed by Applied Expert Systems, is an expert system that takes into account a company's financial situation, then matches needs with the most appropriate financial products and services. The system will run scenario spreadsheets showing the income tax situation, cash flows, net worth, and other critical factors based on alternative decisions.
- *GURU,* developed by Micro Data Base Systems, is an expert system shell and spreadsheet providing management advice and financial analysis.
- Peat Marwick is using the advice of an expert system to bring more consistency and precision to the auditing of commercial bank loans. This allows the organization to assess a company's provision for bad debts.
- Anthem Corporation's Financial Crime Investigator helps in identifying fraud in contracts or in purchases.
- *Nortel Wireless Networks Logic Oriented Repair Environment (LORE)* diagnoses production defects, improves repair accuracy, and enhances resource flexibility in the company's manufacturing processes.
- The *Expert Business Impact Analysis System,* developed by Decision Support Systems, provides an appraisal

of business risks and recommendations for strategies to cope with said risks. The focus is on global risks that can threaten a company's operations. Once a key risk is identified, the best defensive strategy is selected.

- *Strohl Systems* provides contingency planning, assessing of potential risks and alternative strategies for preventing business interruptions. The software also aids the decision maker in putting together a contingency plan for recovering from outages, failures, and disasters that cannot be adequately controlled via prevention strategies. Contingency planning is the process an organization goes through to assure that it can get its information systems or operations back up and running in cases of failure or disaster.
- *Internal Operations Risk Analysis,* a system by Business Foundations Software, uses 180 interview questions to assess the control strengths and weaknesses of an organization's business operations. The software provides an overall rating of controls strength that can be broken down by operational area. A similar system available from Price Waterhouse Cooper is known simply as *controls.*

Fuzzy Logic

Fuzzy logic deals with uncertainty. This technique, which uses the mathematical theory of fuzzy sets, simulates the process of normal human reasoning by allowing the computer to behave less precisely and logically than conventional computers. Fuzzy logic is a type of mathematics. It deals with nonprecise values with a certain degree of uncertainty. This technology allows logistics to be utilized by nonprecise information. Fuzzy logic can be advantageous for the following reasons:

- It provides flexibility: It gives you options.
- It gives you imagination.
- It is more forgiving.
- It allows for observation.

One example where fuzzy logic is being used extensively is in consumer products where the input is provided by sensors rather than by people.

Automatic Programming

Automatic programming is described as a "supercompiler," or a program that could take in a very high-level description of what the program is to accomplish and produce a program in a specific programming language. One of the important contributions of research in automatic programming has been the notion of debugging as a problem-solving strategy. It has been found that it is often much more efficient to produce an inexpensive, errorful solution to a programming or robot control problem and modify it than to insist on a first solution completely free of defects.

Functional Area Applications

In addition to the applications previously described, expert systems are used in accounting-related systems, financial ratio analysis, capital resource planning, loan applications, strategic marketing, and development of strategic objectives for the organization.

Accounting Systems

Internal accounting systems are an ideal area for expert systems applications. Expert systems can be developed to analyze cash flows, accounts payable, accounts receivable, and the appropriate use of general ledger entries. The knowledge base can include information from accounting organizations, such as the American Institute of Certified Public Accountants (AICPA). Current tax laws, Securities and Exchange Commission requirements, and generally accepted accounting practices can also be entered into the knowledge base. The inference engine for the accounting expert system can assist in many important decisions, including financial accounting approaches, the management of cash flows, and other related accounting practices. Four areas of accounting in which expert systems can be used are accounting standards, taxation, management and control, and auditing.

In the area of accounting standards, an expert system would apply standards in a consistent manner when preparing accounts or performing audits. This task would probably be performed more often by external auditors than by internal auditors.

Taxation is an area restricted by a complex set of rules and procedures. Expert systems make compliance with these rules much easier, since all rules can be programmed into the computer. Tax planning is an area that has also benefited. More on this is explained later.

In the area of management and control, expert systems are used to supplement management information systems. Expert systems provide decision models used for planning and control. As with any new management system, the internal auditor should evaluate the potential benefits and control areas. Furthermore, the auditor must periodically evaluate established expert systems to determine whether the systems continue to meet the objectives they were designed to meet.

Auditing is the final area of accounting where expert systems can be very useful. Expert systems can choose an audit program, choose a test sample, determine the level of error, perform an analytical review, then make a judgment based on the findings.

Expert systems aid in internal control evaluation, risk analysis, disclosure compliance, audit assignment scheduling, and auditor behavior evaluation. Examples of audit expert systems dealing with work programs are Arthur Andersen's EASY, Coopers and Lybrand's Expertest, Deloitte and Touche's Audit Planning Advisor, Ernst and Young's Decision Support, and Price Waterhouse's Planet. Examples of expert systems dealing with internal control assessment are Coopers and Lybrand's Control Risk Assessor, Deloitte and Touche's Internal Controls Expert, and Ernst and Young's Flow Evaluator. Examples of expert systems doing risk evaluation are KPMG Peat Marwick's Inherent Risk Analysis, and Coopers and Lybrand's Risk Advisor. Examples of expert systems concentrating on disclosure compliance are Price Waterhouse's Professional Disclosure Requirements, Coopers and Lybrand's Statutory Accounts Checker, and Arthur Andersen's Financial Disclosures. Expert systems can also assist in:

- Preparing working papers
- Maintaining the ledger
- Preparing financial statements
- Planning budgets and forecasts
- Preparing and analyzing payroll
- Analyzing revenue by volume, price, and product/service mix
- Analyzing expenses
- Costing specified in terms of volume, price, and category
- Converting from cash to accrual basis
- Aging accounts receivable
- Analyzing financial statements
- Analyzing financial aspects of the business

Currently, there are few tax expert systems available. This is due to two primary factors. First, if the information in the knowledge base is incorrect and bad decisions are made based on the system, the developer could be sued. Second, many expert systems are developed by large firms that want to protect their investment. It is not difficult to develop an expert system using a shell. The reasons may include the tax code is under constant revision (more change implies higher cost to maintain the expert system), tax practitioners do not believe in the benefits of expert systems, existing CD-ROM tax databases provide a lot of information, and tax-only expert systems are not sufficient to do business planning—more support is needed to make planning decisions.

There are examples of programs used in connection with taxes. *ExperTAX* developed by Coopers and Lybrand is used in tax planning and tax accrual. It uses a question-and-answer format to run a maze of 3,000 rules and outlines a client's best tax options. It will, for example, identify the differences between book and tax values. Coopers and Lybrand's ExempTax and RIC Tax, Ernst and Young's VATIA and PANIC, and Price Waterhouse's COBRA and RIC Checklist are used for tax compliance. *Taxadvisor* is used for estate planning. *Corptax* examines the tax consequences for stock redemptions. CCH Inc. introduced *CCH Tax Assistant.* This software, while not termed an expert system by CCH, performs in many ways like an expert system. Tax Assistant uses user-entered information while making decisions. The software can reduce the time spent by accountants calculating and generating reports. In addition, lower-level accountants can complete more difficult research tasks using the software.

Some believe that expert systems are the future in tax accounting. Expert systems could be used for compliance work—for example, to determine whether an activity is passive. In addition, they could be used for identifying problems and for planning purposes—for example, to determine whether a company is a personal holding company and how to avoid the associated penalty.

Capital Expenditures Planning

Capital investment planning involves making long-term planning decisions for alternative investment opportunities. There are many investment decisions that the company may have to make in order to grow. Examples of capital budgeting applications are product line selection, keeping or selling a business segment, leasing or buying, and which asset to invest in. Resource commitments may also be evaluated in the form of new product development, market research, introduction of a computer, refunding of long-term debt, and so on. Expert systems may be used in mergers and acquisitions analysis in the form of buying another company to add a new product line. *CashValue* is a commercially available expert system in capital projects planning.

Analysis of Credit and Loan Applications

A major part of any lending institution is making sound, profitable loans to business. A large number of risky loans can result in financial losses and potential bankruptcy for the institution. Reliable loans to companies with little chance of defaults can substantially increase a bank's overall profitability. Due to the high degree of analytical skills and experience involved, the analysis of loan applications is quite appropriate for computerized expert systems. Extending loans and lines of credit to businesses involves several key considerations, one of which is management attitudes and style. Does the management have the ability to grow in adverse as well as good times? How will management use the proceeds of the loan? Are there any potential problems with the company or management? The loan analysis expert system can either accept or reject the application for loans and credit. The acceptance can also be conditioned on some criteria. For example, the loan can be made only if the company receiving the funds agrees to make certain changes in its operation, management style, marketing strategy, and so forth. The expert system can also identify questionable loans in terms of default risk. The result could be a higher interest rate, a lower loan amount, an altered repayment structure, or higher collateral requirements.

MARKETING APPLICATIONS

Marketing expert systems can be developed to allow marketing managers to make strategic marketing-related decisions and to plan activities. The ES can help in establishing sales and profit goals, determining which products and services to promote, and updating prospective customer profiles. The marketing expert system requires a knowledge base covering relevant data on customers, the overall market structure, diverse internal and external factors, and the competition.

Once the overall strategic marketing plan has been mapped out, the expert system can explore specific goals. The types of marketing mix—that is, what products and services are to be produced, promotional efforts, pricing considerations, and the distribution system—are resolved at this level. The product quality, style, packaging, warranties, customer services, features and options, and return policies are analyzed. Pricing policy decisions are equally important. The list price, discounts, and credit terms are determined as a part of price analysis. Advertising, the role of sales representatives, direct marketing, publicity, the use of marketing research firms, and using professional marketing companies are important decisions for promotion. Finally, the distribution channel of delivering products and services to customers is examined.

Applications in Finance

Insurance

- *Underwriting:* Expert systems will increase the consistency of applying company standards in evaluating various risks (fire, flood, theft, etc.).
- *Claims processing:* Fraud detection is particularly difficult in medical insurance due to the complexity of claims. Expert systems will substantially reduce labor cost by quickly evaluating claims and improving the detection of suspicious information.
- *Reserving:* Deciding how much reserve funding to set aside for future claims and ongoing payout is similar to factory inventory schedules in many ways. ES will provide the means to consistently allocate resources to meet uncertain demands.

Portfolio Management

- *Security selection:* With over 100,000 stocks and bonds to choose from, selecting the right securities is a substantial challenge. More information is available than can be intelligently digested. The ES will analyze data and provide recommendations. For example, Unitek Technologies' *Expert Strategist* performs financial statement analysis.
- *Consistent application of constraints:* Managers of multiple portfolios must consistently apply multiple constraints on different portfolios. The constraints include compliance with legal SEC rules, clients' guidelines, and consistency across related accounts. ES will help financial professionals in applying different portfolio designs under the multiple constraints.
- *Hedge advisor:* The number of financial instruments available and the complexity of their relationship is increasing rapidly. These instruments vary in margin, liquidity, and price. They can be combined to create "synthetic securities," thereby hedging against market risk. An ES will help with the process of creating synthetic securities.

Trading Advisor

- *Real-time data feed:* Timely information is critical in any trading application. Expert systems will integrate multiple real-time external/internal data sources and provide timely information.
- *Trading rules and rule generators:* The conventional knowledge/engineering approach to rule writing will be replaced by rule generators. A rule generator ES will recognize data patterns and generate immediate hypotheses (trading rules) that lead to trading recommendations.

- *Critics and neural nets:* Critic ESs will review and evaluate system-recommended trades, process explanations of those trades, and find out culprits and heroes.

ESs in the Global Financial Market

- *Financial statement advice for multinational companies:* Multinational firms have unique problems with regard to reporting and legal requirements. These firms must deal with inconsistencies such as varying reporting formats, regulatory requirements, and account types. These problems will be solved by ESs.
- *24-hour trading programs:* Individual human traders cannot work for 24 hours without resting. However, ESs can. With traderless expert systems, smaller companies will have a better chance of entering global markets and foreign exchange trading.
- *Hedges:* In the international security markets, many different types of hedges are possible, including interest rate swaps, currency swaps, options, and futures. An ES can take advantage of those hedges.
- *Arbitrage:* ES will quickly identify and evaluate arbitrage opportunities and trigger transactions.

Benefits and Disadvantages of Expert Systems

The following benefits are offered by expert systems:

- They increase output and productivity, and improve accuracy and reliability.
- They reduce personnel costs.
- They can function as tutors, since they distill expertise into clearly defined rules.
- They capture and document scarce expertise.
- The system will be available to provide second opinions within the domain, as well as provide what-if analysis where results are sought on variable changes.
- They feature a shorter decision time. Routine decisions are rapidly made by the systems.
- An ES enhances problem-solving capabilities.
- They unravel a maze of rules and reduce business risk.
- They are complete and timely in reviewing transactions.
- They have a breadth in application.
- They have differentiation attributes such as to a product or focus of a company.
- Expert systems do not forget, are reproducible, and are consistent in handling similar transactions.

- The systems are more secure than an expert employee who may be hired by a competitor. Further, they create entry barriers to potential competitors.

The drawbacks to expert systems are:

- They are unable to respond creatively to unusual situations.
- They fail to adapt to a continually changing environment. They must be explicitly updated.
- They are usually confined to a very narrow domain and may have difficulty coping with broad-discipline knowledge decisions. It is not yet known how to give expert systems common sense.
- They are dependent on symbolic input.

Neural Networks

Expert systems typically require huge databases of information gathered from recognized experts in a given field. This system will then ask questions of the user and deduce an answer based on the responses given and the information in the database. These answers are not necessarily right but should be a logical conclusion based on the information provided.

Neural networks are a developing technology in which computers actually try to learn from the database and operator what the right answer is to a question. The system gets positive or negative responses to output from the operator and stores that data so that it will make a better decision the next time. Neural networks are based on pattern recognition. While still in its infancy, this technology shows promise for use in credit assessment, fraud detection, economic forecasting, and risk appraisals.

The idea behind this software is to convert the order-taking computer into a "thinking" problem solver. This would allow computers to take over some of the more mundane decision-making jobs of accountants such as determining if a lease is operating or capital. Neural networks are software programs that simulate human intelligence. They are designed to "learn" from experience. For example, each time a neural network program makes the right decision (which is predetermined by a human instructor) on recognizing a number or sequence-of-action pattern, the programmer reinforces the program with a confirmation message that is stored. In the event of a wrong decision, a negative message is reinforced. Thus, it gradually builds experimental knowledge in that subject.

Today, most neural networks take the form of mathematical simulations embedded in software that runs on ordinary microprocessors.

NEURAL NETWORK APPLICATIONS IN BUSINESS

Currently, a neural computer network is being employed at the Mellon Bank's Visa and MasterCard operation in Wilmington, Delaware, which keeps a daily track of millions of accounts. One of the functions of this operation's computer is to scan customer purchases and look for spending patterns that may indicate stolen credit cards. The neural network compares purchases with customer behaviors. It also generates data without being told to do so because the system has been programmed to take the initiative and "think" like a human.

Oracle Corporation's Oracle Special Investigative Unit Support System (SIUSS) aids in fraud investigations by detecting hidden patterns within large volumes of data. Information is compared to predetermined criteria.

One way in which neural networks will help accountants is in internal audits. Ernst & Young in Dallas is working on this application that would allow financial managers to improve their handling of working capital.

Neural networks are beginning to be helpful in many business problems when information is not easy to quantify. Besides bankruptcy, they are being used in the management of portfolios. A portfolio manager must continuously scan for nonperforming stocks while stock analysts are looking for undervalued stocks. Neural networks are particularly good for problems when deductive reasoning gives mixed results. The inductive reasoning of neural networks can do a better job. There is a large store of historical information about good and bad investments that can be analyzed for relationships that may be quite subtle. Shearson-Lehman is using neural networks to predict stock patterns.

Further, neural networks appear to be a useful tool in bankruptcy prediction. They can use some of the tools already in place to improve prediction. If the ratios chosen for the Z-model (discussed in Chapter 11) are used but the neural network is allowed to form its own functions, the predictive abilities of the Z-formula can be much improved upon. This is of significant value to managers, creditors, and investors, since misclassification, particularly of a firm that is going bankrupt, has huge monetary implications.

Applications of neural networks are language processing (text and speech), image processing, character recognition (handwriting recognition and pattern recognition), and modeling.

1. At Signet Bank, neural networks read and automatically process student loan applications and canceled checks.
2. A neural network helps manage the Fidelity Disciplined Equity Fund, a fund that has consistently beat the Standard & Poor's 500 Stock Index.

3. Neuroscope is a neural network diagnostic tool that provides early warning of failure in industrial machinery.
4. Foster Ousley Conley uses a neural network–based system for residential real estate appraisal. The system performs better than humans because it can review data from hundreds of houses and analyze the data in many different ways.
5. At Mellon Bank's Visa and MasterCard operations, neural networks outperform expert systems—and the experts themselves—in detecting credit card fraud. Since the neural network can learn by experience, it can find incidences of fraud not anticipated by an expert.
6. Neural networks can be used to forecast a client's earnings. By comparing this forecast to actual results, the auditor can make a judgment as to the reasonableness of the actual results. The forecasted earnings can also indicate to the auditor if the client is likely to continue as a going concern.
7. A cost accountant/consultant can use a neural network to determine optimal resource allocation and production schedules. The manipulation of the hundreds of variables and constraints has traditionally been undertaken using operations research models.
8. The IRS in Taiwan is using a neural network to determine the likelihood of tax evasion and the necessity of further investigation.

The following is a list of some popular neural network software:

NeuroSolutions
NeuroDomension, Inc.
www.neurosolutions.com

NeuroXL Predictor
FRANZ AG
www.neuroxl.com

NeuralWorks Predict
NeuralWare
www.neuralware.com

CHAPTER 16

COMPUTER SECURITY

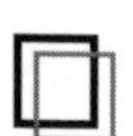

THREATS AND ATTACKS ON COMPUTER TECHNOLOGY

Every day there are news stories about computer-related data errors, thefts, burglaries, fires, and sabotage. Although considerable efforts have been made to reduce vulnerability to such events, much more effort is needed. Weak computer security and lack of internal controls tremendously increase an organization's vulnerability to the following:

- Commission of fraud
- Theft of electronic information
- Theft of physical information, such as printed outputs or computer disks/tapes
- Invasion of privacy
- Damage to computers and peripherals
- Interception of communications
- Illegal recording of electromagnetic emanations from computers and peripherals
- Unintentional data errors due to carelessness or negligence
- Loss of information integrity through unauthorized alterations and modifications to data
- Sabotage by disgruntled employees or competitors
- Power failure

Crime insurance policies should be taken out that cover such areas as theft, fraud, intentional destruction, and forgery. Business interruption insurance covers lost profits during downtime. Insurance should also cover computer equipment in transit.

A risk analysis should be performed in planning computer security policies and financial support. Computer security risks fall into one of three major categories: destruction, modification, and disclosure. Each of these may be further classified into intentional, unintentional, and environmental attacks. The threat comes from computer criminals and disgruntled employees who intend to defraud, sabotage, and "hack." It also comes from computer users who are careless or negligent. Lastly, the threat comes from the environment; an organization must protect itself from disasters such as fire, flood, and earthquakes. An effective security plan must consider all three types of threats: intentional attacks, unintentional attacks, and environmental attacks. What is the company's degree of risk exposure?

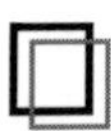

FINANCIAL LOSS AND THE COST-BENEFIT CRITERION

The danger of financial loss to a company can be greatly reduced by increasing computer security. In all likelihood, not investing in appropriate security measures will prove to be far more expensive for a company than investing in the appropriate security measures. It would even be appropriate for a company to consider the cost of investing in computer security as a form of insurance.

The cost of security measures must always be compared with the benefits received. As Exhibit 16.1 illustrates, the optimal level of security expenditure is when the combined cost of security measures and financial loss is minimized. The law of diminishing returns clearly applies here. Beyond a certain point, additional expenditures on security measures are not likely to be cost-effective. While appropriate security measures can greatly reduce the likelihood of a financial loss, security measures by themselves cannot guarantee against every kind of damage and accident; a certain degree of risk will always have to be accepted.

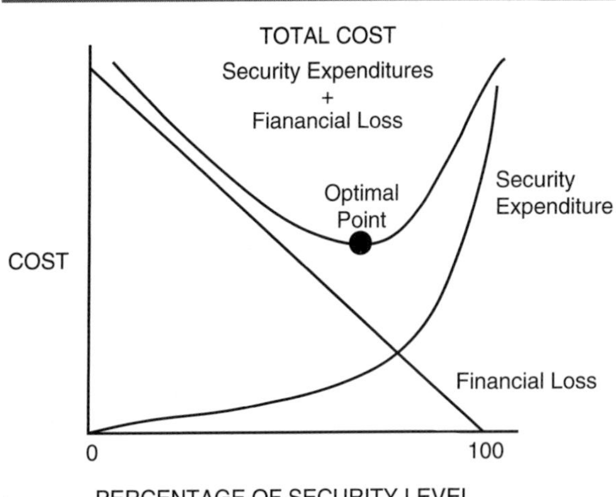

Exhibit 16.1 OPTIMAL SECURITY EXPENDITURE AS A FUNCTION OF FINANCIAL LOSS AND SECURITY EXPENDITURE

Amount of Loss	High	Low
High	A	B
Low	B	C

Exhibit 16.2 LOSS EXPECTANCY

The cost-benefit criterion dictates that a company formally assess the risks it faces. The following questions must be answered by the organization:

- What type of threats may affect our organization?
- What is the probability that a threat will occur?
- What is the potential liability for each threat?

For each type of threat, expected loss may be calculated as follows:

Loss expectancy = Probability of loss × Amount of loss

Using the above formula, expected losses may be classified into three categories. As shown in Exhibit 16.2, loss expectancy is highest for category A and lowest for category C. Clearly, considerable attention must be directed toward category A, since there is both a high amount and a high probability of loss. In contrast, little attention needs to be given to category C items, which seldom occur, and the associated loss is small. Professional judgment will be required to determine which items in category B require attention and which do not.

While the above model is theoretically appealing, it does have serious practical limitations. The model relies heavily on estimating future probabilities and costs; it is extremely difficult to make such estimates with reasonable accuracy. When implementing the model, it is also possible for the user to overlook many serious indirect consequences of the threat.

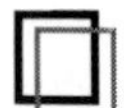

PHYSICAL SECURITY AND DATA SECURITY

Physical security is the first line of defense in protecting a computer system; it encompasses the plant, equipment, and personnel. Data security is also of vital concern to an organization; data integrity, data accuracy, and data privacy are of paramount importance. Physical and data security considerations are equally important. An effective security system will prevent a security breach. However, if in spite of proper protection, a system is successfully attacked, the system should create an audit trail to allow prompt investigation.

The computer room is the structure that houses the computer facilities. Unauthorized access to the computer room should be restricted. Sensing and surveillance devices may be installed. The plant should also be designed to protect the computer environment, including heating, cooling, dehumidifying, ventilating, lighting, and power. Air ducts of air-conditioning units should be secured against access with heavy-gauge screens. Appropriate care must also be taken to protect the plant from harm from accidents and disasters such as fire and floods. Adequate emergency lighting should be available for safe evacuation in case of fire or other disaster.

Consideration must be given to loss or damage to computer equipment and peripherals. Media, such as disks, tapes, and output, should be protected. User manuals for equipment and software must be protected to maintain continuity of proper operations. Surge protectors should be used to protect the computer system against power line disturbances. Finally, the organization must consider loss of or injury to its personnel. Not only must the organization be concerned about the physical safety of its employees, it must also consider the threat of psychological dissatisfaction. Disgruntled employees may do intentional damage. Moreover, job turnover associated with dissatisfied employees disrupts the routine operation and maintenance of computer systems.

The integrity, accuracy, and privacy of data must be protected. Data integrity is essential to computer security. Data lacks integrity if it is missing, incomplete, inconsistent, or if it is stored in a poorly designed database environment. The concept of accuracy is distinct from that of integrity. Data is accurate if it is reliable and the data is what it purports to be. Privacy means that only authorized individuals have access to data. Programmers should not have free access to the computer area or library due to possible data manipulation. Important CDs should be locked up.

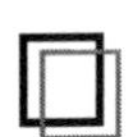

CONTROLLING PHYSICAL ACCESS

Access controls guard against improper use of equipment, data files, and software. To limit physical access, a security system must be able to discriminate between authorized and unauthorized individuals. Physical access can be limited using these general methods:

- *Identification:* Identification is based on comparing the physical characteristics of the individual with previously stored information. For example, an individual's signature, personnel number, code, voice print, palm print, fingerprint, teeth print, or other personal trait could be verified before allowing access. Secondary authentication, such as the user's place of birth, may be required for highly sensitive information.

- *User's name and passwords:* Passwords are based on some memorized combination of letters or numbers. There should be no logic to the password so that it cannot be easily guessed. Individuals are authorized based on what they know. Passwords should be changed regularly. Inactive passwords (e.g., more than four months old) should be deleted. Passwords should be changed and confidential data withdrawn from terminated employees. If a user changes a password, controls must exist to assure the user does not use his or her old password. Passwords should not be shared. Access control software may be used to have a minimum password time period in which a new password cannot be changed or a new password matching an old one will be rejected.
- *Cards/keys:* Access can also be limited through the use of cards, keys, or badges; individuals are authorized based on what they possess. Improper access may be signaled by an alarm, and unauthorized access patterns should be investigated. Smart cards may be used in which the user enters both his or her identification number and a random generated code that changes each time the card is used or over a stated time period.

Within the plant, areas containing sensitive data should be accessible only to authorized personnel. These areas, including the computer room, should have only a single entry door that can be operated by an appropriate encoded magnetic-strip ID card. Physical controls might include having a librarian keep a log. A lockout should occur with repeated errors. Logs should automatically be kept of the ID number, time of access, and function performed. Further, data dictionary software provides an automated log of access to software and file information. Intrusion detection devices such as cameras and motion detectors should be used to monitor sensitive and high-risk areas against unauthorized individuals.

Are controls being diligently followed over processing, maintaining records, and file or software modification? Each individual function (e.g., accounts receivable, payroll) may have its own password so that users have access to limited areas of the database. The computer can keep an internal record of the date and time each file was last updated, and this internal record can be compared against the log. The hours to access key microcomputer files can be limited to prevent unauthorized access after normal working hours. Files should be displayed in terms of different levels of confidentiality and security such as top secret, confidential, internal use only, and unrestricted. Confidential information should not be displayed on the screen. To control access to sensitive data, there should be a mapping of access requirements to the system components. Access rights should be based on job function, and an appropriate segregation of duties should exist. Temporary employees should be restricted to a specific project, activity, system, and time period.

FIRE SECURITY

According to insurance companies, fire is the most frequent cause of damage to computer centers. Simple steps can reduce the damage caused by fire and, in the process, reduce insurance premiums.

- Safes for storage of documents should have a minimum four-hour fire rating.
- Walls, floors, and ceilings of computer facilities should have a minimum two-hour fire rating.
- The fire alarm should ring simultaneously at the computer facility and the nearest fire department. In addition, fire alarm signals should be located where prompt response is assured.
- Vaults used for storing backup data and records should be located in a separate building at sufficient distance.
- Smoke and ionization detection systems should be installed throughout the ceiling of the computer facilities. Water detection systems should also be installed under the floor of computer facilities.
- Halon or a similar fire extinguishing system should be installed throughout the computer facilities. Automatic sprinkler systems can be used in the supply and support areas. In case of destruction, there should be a disaster recovery plan.
- Adherence to building code and fire marshal regulations is a must.

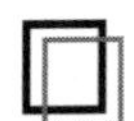

SABOTEUR'S TOOLS

While in recent years ingenious procedures have been developed to preserve computer security, many computer systems are still astonishingly insecure. Saboteurs may use a wide variety of tools and techniques to overcome security. Some of the methods are as follows:

- *Trojan horse:* The saboteur places a hidden program within the normal programs of the business. The computer continues to function normally, while the hidden program is free to collect data, make secret modifications to programs and files, erase or destroy data, and even cause a complete shutdown of operations. Trojan horses can be programmed to destroy all traces of their existence after execution.

- *Salami techniques:* The perpetrator can make secret changes to the computer program that cause very small changes that are unlikely to be discovered, but the cumulative effect can be very substantial. For example, the perpetrator may steal 10 cents from the paycheck of each individual and transfer it to his own account.
- *Back door or trap door:* During the development of a computer program, programmers sometimes insert a code to allow them to bypass the standard security procedures. Once the programming is complete, such a code may remain in the program either accidentally or intentionally. Attackers rely on their knowledge of this extra code to bypass security.
- *Time bomb/logic bomb:* A code may be inserted into a computer program that causes damages when a predefined condition occurs, such as a date or time.
- *Masquerade:* A computer program is written that masquerades or simulates the real program. For example, a program may be written to simulate the log-in screen and related dialogue. When a user attempts to log in, the program captures the user's ID and password and displays some error message prompting the user to log in again. The second time, the program allows the user to log in and the user may never know that the first log-in was fake.
- *Scavenging:* A computer normally does not erase data that is no longer needed. When the user "deletes" some data, that information is not actually destroyed; instead, that space is made available for the computer to write on later. A scavenger may thus be able to steal sensitive data that the user thought had been deleted but was actually still available on the computer.
- *Viruses:* Viruses are similar to Trojan horses, except the illegal code is capable of replicating itself. A virus can rapidly spread throughout the system, and eradicating it can be expensive and cumbersome. To guard against viruses, there should be care in using programs on disk or in copying software from bulletin boards or other sources outside the company. The best precaution is to use a commercial virus scanner on all downloaded files from unreliable Internet sources before using them. An example is McAfee's virus scan. Virus protection and detection is crucial.

- *Data manipulation:* The most common and easiest way of committing fraud is to add or alter the data before or during input. The best way to detect this type of computer crime is the use of audit software to scrutinize transactions and review audit trails that indicate additions, changes, and deletions were made to data files. The use of batch totals, hash totals, and check digits can also help prevent this type of crime. A batch total is a reconciliation between the total daily transactions processed by the micro and manually determined totals processed by an individual other than the computer operator. Material deviations must be investigated. A hash total is adding values that would not typically be added together, so the total has no meaning other than for control purposes. Examples are employee and product numbers. A check digit is used to ascertain whether an identification number (e.g., account number, employee number) has been correctly entered by adding a calculation to the identification number and comparing the outcome to the check digit.
- *Piggybacking:* Piggybacking is frequently used to gain access to controlled areas. Physical piggybacking occurs when an authorized employee goes through a door using his magnetic ID card, and an authorized employee behind him also enters the premises. The unauthorized employee is then in a position to commit a crime. Electronic piggybacking may also occur. For example, an authorized employee leaves her terminal or desktop and an authorized individual uses that to gain access.

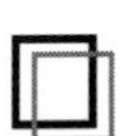

COMMUNICATIONS SECURITY

Attacks on computer security that do not require physical access fall under the domain of communications security. The increased use of computer technology has also increased dependence on telecommunications. All types of data, including sound, video, and traditional text data, are transferred between computers over networks. Communications security means ensuring that the physical links between the computer networks function at all times. This also means that breakdowns, delays, and disturbances are prevented during data transmission. Care must be taken to prevent unauthorized individuals from tapping, modifying, or otherwise intercepting data transmission. Six considerations in communications security are:

- *Line security:* Line security is concerned with restricting unauthorized access to the communication lines connecting the various parts of the computer systems.

- *Transmission security:* Transmission security is concerned with preventing unauthorized interception of communications.
- *Digital signature:* This is used to authenticate the sender or message integrity to the receiver. A secure digital signature process is a method of signing a document and making forgery infeasible, then validating that the signature belongs to the authorized individual.
- *Cryptographic security:* Cryptography is the science of secret writing. The purpose of cryptographic security is to render the information unintelligible if transmission is intercepted by unauthorized individuals. When the information is to be used, it can be decoded. Security coding (encryption) of sensitive data is necessary. A common method is the data encryption standard (DES). For even greater security, double encryption may be used in which encryption is processed twice using two different keys. (You may also encrypt files on a hard disk to prevent an intruder from reading the data.)
- *Emission security:* Electronic devices emit electromagnetic radiation that can be intercepted without wires by unauthorized individuals. Emission security is concerned with preventing the emission of such radiation.
- *Technical security:* Technical security is concerned with preventing the use of devices such as microphone, transmitters, or wiretaps to intercept data transmission. Security modems may be used that allow only authorized users to access confidential data. A modem may have graduated levels of security, and different users may be assigned different security codes. There can be password and callback features. There may be built-in audit trail capabilities, allowing you to monitor who is accessing private files.

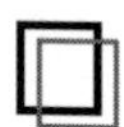

CONTROLS

Controls are used to reduce the probability of attack on computer security. As additional controls are placed, the overall operating costs are likely to increase. As discussed earlier, cost-benefit considerations require a careful balance of controls. There are four main classes of controls:

- *Deterrent controls:* The aim of deterrent controls is to create an atmosphere conducive to control compliance. For example, the organization could impose penalties whenever a control is disregarded, regardless of the actual damage. Deterrent controls are inexpensive to implement. However, their effectiveness is difficult to measure. These controls complement other controls and are not sufficient by themselves.

- *Preventive controls:* Preventive controls are designed to reduce the probability of an attack. They serve as the first line of defense. Effective preventive controls will thwart a perpetrator from getting access to the computer system.
- *Detective controls:* Once a system has been violated, detective controls help identify the occurrence of harm. These controls do nothing to insulate the system from harm; they only serve to focus attention on the problem. For example, a bait file will identify unauthorized use. Here, a "dummy" nonexistent record is put into processing. There may be a comparison between standard run time and actual run time for an application to spot possible misuse.
- *Corrective controls:* After a loss has occurred, corrective controls serve to reduce the impact of the threat. Their purpose is to aid in recovering from damage or in reducing the effect of damage. For instance, lost information on CDs may be restored with utility programs.

Application Controls

Application controls are built into software to deter crime and minimize errors. Application controls typically include input controls, processing controls, change controls, testing controls, output controls, and procedural controls.

- *Input controls:* The purpose of input controls is to ensure that each transaction is authorized, processed correctly, and processed only once. An edit program substantiates input by comparing fields to expected values and by testing logical relationships. A missing data check assures that all data fields have been used. A valid character check verifies that only alphabetical, numeric, or other special characters are present in data fields. "Dual read" is an input control in which duplicate entry or key verification verifies the accuracy of some critical field in a record by requiring that a data item is entered twice. A valid code check compares a classification (e.g., asset account number) or transaction code (e.g., credit sale entry) to a master list of account or transaction codes (master file reference). Input controls include rejecting, correcting, and resubmitting data that were initially wrong. Is input information properly authorized? Character validation tests may also be programmed to check input data fields to see if they contain alphanumerics when they are supposed to have numerics. A preprocessing edit check verifies a key entry by a second one or a visual examination. There may be a limit test check of input data fields to make sure that some predetermined limit has not been exceeded (e.g., employee weekly hours should not be automatically processed if the sum of regular and overtime hours per individual exceeds 60).

- *Processing controls:* Processing controls are used to ensure that transactions entered into the system are valid and accurate, that external data are not lost or altered, and that invalid transactions are reprocessed correctly. Sequence tests may be performed to note missing items. In batch or sequential processing, batch totals are used to ensure that the counted and total number and value of similar data items are the same before and after processing. In a parity check, because data are processed in arrays of bits (binary digits of 1 or 0), we add a parity bit, if needed, so as to make the total of all the "1" bits even or odd. The parity bit assures that bits are not lost during computer processing. Parity checks prevent data corruption. External and internal file identification labels may be used. The program may check to see if an item in a record is within the correct range. Crossfooting tests apply to logical tests for information consistency (e.g., sum totals to column totals). Application reruns assure the initial run was correct.
- *Change controls:* Change controls safeguard the integrity of the system by establishing standard procedures for making modifications. For example, a log file can be maintained to document all changes. A report may be prepared showing the master file before and after each update.
- *Testing controls:* Testing controls ensure that reliance can be placed on a system before the system becomes operational. For example, limited test data could be processed and tested using the new system. Utility programs can be used to diagnose problems in application software.
- *Output controls:* The purpose of output controls is to authenticate the previous controls; this is used to ensure that only authorized transactions are processed correctly. Random comparisons can be made of output to input to verify correct processing. For example, an echo check involves transmitting data received by an output device back to its source. Output controls presume information is not lost or improperly distributed. Errors by receivers of output, such as customers, should be investigated.
- *Procedural controls:* Procedural controls safeguard computer operations, reduce the chance of processing mistakes, and assure continued functioning if a computer failure occurs. Processing errors must be thoroughly

evaluated. Output should be distributed to authorized users of such information. A record retention and recovery plan must also exist.

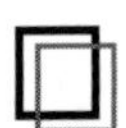

ELECTRONIC DATA INTERCHANGE

Electronic data interchange (EDI) is the electronic transfer of business information among trading partners. Thousands of businesses use EDI to exchange information with suppliers and customers. The benefits of EDI are clear. The paperwork is greatly reduced and the efficiency in accounting and processing functions is greatly enhanced.

The risk inherent in EDI is much greater than in standard computer processing systems. An EDI security system is only as strong as the weakest link among the trading partners. Some risks of EDI are:

- Data could be lost in the interchange.
- Unauthorized changes may be made to the data.
- The lack of paperwork means a greater likelihood that the audit trail may not be maintained.
- Authorized individuals can initiate unauthorized transactions.
- Unauthorized individuals can gain access to the system through the weakest link among the trading partners.

PERSONNEL SECURITY

Each employee should sign a nondisclosure agreement not to reveal computer security information to those outside the business or to unauthorized staff within the firm. If a staff member leaves the company, certain control procedures are required, including returning all badges, keys, and company materials. Access codes, passwords, and locks may need to be changed.

Specific procedures should be established for recruiting and hiring computer data processing professionals. A security investigation should include contacting the applicant's work references, checking the applicant's background with appropriate authorities, and verifying the applicant's school references. The importance of computer security with respect to every phase of computer data processing should be emphasized to new employees. For example, to indoctrinate new employees, educational seminars can be scheduled where security professionals can communicate the company's rules and procedures.

In addition, formal performance evaluation systems should be in place to ensure that employees' performances and skills are routinely reviewed. An effective review procedure can help prevent job frustration and stress. It can also help maintain employee morale. Discontentment often acts as a catalyst for computer crime. Possible indicators of discontentment include excessive absenteeism, late arrival, low quality or low production output, complaints, putting off vacations, and excessive unwarranted overtime. Quick action, such as communicating with the employee on a one-to-one basis, can minimize if not eliminate job discontentment.

Segregation of duties among staff is needed. For example, a programmer should not also serve as an operator. Rotation of assignments should also exist, such as programmers doing different assignments and operators working different shifts. A function may be designed to require more than one operator to make it more difficult for an individual to perpetrate an improper act, since others are involved. The development and testing of software should also be separate.

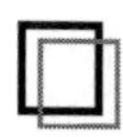

AUDIT TRAIL

Audit trails contain information regarding any additions, deletions, or modifications to the system, providing evidence concerning transactions. An effective audit trail allows the data to be retrieved and certified. Audit trails will give information regarding the date and time of the transaction, who processed it, and at which terminal.

To establish an adequate audit trail, you must analyze transactions related to the physical custody of assets, evaluate unusual transactions, and keep track of the sequential numbering of negotiable computer forms. Controls should be periodically tested. For example, the audit trail requires the tracing of transactions to control totals and from the control total to supporting transactions. Computer-related risks affect the company's internal control structure and thereby affect the company's audibility.

Electronic data interchange (EDI) systems are online systems where computers automatically perform transactions such as order processing and invoice generation. Although this can reduce costs, it can adversely affect a company's audibility because of the lessened audit trail.

The AICPA has issued control techniques to ensure the integrity of an EDI system. The AICPA recommends controls over accuracy and completeness at the application level of an EDI system to include checking on performance to determine compliance with industry standards, checking on sequence numbering for transactions, reporting irregularities on a timely basis, verifying adequacy of audit trails, and checking embedded headers and trailers at interchange, functional group, and transaction set level. Control techniques at the environmental level include reviewing quality assurance of vendor software, segregating duties, ensuring that software is virus-free, procuring an audit report from the vendor's auditors, and obtaining evidence of testing. To ensure that all the EDI transactions are authorized, the AICPA provides these authorization controls: operator identification code, operator profile, trading partner identifier, maintenance of user access variables, and regular changing of passwords.

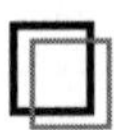

NETWORK SECURITY

Network security is needed for both local area networks (LANs) and wide area networks (WANs). There must be positive authentication before a user can gain knowledge of the online applications, network environment, nature of applications, terminal identification, and so on. Information should be provided on a need-to-know basis only.

Access controls should exist to use a specific terminal or application. Date and time constraints along with restricted file usage may be enumerated. Unauthorized use may deactivate or lock a terminal. Diskless workstations may result in a safer network environment.

There must be a secure communication link of data transmission between interconnected host computer systems of the network. A major form of communication security on the network is cryptography to safeguard transmitted data confidentiality. Cryptographic algorithms may be either symmetric (private key) or asymmetric (public key). The two popular encryption methods are link-level security and end-to-end security. The former safeguards traffic independently on every communication link while the latter safeguards messages from the source to the ultimate destination. Link-level enciphers the communications line at the bit level; data is deciphered upon entering the nodes. End-to-end enciphers information at the entry point to the network and deciphers at the exit point. Unlike link-level, security exists over information inside the nodes.

Security should be provided in different layers. Security must exist over networking facilities and telecommunication elements. Controls must be placed over both host computers and subnetworks.

Network traffic may travel over many subnetworks, each having its own security levels depending on confidentiality and importance. Therefore, different security services and controls may be required. Security aspects of each subnetwork have to be distributed to the gateways so as to incorporate security and controls in routing decisions.

The architecture of a network includes hardware, software, information link controls, standards, topologies, and protocols. A protocol relates to how computers communicate and transfer information. Security controls must exist over each component within the architecture to assure reliable and correct data exchanges. Otherwise, the integrity of the system may be compromised. Communication security may be in the form of:

- *Access control:* Guards against improper use of the network. For example, KERBEROS is commercial authentication software that is added to an existing security system to verify a user's existence and assure he or she is not an imposter. KERBEROS does this by encrypting passwords transmitted around networks. Password control and user authentication devices may be used such as Security Dynamics' SecurID (800-SECURID) and Vasco Data Security's Access Key II (800-238-2726). Do not accept a prepaid call if it is not from a network user. Hackers do not typically spend their own funds. Review data communications billings and verify each host-to-host connection. Review all dial-up terminal users. Are the telephone numbers unlisted and changed periodically? Control specialists should try to make unauthorized access to the network to test whether the security is properly working.
- *Identification:* Identifies the origin of a communication within the network through digital signals or notarization.
- *Data confidentiality:* Maintains confidentiality over unauthorized disclosure of information within the communication process.
- *Data integrity:* Guards against unauthorized changes (e.g., adding, deleting) of data at both the receiving and sending points such as through cryptographic methods. Antivirus software should be installed at both the network server and workstations. Detection programs are available to alert users when viruses enter the system.
- *Authentication:* Substantiates the identity of an originating or user entity within the network. The authenticator verifies that the entity is actually the authorized individual and that the information being transmitted is appropriate. Examples of security controls are passwords, time stamping, synchronized checks, nonrepudiation, and multiple-way handshakes. Biometric authentication methods measure body characteristics with the use of equipment attached to the workstation. Retinal laser beams may also be used. Keystroke dynamics is another possibility for identification.
- *Digital signature:* Messages are signed with a private key.

- *Routing control:* Inhibits data flow to insecure network elements such as identified unsecure relays, links, or subnetworks.
- *Traffic padding:* A traffic analysis of data for reasonableness.
- *Interference minimization:* Radar/radio transmission interference must be eliminated or curtailed. There are various ways to back up data in networks. For a small network, one workstation may be used as the backup and restore for other nodes. In a large network, backup may be done by several servers, since the failure of one could have disastrous effects on the entire system. Access to backup files must be strictly controlled.

An example of a network security package is Intrusion Detection Incorporated's Kane Security Analyst, which assesses existing security.

Protect Your Company from Internet Dangers

1. **Have a firewall.** A firewall is simply a device that prevents hackers from gaining access to your company network. For small companies, use a broadband router, like those made by Netgear, Linksys or D-Link, that has a firewall built in.
2. **Use an anti-virus program and keep it current.** Any of the popular brands will work (e.g., Norton, McAfee, etc.). Renew your subscription every year or upgrade to the latest version. Make sure that your computers are automatically getting the latest virus definitions.
3. **Get Microsoft Windows and Office updates.** Microsoft has introduced significant security improvements in Service Pack 2 for Windows XP that can be updated for free. Older versions of Windows are more susceptible to spyware and Internet worms. Consider upgrading PCs to Windows XP or Longhorn.
4. **Use anti-spyware and anti-spam programs.** Microsoft offers a free anti-spyware program for Windows 2000 and XP. Many Internet service providers (e.g., Cox Communications, AOL, etc.) offer complimentary anti-spam services. If your provider doesn't, there are spam filter programs that work with Outlook and Outlook Express.
5. **Secure your network.** A firewall won't protect you if a hacker can figure out the password. Make sure your computer technician has changed the default password on your router. If you have a wireless network, make sure it is using WEP or WPA encryption to prevent unauthorized access.

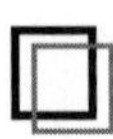

THE SECURITY ADMINISTRATOR

The size and needs of the company will dictate the size of the security administration department. This department is responsible for the planning and execution of a computer security system. It ensures that the information system's data is reliable and accurate. The security administrator should possess a high level of computer technical knowledge as well as management skills and a general understanding of the organization's internal control structure.

A security administrator should interact with other departments to learn about the organization's changing needs and to be able to maintain and update the security system efficiently. The security administrator is responsible for enacting and customizing policies and standards for the organization based on specific needs. Checks on performance and monitoring of staff should be done to ensure compliance with these policies and standards. In developing these policies and procedures, as well as the overall information computer security system, the security administrator must perform a risk assessment (see Exhibit 16.3).

(A no response indicates a potential vulnerability.)

Organizational

1. Is management's attitude toward microcomputer security, as reflected by its actions, appropriate?
2. Has the organization prepared a coordinated plan of implementation for microcomputers, addressing such factors as:
   - Hardware compatibility within and between departments?
   - Software compatibility within and between departments?
   - Future expansion?
   - A manual of standard practices?
3. Is rotation of duties utilized to increase the chance of exposure of errors and irregularities and to give depth to microcomputer operations?
4. Are vacations mandatory to reduce the likelihood of fraud or embezzlement resulting from increased chance of exposure?
5. Do personnel policies include background checks to reduce the likelihood of hiring dishonest employees?

Exhibit 16.3 MICROCOMPUTER SECURITY CHECKLIST

6. Have employees who have access to sensitive data been bonded?
7. Is there a quality-control program in existence?
8. Are exception reports to procedures and policies prepared?

Hardware

1. Is theft and hazard insurance covering microcomputers adequate?
2. Which of the following theft deterrence techniques are in operation:
   - Limiting computer access to employees with a defined need?
   - Installing computers only in areas that are locked and kept under surveillance when not in use?
   - Bolting computers to desks or tables?
   - Placing lockable covers on computers?
   - Installing alarms and motion detectors in areas with a high concentration of computer equipment?
   - Placing internal trip alarms inside computers?
3. Which of the following factors for the physical protection of hardware are present:
   - Elementary surge suppressors or noise-filtering devices to protect against surges and spikes?
   - Line conditioners to smooth out power?
   - Uninterruptible power supply units to supply power during power outages?
   - Antistatic mats and pads to neutralize static electricity?
   - Halon fire extinguishers to reduce losses from fire?
   - Placement away from the sprinkler system to avoid water damage?
   - Waterproof covers to avoid water damage?
   - Implementation of a smoking ban, or the use of a small fan around the computer to blow any smoke away from the system?
   - Avoidance of other potential pollutants (e.g., dust, food, and coffee) around the computer?
4. In the event of equipment breakdown, is substitute equipment available?

Exhibit 16.3 MICROCOMPUTER SECURITY CHECKLIST *(continued)*

Software

1. Does present insurance cover software?
2. Is insurance carried to cover the cost of a business interruption resulting from a computer mishap?
3. Are backups and working copies maintained on site?
4. Do software backups, like originals, have write-protect tabs in place?
5. Are originals placed in off-site storage (e.g., a safe-deposit box or the home of the owner or chief executive officer)?
6. Are steps taken to avoid unauthorized copying of licensed software?
7. Are steps taken to avoid the use of bootleg software?
8. Is software tested before use?

Data and Data Integrity

1. Are backups in data files routinely prepared?
2. Is documentation duplicated?
3. Are backups placed in off-site storage (e.g., a safe-deposit box or the home of the owner or chief executive officer)? For particularly important files, a third copy may be kept.
4. Are backups of sensitive data that are stored off site encrypted to reduce the chance of unauthorized exposure?
5. Do hard disks include an external hard disk or a cassette tape as a backup?
6. Is a program such as Ship or Park used when removing the read/write head from the hard disk to reduce the likelihood of a crash?
7. Has the Format command been left off the hard disk?
8. Have Debug and other utilities that provide a means of accessing restricted software or data been left off the disk?
9. Has data encryption been considered for sensitive data (e.g., payroll)?
10. Is work on sensitive data limited to private offices to reduce the likelihood of exposure?
11. Is sensitive data only placed on distinctly marked diskettes or removable hard disks?
12. Are diskettes or cartridges removed from unattended computers?

Exhibit 16.3 MICROCOMPUTER SECURITY CHECKLIST *(continued)*

13. Does the organization have a designated custodian for sensitive data disks?
14. Are unattended microcomputers turned off when data is removed from the system?
15. Is reformatting of the disk or overwriting of the file required for destruction of sensitive data?
16. Have legally binding confidentiality agreements been drafted by the employer and signed by microcomputers users with access to sensitive data (e.g., customer lists)?
17. Are diskettes or cartridges stored in a secure cabinet or fire-rated safe?
18. Which of the following are required before decisions are made based on microcomputer-generated reports:
    - Validating the accuracy of customized microcomputer programs and embedded formulas?
    - Dating changes to databases?
    - Dating reports with the date of production and the date of the database?
    - Independent validation of the data input?
19. In the event of downtime, are there alternative processing arrangements with service bureaus?
20. Does a preventive maintenance program exist?
21. Have data been processed out of sequence or priority?
22. Do transactions not fit a trend (e.g., too little, too much, too often, too late, illogical)?
23. Are compiled data in conformity with legal and regulatory dictates?
24. Did anyone attempt access above their authorization level?

Exhibit 16.3 MICROCOMPUTER SECURITY CHECKLIST *(continued)*

Source: Buttress, T. E., and M. D. Ackers, "Microcomputer Security," *Journal of Accounting and EDP*, Spring 1990.

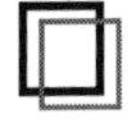

HOW TO AVOID SPAM

Spam is a computer term for unwanted e-mail. In a Monty Python television skit, a group of Vikings in a restaurant sing about the meat product, "Spam, spam, spam, spam, spam, spam, spam, spam, lovely spam! Wonderful spam!" until told to shut up. As a result, something that keeps being repeated to great annoyance is called spam, and computer programmers have picked up on it. The spam problem has reached epic levels, with users continuously barraged with unwanted mail. Begin fighting the problem by learning the basics of stopping spam and getting resources at your disposal.

- *Protect your e-mail address:* Spammers either buy lists of e-mail addresses or use software programs that mine the addresses from the Internet. If your address is posted in discussion groups, on Web sites, in chat rooms, and so on, chances are it will end up on one or more of these lists. Only post your address publicly when absolutely necessary.
- *Set up multiple e-mail accounts:* If you do participate regularly in online activities where you post your address, set up another e-mail account. Reveal it only to close friends and family.
- *Use spam filters:* Many e-mail programs, such as Outlook Express, have built-in tools that block messages sent from certain addresses or that filter messages based on key words you define. Check the online help files for your e-mail software.
- *Use antispam software:* You can install software designed to eliminate spam. Some programs work by matching incoming messages against a list of known spammers; others block messages that do not match an approved list of acceptable addresses. Check out the latest antispam programs at Download.com.
- *Report violators:* A number of government agencies and private groups accept complaints. Whether they can do anything to stop the deluge is an unanswered question. Forward spam to the Federal Trade Commission at uce@ftc.gov.

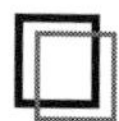

THE LAW

The Computer Fraud and Abuse Act of 1996 (www.usdoj.gov) is a federal law making it a crime for any unauthorized use (copying, damaging, obtaining database information, etc.) of computer hardware or software across state lines. Offenders can be sentenced to up to 20 years in prison.

CHAPTER 17

WIRELESS TECHNOLOGY

Wireless networking is fast becoming a viable alternative r companies that can utilize its advantages. It can provide hanced connectivity and flexibility for companies seeking expand a computer network or make their employees ore mobile. Major technology companies are behind its andards, and the price and choice of products should only nprove.

Two major developing technologies are changing the mputer networking landscape: Wi-Fi (Wireless Fidelity) d Bluetooth. These two forms of wireless technology can ange the entire infrastructure of business networks. lany new hardware and software products produced by any big-name technology companies are equipped for se with Bluetooth and Wi-Fi. The Bluetooth Special Intert Group (SIG; www.bluetooth.com) and the Wi-Fi Allice (www.weca.net) help effectively develop, integrate, d implement these wireless technologies globally. These vo groups have created global standards for each technolgy that must be met by any company producing hardware software to operate with Bluetooth or Wi-Fi.

BLUETOOTH

luetooth is a radio frequency specification for short-range ata transfer. Any device containing Bluetooth technology, hether it be a handheld PC, cell phone, laptop, or stanard PC, receives the signal broadcasted by the network. s mentioned, the Bluetooth SIG was formed to develop d maintain a global standard for Bluetooth wireless techlogy. This facilitates interoperability, advancement, and evelopment of the technology. Over 2,000 companies from ound the globe are members of this industry group. The uetooth SIG consists of leaders in telecommunications d computing including such household names as Ericsn, IBM, Intel, Microsoft, Motorola, Nokia, and Toshiba. e Bluetooth specified standard contains the information necessary to ensure that all devices supporting Bluetooth are able to communicate with each other globally, so it does not matter who manufactures a device. As long as it has the Bluetooth logo or label on it, it can be fully synchronized with any other Bluetooth device. This is a huge step toward full integration. Instead of using many independently operating devices to accomplish one task, businesses may utilize these devices as one tool by integrating their performance. Using Bluetooth can also give a business many more options in terms of purchasing new hardware and upgrades. Because all Bluetooth devices are fully interoperable, businesses are not forced to go back to the same manufacturer. They can look for the best prices as long as the alternative device supports Bluetooth.

The current Bluetooth specified standard calls for the support of several elements. First, there must be general access among devices so that they can link, synchronize, and communicate with each other. Next, cordless telephony must be supported. Cell phones with Bluetooth must be able to operate as cordless phones when they are in proximity to their base station. For example, the cell phone would act as a cordless phone and a laptop or desktop at the base station. The serial ports on Bluetooth supportive devices will act similar to wire serial ports. Each device will also be able to receive and transmit voice data as well as send faxes. Dial-up networking between a cell phone and a laptop computer are part of the standard. As already mentioned, Bluetooth devices will have full wireless personal area network (WPAN) access with the ability to transfer files.

Bluetooth Networks

Bluetooth provides a 10-meter personal bubble. It supports the simultaneous transmissions of information and voice data. A network of Bluetooth devices is called a piconet. Each piconet can support a maximum of eight devices and a minimum of two. Any and all devices containing Bluetooth can be potentially networked with each other. Each piconet has a master unit and slave units. The master unit synchronizes all of the slave units. The slave units are all of the other networked devices besides the master unit. Piconets may be integrated to form a scatternet by setting up a master device to synchronize several piconet master devices. Therefore, the master device of a piconet can also be a slave in a scatternet. The gross data transfer of Bluetooth devices is 1 megabyte per second, while the actual data rate is 432 kilobytes per second. Bluetooth technology is as secure as a wire with up to 128-bit public/private key authentication. Furthermore, it supports good encryption. Bluetooth transmits its signal for up to 10 meters when a 0 dBm radio is used. When a +20 dBm radio is used, the link range can be increased to up to 100 meters.

Practical Uses

The most attractive feature of Bluetooth is that all products containing this technology will work together. All manufacturers implementing Bluetooth into their products must get them tested and certified to ensure interoperability. Accordingly, this feature is perhaps the most attractive for your client's business. All of a company's hardware will be integrated and able to share information. You will be able to synchronize your mobile computer with your desktop simply by placing the mobile computer near the desktop. This will save much time plugging and unplugging. This technology is also useful outside of the office. You can leave your cell phone in your pocket and dial up to the Internet using your laptop, as opposed to lining up the phone's infrared port with that of your mobile computer. The best part is this synchronization will be unconscious and automatic when the devices are within a certain range of each other.

Currently, Bluetooth's most practical usages are its ability to wirelessly synchronize devices and to serve as small networks. Its range limits its ability to serve the needs of large networks. For small business or sole practitioners requiring smaller networks, Bluetooth can serve this purpose. The main advantage of Bluetooth, though, is the ability a CPA and businessperson has when making use of this technology. A person can coordinate each piece of his or her equipment to create a more powerful and efficient business tool. For more information about Bluetooth technology, see www.bluetooth.com/ or see the Web sites of any of the Bluetooth SIG member companies. To learn more about the Bluetooth SIG and its members, go to www.bluetooth.com/sig/about.asp.

WIRELESS FIDELITY (Wi-Fi)

Wireless Fidelity (Wi-Fi), also known as 802.11b, has a range that is longer than that of Bluetooth. Wi-Fi transfers data at 11 megabytes per second. (However, note that Wireless-G operates at speeds almost five times faster than 802.11b.) Wireless-G is compatible with 802.11b products. Many large corporations use Wi-Fi wireless devices to extend standard wired networks to areas such as training classrooms and large public spaces. In addition, many companies make use of Wi-Fi to provide wireless networks to their workers. These wireless networks may also be accessed remotely from workers' homes or other offices. Wi-Fi is also used to bridge the information flow between two or more offices in different buildings.

Wi-Fi networks are found in public places such as hotels and airports. When in an area that supports Wi-Fi, a Wi-Fi certified product is automatically linked to the network when the device is turned on. Wi-Fi is ideal for mid- and large-size companies. It enables businesses to boost productivity and efficiency through constant real-time information flows, full sharing of data, and constant, uninterrupted communication. People are able to continue to work on projects or prepare for meetings in the airport while they are waiting to board their flight. With wireless technologies such as Wi-Fi, companies can keep their employees, whether they are in or out of the office, up-to-date at all times. Costly omissions of information will be virtually unheard of. As time progresses, Wi-Fi networks will be just about everywhere. Members of the Wi-Fi Alliance plan to bring Wi-Fi to urban areas, central cities, and even some major highways. Now, in reading this, you might be reluctant to believe that such an implementation will take place. Just take a look at some of the members of the Wi-Fi Alliance. They are all major players in their respective markets. The site is www.weca.net/OpenSection/index.asp.

Another advantage of Wi-Fi is mobility. Having a wireless network gives your client company many options. It is easy to add other computers to the network. To add another wireless computer to a Wi-Fi network, just plug in your card or universal serial bus (USB) connection and the computer is instantly networked. Computers can just as easily be removed. Furthermore, if your client's business needs to move, the company will not have to abandon its network infrastructure or hire someone to rewire its new office location. Simply unplug at the old office and plug in the base station to a power outlet at the new office. Then turn on the other devices. Presto! A wireless network has been assembled.

Range and Security

When a Wi-Fi computer is close to the base station, it is capable of transferring and receiving data at a rate of up to 11 megabytes per second. As the Wi-Fi device is moved farther away from the base station, the data rate will drop to around 5.5 megabytes per second. Generally, the lowest data transfer rate at the maximum range from a base station will not drop below 1 or 2 megabytes per second. This is a drastic deterioration from the 11-megabyte maximum transfer rate. However, transferring information at 1 megabyte byte per second is still an acceptable performance level compared to other connection types. For instance, 1 megabyte per second is faster than most DSL and cable connections. Therefore, it is still an above average high-speed transmission. This makes it more than adequate for such tasks as sending and receiving e-mail, browsing the Internet, and entering data from a mobile computer. A standard Wi-Fi antenna broadcasts from 750 to 1,000 feet outdoors in open spaces. In an office or other workplace setting with other stimuli that could interfere with the signal, the standard antenna broadcasts from 150 to 350 feet. Keep in mind that dense materials such as certain metals may affect the transmission of radio waves and therefore affect a Wi-Fi broadcast. If the walls in your office are heavily reinforced with such materials as metal, heavy wood, brick, or stone, Wi-Fi devices may have difficulty transmitting from one room to another.

Wired Equivalent Privacy (WEP) is 802.11's encryption standard. WEP works by encrypting the data transferred between the Wi-Fi computer and the Wi-Fi access point. A Wi-Fi access point (AP) is a hardware device or software that acts as a communication hub for wireless devices to connect to a wired local area network (LAN). It provides wireless security while extending the service range that a user of wireless can access. Data is sent to the access point via the public Internet. Therefore, unless it is encrypted, the data is unprotected during its transmission. When the data reaches the access point, it is encrypted and transferred to a Wi-Fi device by WEP. Other wireless technology standards with better security are in development. IEE 802.1X is a more secure wireless access that makes use of an Extensible Authentication Protocol (EAP). There have been several security problems with WEP. Therefore, the Wi-Fi Alliance is planning on implementing a new security standard that implements 802.1X and the EAP: Wi-Fi Protected Access (WPA).

Many corporations use virtual private networks (VPNs) to protect remote access to their WLANs. The VPNs also protect their connections. A VPN creates a secure virtual tunnel from the worker's computer all the way to the corporation's server. A secure connection is established from the worker's Wi-Fi hardware, through his or her Wi-Fi access point, over the public Internet, through the corporation's access point, to the corporation's hardware. Existing systems can be modified to make use of VPN to support a Wi-Fi network. There are many different types of VPNs, some of which are very expensive. Microsoft, however, provides a very basic VPN technology that is free. The VPN is provided with Microsoft's advanced server operating systems. For more information, visit the question-and-answer site: microsoft.com/ntserver/support/faqs/VPNSecFAQ.asp.

A VPN works through a company's server. It encrypts any data transferred to company computers from outside the office. VPN software also operates on remote computers and laptops. Virtual privatel networks enable the transfer of data while protecting that data from being viewed by intruding parties. Setting up a VPN gives a company a lot of mobility. It supports communications from areas such as airports and hotels, enabling people to stay abreast of developing situations that may be crucial to a client's company. Individuals can access information in company networks from anywhere. Companies can expand their networks to the homes of their employees. Therefore, through the use of a WLAN with a VPN, part-time employees can do more from the personal computers in their homes. In addition, full-time employees can spend more time with their families because they can perform a variety of tasks from their homes. Another important aspect of Wi-Fi security is its ability to provide different levels of access. For example, a company can provide top-notch security while allowing open access to the Internet and e-mail accounts for guests on the network. This is accomplished by granting network access at different levels.

In addition to a VPN, wireless networks have a standard technology called Remote Access Dial-Up User Service (RADIUS). RADIUS is used to protect access to wireless networks. Remote Access Dial-Up User Service is security that allows only approved users to access the network. In order for someone to access the network and the corresponding files contained on the network, he or she must input a user name and password. The RADIUS server then verifies the name and password, and if correct, allows that person to access the network. A key feature to RADIUS is that it may be used to provide different types of access levels. A company may use a RADIUS server to provide access to the Internet, another one for network databases, and another one for access to e-mail. Microsoft provides a basic RADIUS server with its advanced server operating systems for free. Other RADIUS servers may be purchased in the forms of software and hardware but can be rather pricey.

One of the most formidable lines of system defense is the firewall. Firewalls work by blocking unwanted and unauthorized people from viewing company databases. Many Wi-Fi access points have built-in firewalls. In addition, all Wi-Fis include a network capability, enabling a group of devices to share one Internet provider (IP) address regardless of whether the IP is from a dial-up, cable, or digital service line (DSL) connection. This capability is called network address translation (NAT). NAT works by creating new IP addresses for each computer of the group from the original single IP address. Therefore, the new IP addresses are invisible to users of the public Internet. The new IP addresses function separately under the cover of the original one.

Public Wi-Fi

Wireless networks are not only making their way into today's businesses, they are steadily becoming a reality in many public areas as well. Companies such as Wayport, which provides Wi-Fi to hotels, airports, and other public areas around the United States, are teaming up with major companies such as 3Com, Sony, Sharp, and other members of the Wi-Fi Alliance to provide wireless fidelity. Major hotels such as the Four Seasons, Holiday Inn, Hampton Inn, Ramada, and many others are also teaming up to provide wireless fidelity in their hotel chains through Wayport. With members of industry groups such as the Bluetooth SIG and the Wi-Fi Alliance pushing the development and advancement of a global wireless infrastructure, more hardware will be built on this standard. Cellular phones and laptops equipped with Bluetooth and Wi-Fi certification are already on the market.

Eventually, wired connections will be a thing of the past. With hotels and airports around the world upgrading to wireless, companies that go wireless will be a step ahead. They will have the up-to-the-minute information needed, full integration of technological equipment, full access to their network databases, and the infrastructure to make it possible from anywhere in the world. An interested party's best bet is to begin researching the benefits and detriments of going wireless. The benefits of going wireless are (1) it is cost-effective because you do not incur the cost of wiring and the cost of labor to do so (you only have to set up a software protocol); (2) it is a portable network, so you can just move computers around the wireless router (a radio transmitter); and (3) it is peer-to-peer flexible because of the absence of wires, so a traditional wired router is not needed. The detriments of going wireless are (1) transmission time is slower than the fastest wired networks; (2) radio frequency transmission is believed by some to cause health problems similar to microwaves (this is controversial); and (3) there may be security problems. Of course, a wireless network may be hooked up to a wired network with the use of a bridge. Therefore, a company's system may have an integration of wired and wireless networks. Beginning to upgrade now may be beneficial in the long run.

WIRELESS VERSUS WIRED

Mobility and efficiency are the advantages of using wireless. Other network technologies such as wired, phone line, or power line–based networks require connections through wire or cable. Wireless uses radio waves that are capable of traveling through walls and floors. Furthermore, you can connect from anywhere, regardless of whether you are inside or outdoors. Wireless networks do not require phone jacks to be close to the devices for them to be networked with the rest of the system. This completely eliminates the inefficient and expensive task of hiring people to rewire an office to support a wired network. Furthermore, wireless technology simply eradicates the clutter of wires around offices. In addition, power line networks are generally more expensive than Wi-Fi networks. Plus, transformers, large appliances, and surge protectors may interfere with power line networks (a type of wired network). Lastly, no wired network is portable. It is completely fixed when it is intact.

An employee at an office with a wired network cannot pick up his or her laptop and go to another part of the office to continue working, unless there is an available connection. With wireless networks, having a limited number of connections in an office will not be an issue, because everywhere is a connection. You probably already have an expensive wired network in your office and might like to add wireless components. This would not be a problem. Wireless components can be added to your existing wired network. Many wireless access points and gateways allow users to connect to wired equipment as well. Many corporations frequently do this. Companies can extend their wired networks by adding Wi-Fi networks. By connecting wireless access points to an existing wired network, a company can provide wireless access to all areas of its office.

The major problem with wireless technology is its price tag. The components for wired networks are still cheaper than those for wireless networks. Access points are just a few hundred dollars. Therefore, the cost of hardware that supports wireless connections can easily be two to four times more expensive than wired network components. The argument, however, is that this higher cost for hardware is offset by the ease of installation and maintenance. Accordingly, long-run costs to maintain the equipment are lower. There will be no expenditures to replace old wires. Furthermore, companies using wireless will never have to hire an electrician to run electrical wiring or install outlets to make a part of the office networkable. For a wireless network, the major expenditures will be for new hardware to add to the network. Lastly, companies will not have to drill holes or run wires through floors and ceilings when installing a wireless network.

Access points are a bit pricey, but in most instances the purchases of additional access points will be few and far between. The only foreseeable instance in which the purchase of a new access point will be necessary is when a company needs to significantly expand its network. Another point to keep in mind is that wireless technology is still relatively unknown. Therefore, as more and more hardware is produced to support wireless, more and more people will switch to this newer technology. As demand grows, the price will decline. Also offsetting the higher costs of wireless are the savings the technology generates. As a result of lower maintenance costs, companies will spend less on information technology (IT). Coupled with greater efficiency and a higher level of productivity (generated through the use of wireless), this will mean higher bottom lines.

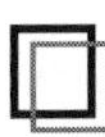

EXPECTED GROWTH OF WIRELESS

The following section contains supplemental information. Keep in mind that the independent study discussed in this section is displayed on the Bluetooth Web site. Read about it at www.bluetooth.com. The information contained in the study is significant when you consider the size and composition of the Bluetooth SIG. The companies that make up this industry group are household names. Furthermore, many of them are also members of the Wi-Fi Alliance.

Promoter Members of the Bluetooth SIG

- 3Com
- Agere
- Ericsson Technology Licensing AB
- IBM Corporation
- Intel Corporation
- Microsoft Corporation
- Motorola, Inc.
- Nokia
- Toshiba Corporation

For a complete list of the group's members, please see www.bluetooth.com/sig/membership/promoter.asp.

Some Members of the Wi-Fi Alliance

- 3Com
- Agere
- Apple
- Epson
- Ericsson Technology Licensing AB
- Hewlett Packard
- Intel Corporation
- Microsoft Corporation
- Motorola, Inc.
- Nokia
- Sharp
- Sprint
- Toshiba Corporation
- U.S. Robotics
- Yamaha

For a complete list of the group's members, please see www.weca.net/OpenSection/members.asp?TID=2.

Recently, the Bluetooth Special Interest Group contracted with a research firm to project future demand for wireless technology. The group that performed the independent study is the Zelos Group LLC, which is an advisory service firm that helps assess the nature and timing of the adoption of new products and services by consumers. The group serves technology industries. Its Web site is www.zelosgroup.com. The Zelos Group LLC predicts that Bluetooth technology will generate around $12 billion over the next four years. The majority of this revenue will be the result of purchases of Bluetooth-enabled equipment used to link pocket computers with mobile handsets, equipment used to wirelessly view and download personal data assistant (PDA) files, and other equipment capable of wirelessly accessing e-mail and the public Internet. The United States and Western Europe were covered in the studies for the years 2001 through 2006. The study assessed likely usages of Bluetooth for PDAs, headsets, handsets, notebook PCs, and automobiles. This information is not just beneficial to businesses seeking to go wireless but also to businesses that distribute hardware, software, and the like. Please view the Web site for more information.

UPS Going Wireless

Shipping giant United Parcel Service has decided to implement a wireless tracking system into its operations. The company has begun to deploy a wireless tracking system that combines Bluetooth with Wireless Fidelity. UPS plans to issue Bluetooth bar code readers to 55,000 of its package handlers. This is the first major wireless implementation of such a system. The project will cost around $120 million.

This large-scale implementation, which combines Bluetooth with Wi-Fi to create one system, may be an indication of future trends. Bluetooth's strength seems to be in its capabilities to facilitate communication between devices. Wi-Fi is more adept at providing wireless and remote access to the public Internet and private networks. Combining these technologies may prove to be the most efficient means of building a company's network. Wi-Fi access points could be used to provide access to a network, and Bluetooth could be used to connect devices. For example, a person would be able to access his e-mail from his laptop wirelessly through Wi-Fi. He could then download it, forward it, or edit it. Suppose he wanted to print it. Bluetooth would enable the transmission of information from the laptop to a printer and command the printer to print the document wirelessly. It is kind of like a one-two wireless punch. There must be a reason for a company the size of UPS, which must keep track of a huge number of shipments daily, to spend $120 million on this new technology. Furthermore, a significant number of blue-chip technology companies are members of both the Bluetooth SIG and the Wi-Fi Alliance. Perhaps they too see the potential relationship between Bluetooth and Wi-Fi.

Wireless Networks and Your Client's Business

Wireless systems have all the aspects needed to alter the way in which people work. More can be done from the home and on the road through remote access. Important information can be received in real time virtually anywhere. The need to spend long hours in the office over weekends is greatly decreased by Wi-Fi. Small and medium-size businesses can now obtain the same, and many times better, technology to keep track of their inventory as their larger competition. The best part is that a small business can install the wireless network itself instead of enlisting outside help. Businesses can now have live streaming, real-time inventory data. This type of wireless technology is ideal for retail, wholesale, shipping, and manufacturing companies.

The Accountant's Role

The accountant must be abreast of the latest developments in wireless networks for practical use within the CPA firm and for properly advising client companies. The CPA must be familiar with the various business applications of wireless networks, the benefits, the drawbacks, and how to get the most out of the system to enhance efficiency, productivity, timeliness, and profitability. The use of wireless networks will optimize computer operations and corporate activities. A wireless network adapter is installed in each computer so that there is no need to drill holes and run cables. However, the farther the wireless network computer is from a wireless access point and the greater the number of solid objects standing in the way, the slower will be the connection. To optimize network speed and range, the wireless access point should be positioned at least a few feet above the floor away from metal objects. The access point should be in the center of the coverage area. However, another approach is to position the access point so that it is as close as possible to the largest number of computers. With larger areas or those with many obstructions, multiple access points are needed. Make sure the access points have the same settings. Almost all wireless network adapters support roaming. When access point coverage areas overlap, the adapter will latch on to the strongest signal.

Reliability, performance, and range depend on signal quality. Add an extra antenna to your network adapter and access point to materially improve the quality of the signal. Signal strength—your card's ability to receive data under different conditions—is crucial. As you move away from the gateway, there is a degradation of the signal strength and performance. The measure of gateway performance is the combination of range and throughput. Range means how far you can go from the gateway and still have an acceptable signal. Throughput measures the amount of work performed by a computer system over a specified time period. Throughput decreases dramatically when several users access the gateway simultaneously. The card in the gateway has a fixed bandwidth that all client cards must share. For security reasons, mix numbers and letters in your wireless network's service set identifier used by each wireless device on your network to log in.

What Does It All Mean for CEOs, CIOs and Users?

CEOs

Mobile working can dramatically boost productivity and improve an organization's responsiveness and flexibility, but it also poses challenges for the chief executive. As the trend toward mobile working gathers pace, these are issues that executives cannot afford to ignore. As wired and wireless network–enabled notebook PCs, personal digital assistants (PDAs), and smart phones proliferate, mobile working is becoming a reality not just for a select few corporate road warriors, but for a much larger group of employees.

This expansion has significant advantages and risks for corporate management. On the positive side, mobile and remote access to corporate systems such as e-mail, enterprise portals, and applications such as contact management and customer relationship management systems often provides a competitive edge for companies while improving both customer and employee satisfaction. On the negative side, mobile technologies and services tend to come with premium price tags, pushing costs up at a time when chief executives are still under pressure to improve margins and show rapid returns on investments.

Mobile systems are also notoriously difficult to manage and control. Perhaps most seriously, ad-hoc arrangements can represent a real threat to enterprise system security. Balancing the risks and rewards of mobile working and establishing a corporate policy framework to cover, for example, remote access to corporate networks has become an important issue for chief executives—an issue that they ignore at their peril.

CEOs will want to ensure that they are getting value for their money when they invest in mobile working infrastructure, so they will probably want to see estimates—and subsequently evidence—of productivity gains and other tangible improvements. They will also want to see investment return projections and will probably want to be involved in making choices about competing projects.

CEOs may be concerned with how to ensure that mobile and remote workers are earning their keep when they are out of the office. Most consultants suggest that trust plays a key role in enabling a mobile workforce. They add that it is important to lay down guidelines and keep a watch on costs to ensure they do not spiral out of control. Given the growing threat posed by e-mail viruses, spyware, and other unwelcome network intrusions, most CEOs are well advised to take steps to ensure that the benefits of mobile working are not negated by the threat it can pose to corporate security. But while it may be tempting to use security as an excuse for inaction, the competitive and financial risks of not adopting mobile working practices when competitors are pushing forward may be even greater.

CIOs

Like it or not, mobile devices ranging from Wi-Fi–enabled notebook PCs and PDAs to datacentric communicators such as the Treo 600 or RIM's Blackberry are finding their way into the corporate environment. Sometimes they are part of a corporate rollout and can therefore be planned and controlled. But more often than not they are surreptitiously introduced by individuals who have tasted the benefits of remote access and mobile working as consumers and now want to use the same devices and services at work.

One of the key challenges for CIOs in either case is to find ways to accommodate a diverse group of mobile devices while protecting the corporate IT infrastructure and minimizing the network security threat they can pose. Given the fast pace of change in the technology industry, particularly in the mobile device sector, it is often a challenge for a CIO to keep up with hardware, software, and service developments and to provide the level of support—often with reduced resources—that users have come to expect.

One way to minimize the support overhead is to standardize a set of devices such as notebook PCs, PDAs, mobile phones, and communicators. However this often delays deployment and can lead to end user frustration. Another option is to outsource the provision of devices and services. For example, U.S.-based Aruba, which supplies secure Wi-Fi networks for corporate customers, says many of them also want services to manage the deployment and maintenance of the Wi-Fi system.

One of the fastest-growing areas in the mobile technology sector is security. Typically, larger companies will deploy virtual private networks to a corporate network to facilitate secure access for mobile and remote users such as home office workers. However, there are secure alternatives including remote access programs such as LapLink and the GoToMyPC remote access service that can be rolled out across an enterprise or made available to a few users. There is also a growing market for software and hardware such as mini-USB drives and biometric devices such as fingerprint readers designed to protect confidential or sensitive data stored on a portable PC. Other vendors have developed systems designed to enable secure access to e-mail and other corporate services from Internet public access points such as hotels, conference centers, and even Wi-Fi hotspots.

Most CIOs have already discovered that the trend toward mobile working is like a runaway steamroller—it is not about to stop. So while it makes sense to lay down guidelines about which mobile devices are supported and how they should be used, ultimately the CIO has to deal with the realities of mobile working.

USERS

The rapid growth of mobile working and the proliferation of new hardware devices, software, and services designed to enable mobile workers to do their jobs from virtually anywhere pose both great opportunities and challenges. For many employees, the availability of basic tools such as portable PCs, pocket-size PDA organizers, and the now nearly ubiquitous mobile phone gives them much greater freedom and flexibility. For example, salespeople can use mobile technologies to update customer profiles, download price quotes, and provide their audiences with dazzling multimedia presentations. Executives can send and receive e-mail messages, peer into the corporate ERP system, or check share prices and competitors' Web sites while traveling using Wi-Fi or W-LAN wireless connections. A recent study conducted by Intel, the U.S. chipmaker, showed that technology has dramatically changed the lives of mobile professionals, making it much easier to stay in touch while traveling and to respond to colleagues and customers in a more timely fashion.

Meanwhile, a growing number of employees now have broadband Internet access at home or work in remote local offices, yet they can tie back into corporate headquarters securely via a virtual private network connection. But while more and more employees have "always-on" wired and wireless Internet access, they are also finding that they need to set boundaries in order to ensure that they retain a balance between home and office lives and that they are the masters of technology rather than its slave.

Individual attitudes toward mobile technology also vary. While some employees relish the idea of being able to deal with the overnight flood of e-mail using a wireless device on the train before they reach the office, others balk at the idea of work intruding into another part of their life. When the pressure for greater productivity is often unrelenting, balancing the demands of work and private lives in the age of mobile technology has become one of the more interesting issues probed by sociologists.

Fortunately, the wide range of technologies available means that most employees can pick and choose which technologies to adopt and just how much they should intrude into the home. Arguably, however, portable PCs, mobile phones, and PDAs enable employees to work more flexibly and at times that best suit them. Provided a balance is kept, mobile devices and technologies can be valuable tools that enrich both work and private lives.

CHAPTER 18

CAPITAL BUDGETING AND ECONOMIC FEASIBILITY STUDY OF AN IT PROJECT

Capital budgeting is the process of making long-term planning decisions for alternative investment opportunities. There are many investment decisions that the company may have to make in order to grow. Examples of capital budgeting applications are installation of a new information system (IS), lease or purchase, new product development, product line selection, keeping or selling a business segment, and which asset to invest in. A careful cost-benefit analysis must be performed to determine a project's economic feasibility of a capital expenditure project. This chapter covers:

- Several popular capital budgeting techniques
- Effects of the Modified Accelerated Cost Recovery System (MACRS) on capital budgeting decisions
- An economic feasibility study for a new information system

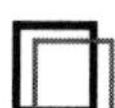

HOW DO YOU MEASURE INVESTMENT WORTH?

Several methods of evaluating investment projects are as follows:

- Payback period
- Net present value (NPV)
- Internal rate of return (IRR)

The NPV method and the IRR method are called discounted cash flow (DCF) methods.

Payback Period

The payback period measures the length of time required to recover the amount of initial investment. It is computed by dividing the initial investment by the cash inflows through increased revenues or cost savings.

EXAMPLE 18.1 PAYBACK PERIOD

Assume:

Cost of investment	\$18,000
Annual after-tax cash savings	\$ 3,000

Then the payback period is:

$$\text{Payback period} = \frac{\text{Initial investment}}{\text{Cost savings}} = \frac{\$18,000}{\$3,000} = 6 \text{ years}$$

Choose the project with the shorter payback period. The rationale behind this choice is that the shorter the payback period, the less risky the project and the greater the liquidity.

EXAMPLE 18.2 PAYBACK PERIOD—TWO PROJECTS

Consider the two projects whose after-tax cash inflows are not even. Assume each project costs \$1,000.

	Cash Inflow	
Year	A (\$)	B (\$)
1	100	500
2	200	400
3	300	300
4	400	100
5	500	
6	600	

When cash inflows are not even, the payback period has to be found by trial and error. The payback period of project A is 4 years (\$1,000 = \$100 + \$200 + \$300 + \$400). The payback period of project B is 1/3 years (\$1,000 = \$500 + \$400 + \$100):

$$2 \text{ years} + \frac{\$100}{\$300} = 2\ 1/3 \text{ years}$$

Project B is the project of choice in this case, since it has the shorter payback period.

The advantages of using the payback period method of evaluating an investment project are that (1) it is simple to compute and easy to understand and (2) it handles investment risk effectively. The shortcomings of this method are that (1) it does not recognize the time value of money and (2) it ignores the impact of cash inflows received after the payback period; essentially, cash flows after the payback period determine profitability of an investment.

Net Present Value

Net present value (NPV) is the excess of the present value (PV) of cash inflows generated by the project over the amount of the initial investment (I):

$$NPV = PV - I$$

The present value of future cash flows is computed using the so-called cost of capital (or minimum required rate of return) as the discount rate. When cash inflows are uniform, the present value would be

$$PV = A \times T2\ (i, n)$$

where A is the amount of the annuity. The value of T2 is found in Exhibit 18.2. T2 is the present value factor of $1 which is found in Exhibit 18.2.

Note: T1 is the present value of $2 which is given in Exhibit 18.1.

If NPV is positive, accept the project. Otherwise reject it.

Periods	4%	6%	8%	10%	12%	14%	20%
1	0.962	0.943	0.926	0.909	0.893	0.877	0.833
2	0.925	0.890	0.857	0.826	0.797	0.769	0.694
3	0.889	0.840	0.794	0.751	0.712	0.675	0.579
4	0.855	0.792	0.735	0.683	0.636	0.592	0.482
5	0.822	0.747	0.681	0.621	0.567	0.519	0.402
6	0.790	0.705	0.630	0.564	0.507	0.456	0.335
7	0.760	0.665	0.583	0.513	0.452	0.400	0.279
8	0.731	0.627	0.540	0.467	0.404	0.351	0.233
9	0.703	0.592	0.500	0.424	0.361	0.308	0.194
10	0.676	0.558	0.463	0.386	0.322	0.270	0.162
11	0.650	0.527	0.429	0.350	0.287	0.237	0.135
12	0.625	0.497	0.397	0.319	0.257	0.208	0.112
13	0.601	0.469	0.368	0.290	0.229	0.182	0.093
14	0.577	0.442	0.340	0.263	0.205	0.160	0.078
15	0.555	0.417	0.315	0.239	0.183	0.140	0.065
16	0.534	0.394	0.292	0.218	0.163	0.123	0.054
17	0.513	0.371	0.270	0.198	0.146	0.108	0.045
18	0.494	0.350	0.250	0.180	0.130	0.095	0.038
19	0.475	0.331	0.232	0.164	0.116	0.083	0.031
20	0.456	0.312	0.215	0.149	0.104	0.073	0.026
30	0.308	0.174	0.099	0.057	0.033	0.020	0.004
40	0.208	0.097	0.046	0.022	0.011	0.005	0.001

Exhibit 18.1 PRESENT VALUE OF $1 = T1 (i, n)

Periods	4%	6%	8%	10%	12%	14%	20%
1	0.962	0.943	0.926	0.909	0.893	0.877	0.833
2	1.886	1.833	1.783	1.736	1.690	1.647	1.528
3	2.775	2.673	2.577	2.487	2.402	2.322	2.106
4	3.630	3.465	3.312	3.170	3.037	2.914	2.589
5	4.452	4.212	3.993	3.791	3.605	3.433	2.991
6	5.242	4.917	4.623	4.355	4.111	3.889	3.326
7	6.002	5.582	5.206	4.868	4.564	4.288	3.605
8	6.733	6.210	5.747	5.335	4.968	4.639	3.837
9	7.435	6.802	6.247	5.759	5.328	4.946	4.031
10	8.111	7.360	6.710	6.145	5.650	5.216	4.192
11	8.760	7.887	7.139	6.495	5.938	5.453	4.327
12	9.385	8.384	7.536	6.814	6.194	5.660	4.439
13	9.986	8.853	7.904	7.103	6.424	5.842	4.533
14	10.563	9.295	8.244	7.367	6.628	6.002	4.611
15	11.118	9.712	8.559	7.606	6.811	6.142	4.675
16	11.652	10.106	8.851	7.824	6.974	6.265	4.730
17	12.168	10.477	9.122	8.022	7.120	6.373	4.775
18	12.659	10.828	9.372	8.201	7.250	6.467	4.812
19	13.134	11.158	9.604	8.365	7.366	6.550	4.844
20	13.590	11.470	9.818	8.514	7.469	6.623	4.870
30	17.292	13.765	11.258	9.427	8.055	7.003	4.979
40	19.793	15.046	11.925	9.779	8.244	7.105	4.997

Exhibit 18.2 PRESENT VALUE OF AN ANNUITY OF $1 = T2(i, n)

EXAMPLE 18.3 NET PRESENT VALUE

Consider the following investment:

Initial investment	$12,950
Estimated life	10 years
After-tax annual cash inflows	$3,000
Cost of capital (minimum required rate of return)	12%

The present value of the cash inflows is:

PV = A × T2(i, n) = $3,000 × T2(12%,10 years) = $3,000(5 × 650)	$16,950
Initial investment (I)	$12,950
Net present value (NPV = PV – I)	$ 4,000

Since the NPV of the investment is positive, the investment should be accepted.

The advantages of the NPV method are that it obviously recognizes the time value of money and it is easy to compute whether the cash flows form an annuity or vary from period to period.

Internal Rate of Return

Internal rate of return (IRR), also called time-adjusted rate of return, is defined as the rate of interest that equates I with the PV of future cash inflows. In other words, at IRR, I = PV or NPV = 0.

Accept the project if the IRR exceeds the cost of capital. Otherwise, reject it.

EXAMPLE 18.4 INTERNAL RATE OF RETURN

Assume the same data given in Example 17-3 and set the following equality (I = PV):

$$\$12{,}950 = \$3{,}000 \times T4(I, 10 \text{ years})$$

$$T4(I, 10 \text{ years}) = \frac{\$12{,}950}{\$3{,}000} = 4.317$$

which stands somewhere between 18% and 20% in the 10-year line of Exhibit 18.2. The interpolation follows:

	PV of an Annuity of $1 Factor T2(i, 10 years)	
18%	4.494	4.494
IRR	4.317	
20%		4.192
Difference	0.177	0.302

Therefore,

$$\begin{aligned} IRR &= 18\% + \frac{0.177}{0.302}(20\% - 18\%) \\ &= 18\% + 0.586(2\%) = 18\% + 1.17\% = 19.17\% \end{aligned}$$

Since the IRR of the investment is greater than the cost of capital (12%), accept the project.

The advantage of using the IRR method is that it does consider the time value of money and therefore is more exact and realistic than the ARR method. The shortcomings of this method are that (1) it is time-consuming to compute, especially when the cash inflows are not even, although most financial calculators and PCs have a key to calculate IRR, and (2) it fails to recognize the varying sizes of investment in competing projects.

Can a Computer Help?

Spreadsheet programs can be used in making IRR calculations. For example, Excel has a function IRR (*values, guess*). Excel considers negative numbers as cash outflows such as the initial investment and positive numbers as cash inflows. Many financial calculators have similar features. As in the following table, suppose you want to calculate the IRR of a $12,950 investment (the value 12,950 entered in year 0 followed by 10 monthly cash inflows of $3,000). Using a guess of 12% (the value of 0.12), which is in effect the cost of capital, your formula would be at IRR(values, 0.12), and Excel would return 19.15%:

Year 0	1	2	3	4	5	6	7	8	9	10
$(12,950)	3,000	3,000	3,000	3,000	3,000	3,000	3,000	3,000	3,000	3,000
IRR = 19.15%										
NPV = $4,000.67										

Note: The *Excel* formula for NPV is NPV (discount rate, cash inflow values) + I, where I is given as a negative number.

HOW DO INCOME TAXES AFFECT INVESTMENT DECISIONS?

Income taxes make a difference in many capital budgeting decisions. The project that is attractive on a before-tax basis may have to be rejected on an after-tax basis, and vice versa. Income taxes typically affect both the amount and the timing of cash flows. Since net income, not cash inflows, is subject to tax, after-tax cash inflows are not usually the same as after-tax net income.

How to Calculate After-Tax Cash Flows

Let us define:

S = Sales
E = Cash operating expenses
d = Depreciation
t = Tax rate

Then before-tax cash inflows (or cash savings) = S – E and net income = S – E – d. By definition,

After-tax cash inflows = Before-tax cash inflows – Taxes = (S – E) – (S – E – d)(t)

Rearranging gives the short-cut formula:

After-tax cash inflows = (S – E)(1 – t) + (d)(t) or
= (S – E – d)(1 – t) + d

The deductibility of depreciation from sales in arriving at taxable net income reduces income tax payments and thus serves as a tax shield:

Tax shield = Tax savings on depreciation = (d)(t)

EXAMPLE 18.5 AFTER-TAX CASH INFLOW

Assume:

S = $12,000
E = $10,000
d = $500 per year using the straight-line method
t = 30%

Then

After-tax cash inflow = ($12,000 – $10,000) (1 – .3) + ($500)(.3)
= ($2,000)(.7) + ($500)(.3)
= $1,400 + $150 = $1,550

Note that a tax-shield = tax savings on depreciation = (d)(t)
= ($500)(.3) = $150

Since the tax shield is dt, the higher the depreciation deduction, the higher the tax savings on depreciation. Therefore, an accelerated depreciation method (such as double-declining balance) produces higher tax savings than the straight-line method. Accelerated methods produce higher present values for the tax savings, which may make a given investment more attractive.

EXAMPLE 18.6 MACHINE PURCHASE DECISION

The Navistar Company estimates that it can save $2,500 a year in cash operating costs for the next 10 years if it buys a special-purpose machine at a cost of $10,000. No residual value is expected. Depreciation is by straight-line. Assume that the income tax rate is 30% and the after-tax cost of capital (minimum required rate of return) is 10%. After-tax cash savings can be calculated as follows:

Depreciation by straight-line is $10,000/10 = $1,000 per year.

Thus,

After-tax cash savings = (S – E)(1 – t)+(d)(t)

= $2,500(1 –.3) + $1,000(.3)

= $1,750 + $300 = $2,050

To see if this machine should be purchased, the net present value can be calculated.

PV = $2,050 T4(10%,10 years) = $2,050 (6,145) = $12,597.25

Thus,

NPV = PV – I = $12,597.25 – $10,000 = $2,597.25

Since NPV is positive, the machine should be bought.

HOW DOES MACRS AFFECT INVESTMENT DECISIONS?

Although traditional depreciation methods can still be used for computing depreciation for book purposes, 1981 saw a new way of computing depreciation deductions for tax purposes. The current rule is called the Modified Accelerated Cost Recovery System (MACRS) rule, as enacted by Congress in 1981 and modified somewhat under the Tax Reform Act of 1986. This rule is characterized as follows:

1. The concept of useful life is abandoned and depreciation deductions are accelerated by placing all

depreciable assets into one of eight age property classes. This method calculates deductions, based on an allowable percentage of the asset's original cost (see Exhibits 18.3 and 18.4). With a shorter asset tax life than useful life, the company would be able to deduct depreciation more quickly and save more in income taxes in the earlier years, thereby making an investment more attractive. The rationale behind the system is that the government encourages the company to invest in facilities and increase its productive capacity and efficiency. (Remember that the higher d is, the larger the tax shield (d)(t).)

2. Since the allowable percentages in Exhibit 18.3 add up to 100%, there is no need to consider the salvage value of an asset in computing depreciation.
3. The company may elect the straight-line method. The straight-line convention must follow the half-year convention, which means the company can deduct only half of the regular straight-line depreciation amount in the first year. The reason for electing to use

	Property Class					
Year	3-year	5-year	7-year	10-year	15-year	20-year
1	33.3%	20.0%	14.3%	10.0%	5.0%	3.8%
2	44.5	32.0	24.5	18.0	9.5	7.2
3	14.8[a]	19.2	17.5	14.4	8.6	6.7
4	7.4	11.5[a]	12.5	11.5	7.7	6.2
5		11.5	8.9[a]	9.2	6.9	5.7
6		5.8	8.9	7.4	6.2	5.3
7			8.9	6.6[a]	5.9[a]	4.9
8			4.5	6.6	5.9	4.5[a]
9				6.5	5.9	4.5
10				6.5	5.9	4.5
11				3.3	5.9	4.5
12					5.9	4.5
13					5.9	4.5
14					5.9	4.5
15					3.0	4.4
16						4.4
17						4.4
18						4.4
19						4.4
20						4.4
21						2.2
Total	100%	100%	100%	100%	100%	100%

[a] Denotes the year of changeover to straight-line depreciation.

Exhibit 18.3 MODIFIED ACCELERATED COST RECOVERY SYSTEM CLASSIFICATION OF ASSETS

Property Class and Depreciation Method	Useful Life (ADR Midpoint Life)[a]	Examples of Assets
3-year property 200% declining balance	4 years or less	Most small tools are included; the law specifically excludes autos and light trucks from this property class.
5-year property 200% computers, declining balance	More than 4 years to less than 10 years	Autos and light trucks, typewriters, copiers, computers, duplicating equipment, heavy general-purpose trucks, and research and experimentation equipment are included.
7-year property 200% and declining balance	10 years or more to less than 16 years	Office furniture and fixtures. Most items of machinery and equipment used in production are included.
10-year property 200% declining balance	16 years or more to less than 20 years	Various machinery and equipment, such as that used in petroleum distilling and refining and in the milling of grain, are included.
15-year property 150% declining balance	20 years or more to less than 25 years	Sewage treatment plants, telephone and electrical distribution facilities, and land improvements are included.
20-year property 150% declining balance	25 years or more	Service stations and other real property with an ADR midpoint life of less than 27.5 years are included.
27.5-year property straight-line	Not applicable	All residential rental property is included.
31.5-year property straight-line	Not applicable	All nonresidential property is included.

[a]ADR midpoint life means the useful life of an asset in a business sense; the appropriate ADR midpoint lives for assets are designated in the tax regulations.

Exhibit 18.4 MACRS TABLES BY PROPERTY CLASS

the MACRS optional straight-line method is that some firms may prefer to stretch out depreciation deductions using the straight-line method rather than to accelerate them. Those firms are just starting out or have little or no income and wish to show more income on their income statements.

4. If an asset is disposed of before the end of its class life, the half-year convention allows half the depreciation for that year (early disposal rule).

EXAMPLE 18.7 MACHINE PURCHASE DECISION UNDER THE MACRS RULE

A machine costs $10,000. Annual cash inflows are expected to be $5,000. The machine will be depreciated using the MACRS rule and will fall under the 3-year property class. The cost of capital after taxes is 10%. The estimated life of the machine is 5 years. The salvage value of the machine at the end of the fifth year is expected to be $1,200. The tax rate is 30%. Should you buy the machine? Use the NPV method.

The formula for computation of after-tax cash inflows (S – E) (1 – t) + (d)(t) needs to be computed separately. The NPV analysis can be performed as follows:

					Present Value Factor @ 10%	Present Value
(S-E)(1 -t):						
	$5,000	$5,000 (1 - .3) = $3,500				
	For 5 years	For 5 years	$3,500		3.791(a)	$13,268.50
(d)(t):						
Year	**Cost**	**MACRS%**	**d**	**(d)(t)**		
1	$10,000 ×	33.3%	$3,330	$999	909(b)	908.09
2	$10,000 ×	44.5		1,335	826(b)	1,102.71
		4,450		444	.751(b)	333.44
3	$10,000 ×	14.8				
		1,480				
4	$10,000 ×	7.4	740	222	.683(b)	151.63
Salvage value:						
	$1,200 in	$1,200(1 -.3)	=	$840	.621(b)	521.64
	Year 5:	$840(c) in year 5	Present value (PV)			$16,286.01

(a) T2 (10%, 4 years) = 3.170 (from Exhibit 18.2).

(b) T1 values (year 1, 2, 3, 4, 5) obtained from Exhibit 18.1.

(c) Any salvage value received under the MACRS rules is a taxable gain (the excess of the selling price over book value, $1,200 in this example), since the book value will be zero at the end of the life of the machine.

Since NPV = PV – I = $16,286.01 – $10,000 = $6,286.01 is positive, the machine should be bought.

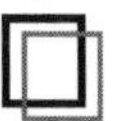

ECONOMIC FEASIBILITY STUDY FOR A NEW INFORMATION SYSTEM

Determining economic feasibility requires a careful investigation of the costs and benefits of a proposed information system. The basic framework for feasibility analysis is the capital budgeting model in which cost savings and other benefits, as well as initial outlay costs, operating costs, and other cash outflows, are translated into dollar estimates.

The estimated benefits are compared with the costs to determine whether the system is cost-effective. Where possible, benefits and costs that are not easily quantifiable should be estimated and included in the feasibility analysis. If they cannot be accurately estimated, they should be listed, and the likelihood of their occurrence and the expected impact on the organization should be evaluated. Some of the tangible and intangible benefits a company might obtain from a new system are cost savings; improved customer service, productivity, decision making, and data processing; better management control; and increased job satisfaction and employee morale.

Equipment is an initial outlay cost if the system is purchased and an operating cost if it is rented or leased. Equipment costs vary from a few thousand dollars for microcomputer systems to millions of dollars for enormous mainframes. They are usually less than the cost of acquiring software and maintaining, supporting, and operating the system. Software acquisition costs include the purchase price of software as well as the time and effort required to design, program, test, and document software. The personnel costs associated with hiring, training, and relocating staff can be substantial. Site preparation costs may be incurred for large computer systems. There are costs involved in installing the new system and converting files to the appropriate format and storage media.

The primary operating cost is maintaining the system. There may be significant annual cash outflows for equipment replacement and expansion and software updates. Human resource costs include the salaries of systems analysts, programmers, operators, data entry operators, and management. Costs are also incurred for supplies, overhead, and other operating expenses. Initial cash outlay and operating costs are summarized in Exhibit 18.5.

During systems design, several alternative approaches to meeting system requirements are developed. Various feasibility measures such as technical, operational, legal, and scheduling feasibility are then used to narrow the list of alternatives. Economic feasibility and capital budgeting techniques, which were discussed earlier, are used to evaluate the benefit-cost aspects of the alternatives.

- Hardware
  - Central processing unit
  - Peripherals
  - Special input/output devices
  - Communications hardware
  - Upgrade and expansion costs
- Software
  - Application, system, general-purpose, utility, and communications software
  - Updated versions of software
  - Application software design, programming, modification, and testing
- Installation
  - Freight and delivery charges
  - Setup and connection fees
- Conversion
  - Systems testing
  - File and data conversions
  - Parallel operations
- Documentation
  - Systems documentation
  - Training program documentation
  - Operating standards and procedures
- Site preparation
  - Air-conditioning, humidity, and dust controls
  - Physical security (access)
  - Fire and water protection
  - Cabling, wiring, and outlets
  - Furnishing and fixtures
- Staff
  - Supervisors
  - Analysts and programmers
  - Computer operators
  - Input (data conversion) personnel
  - Recruitment and staff training
- Maintenance/backup
  - Hardware/software maintenance
  - Backup and recovery operations
  - Power supply protection
- Supplies and overhead
  - Preprinted forms
  - Data storage devices
  - Supplies (paper, ribbons, toner)
  - Utilities and power
- Others
  - Legal and consulting fees
  - Insurance

Exhibit 18.5 INITIAL CASH OUTLAY AND OPERATING COSTS

EXAMPLE 18.8 INFORMATION SYSTEM PROJECT

Sophie, an information systems (IS) project manager for the MYK chain of discount stores, is contemplating installation of a new IS system that is flexible, efficient, timely, and responsive to user and customer needs. The new system aims at improving the company's business processes. After the analysis, Sophie's IS project team members decided they wanted the corporate office to gather daily sales data from each store. Analyzing the prior day's sales will help the company adapt quickly to customer needs. Providing sales data to suppliers will help avoid stockouts and overstocking.

Coordinating buying at the corporate office will help MYK to minimize inventory levels and negotiate lower wholesale prices. Stores will send orders electronically the day they are prepared. Based on store orders, the previous day's sales figures, and warehouse inventory, MYK will send purchase orders to suppliers. Suppliers will process orders and ship goods to regional warehouses or directly to the stores the day that orders are received. Each store will have the flexibility to respond to local sales trends and conditions by placing local orders. Accounts payable will be centralized so that the firm can make payments electronically.

Sophie's team members conducted an economic feasibility study and determined that the project makes excellent use of funds. As shown in Exhibit 18.6, they estimated that initial outlay costs for the system are $4.66 million (initial systems design and new hardware $1.8 million each, software $375,000, training, $185,000, and site preparation and conversion $250,000 each).

The team members estimated what it would cost to operate the system for its estimated six-year life, as well as what the system would save the company. The following recurring costs were identified: hardware expansion, additional software and software updates, systems maintenance, added personnel to operate the system, communication charges, and overhead. The system will also save the company money by eliminating clerical jobs, generating working capital savings, increasing sales and profits, and decreasing warehouse costs. The costs and savings for years 1 through 6, which are expected to rise from year to year, are shown in Exhibit 18.6.

Sophie calculated the annual savings minus the recurring additional costs, then calculated the annual after-tax cash savings under the MACRS tax rule. The $4.66 million system can be depreciated over the six-year period. For example, the depreciation in year 1 of $932,000

EXAMPLE 18.8 INFORMATION SYSTEM PROJECT *(continued)*

reduces net income by that amount. Since the company does not have to pay taxes on the $1 million, at its tax rate of 34% the company ends up saving an additional $316,880 in year 1. Finally, Sophie calculated the net savings for each year.

Sophie used MYK's cost of capital of 10% to calculate the net present value (NPV) of the investment, which is about $3.15 million. The internal rate of return (IRR) is a respectable 26.26%. Sophie realized how advantageous it would be for the company to borrow the money (at 10% interest) in order to produce a 26.26% return on that borrowed money. In addition, payback (the point at which the initial cost is recovered) occurs in the fourth year. NPV and 1RR are calculated as shown in Exhibit 18.6.

Sophie presented the system and its cost-benefit calculations to top management. Challenges to her estimates (various what-if scenarios) were plugged into the Excel model so that management could see the effect of the changed assumptions. This spreadsheet analysis was intended to ensure a positive return of the new system under future uncertainty.

	Initial Outlay			Years			
	0	1	2	3	4	5	6
Initial outlay costs (I)							
Initial system design	$1,800,000						
Hardware	1,800,000						
Software	375,000						
Training	185,000						
Site preparation	250,000						
Conversion	250,000						
Total	$4,660,000						
Recurring costs							
Hardware expansion			$ 250,000	$ 290,000	$ 330,000	$ 370,000	$ 390,000
Software			160,000	210,000	230,000	245,000	260,000
Systems maintenance		$ 70,000	120,000	130,000	140,000	150,000	160,000
Personnel costs		485,000	800,000	900,000	1,000,000	1,100,000	1,300,000
Communication charges		99,000	160,000	180,000	200,000	220,000	250,000
Overhead		310,000	420,000	490,000	560,000	600,000	640,000
Total		$ 964,000	$1,910,000	$2,200,000	$2,460,000	$2,685,000	$3,000,000

Exhibit 18.6 ECONOMIC FEASIBILITY FOR A NEW INFORMATION SYSTEM

Cash savings							
Clerical cost savings		$ 500,000	$1,110,000	$1,350,000	$1,500,000	1,700,000	1,950,000
Working capital savings		1,000,000	1,200,000	1,500,000	1,500,000	1,500,000	1,500,000
Increased sales and profits			500,000	900,000	1,200,000	1,500,000	1,800,000
Reduced warehouse costs			400,000	800,000	1,200,000	1,600,000	2,000,000
Total		$1,500,000	$3,210,000	$4,550,000	$5,400,000	$6,300,000	$7,250,000
Cash savings minus recurring costs		536,000	1,300,000	2,350,000	2,940,000	3,615,000	4,250,000
Less income taxes (34%)	34%	(182,240)	(442,000)	(799,000)	(999,600)	(1,229,100)	(1,445,000)
Cash savings (net of tax)		$ 353,760	$ 858,000	$1,551,000	$1,940,400	$2,385,900	$2,805,000
Tax shield from depreciation		316,880	507,008	304,205	182,206	182,206	91,895
Net cash inflows (net savings) after taxes	$(4,660,000)	$ 670,640	$1,365,008	$1,855,205	$2,122,606	$2,568,106	$2,896,895

Tax savings from depreciation deduction

Year	MACRS	Depreciation	Tax savings
1	20.00%	$ 932,000	$316,880
2	32.00%	1,491,200	507,008
3	19.20%	894,720	304,205

Exhibit 18.6 ECONOMIC FEASIBILITY FOR A NEW INFORMATION SYSTEM *(continued)*

4	11.50%	535,900	182,206
5	11.50%	535,900	182,206
6	5.80%	270,280	91,895

Net present value calculations @ a cost of capital of 10%

Year	Net savings	PV factor	PV
0	$(4,660,000)	1.0000	$(4,660,000)
1	670,640	0.9091	609,679
2	1,365,008	0.8265	1,128,179
3	1,855,205	0.7513	1,393,815
4	2,122,606	0.6830	1,449,740
5	2,568,106	0.6209	1,594,537
6	2,896,895	0.5645	1,635,297
		NPV	$ 3,151,248
		IRR	26.26%

Exhibit 18.6 ECONOMIC FEASIBILITY FOR A NEW INFORMATION SYSTEM *(continued)*

CHAPTER 19

IT PROJECT MANAGEMENT

Information technology (IT) managers must have the organizational skills needed to manage projects. Projects are exceptions to routine work. In a project, you usually deal with unique problems, have a set of constraints, and often work with deadlines. Projects may involve extensive interaction with various departments within your organization. You are likely to encounter the following elements in all projects:

- *Time schedule:* A project has a specific life span. It has a starting point and a stopping point. Controls must be used to ensure that all phases of a project are completed in a timely manner.
- *Budgetary constraints:* A project's budget is often separate from a departmental budget and gives the project team some independence. Capital budgets may be required in addition to expense budgets. The project manager assumes responsibility for the budget and any variance.
- *Results-oriented activities:* Projects are results oriented. They are undertaken to achieve a specific objective. The project manager should identify and define the specific tasks that would lead to the desired results.

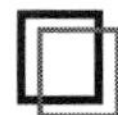

PROJECT MANAGEMENT GOALS

The project manager is responsible for the following goals:

- *Complete the project on time:* The customer expects to receive the system within a predetermined period of time. If time overruns are expected, the project manager should notify the customer ahead of time and explain the reasons for delay.
- *Complete the project within the budget:* Managing the project budget is as important as managing the technical aspects of systems development. As with time

overruns, budget overruns must be communicated and immediately explained to top management. If budget overruns entail a request for changing the price to the client, the new estimate and its consequences must be explained.

- *Meet requirements:* The developers must ensure that the new system complies with the requirements specified at the beginning of the project.
- *Meet expectations:* Beyond the mere compliance with stated requirements and technical specifications, the new system must meet the users' expectations, even if those expectations exceed the work agreed on. If the users' expectations are not met, they will tend to not use the system. Even the best system is a failure when not used.

PLANNING AND CONTROLLING A PROJECT

The purpose of the project should be clearly defined. The management of a project requires proper planning and control of a project's completion time, budgetary resources, and desired results. Without proper planning and control, it is highly unlikely that the project will be completed within the deadline or within resources, or that the desired results will be achieved. In planning and controlling a project, ask the following questions:

Project Objective

- What are the desired results?
- What do we expect to achieve by undertaking this project?
- What problems are likely to be encountered?
- How will those problems be solved?

Time Considerations

- What is the magnitude of the project?
- Is it a large project or a small project?
- If it is a large project, how can it be divided into a series of shorter tasks?
- How long will it take to complete the project?
- What is the project's deadline?
- What are the consequences of a delay in deadline?
- For longer projects, when should each phase of the project be completed?

Financial Considerations

- What is the project's budget?
- What are the major categories of expenses?
- Will capital expenditures be undertaken?
- How much of the budget should be allocated to planned expenses?

- How much of the budget should be allocated to unexpected expenses and contingency planning?
- What are the consequences of going over or under budget?
- What resources, including human resources, are needed to complete the project?
- What tools and methods will be used to ensure that the project is within budget?

Management

- What is my responsibility?
- Who will be on my project team?
- What is the responsibility of each team member?
- Who will manage and coordinate the various activities in a project and ensure that they are proceeding as planned and will be completed before their deadline?
- Who will monitor that the project is proceeding as planned and within budget?
- How will variances be identified and corrected for?

Interim Analysis

- Are the intermediate results consistent with the final desired results?
- Is the project achieving the desired results at each major step along its completion path?
- How will you accelerate the pace of the work if your team falls behind schedule?
- How will you reduce expenses if actual costs exceed the budget?
- If problems are developing, what actions will be taken to correct them?

Final Report

- How will the results of the project be documented?
- What type of final report will be prepared and for whom?

To successfully complete the project, the project manager must have a clear understanding of the desired results and how these results will satisfy the needs of the end user. Project managers should assume a leadership position. Their aim should be not only to supervise but more importantly to coordinate the efforts of the team members. This often requires direct involvement in the major phases of the task so that the team works together, budgets do not show significant variances, schedules are kept, and deadlines are met.

A schedule of work should be prepared outlining responsibilities. Everything should be written down. Checklists should be used to ensure that all team members know their responsibilities and when the job must be completed.

Team members sometimes work on several projects simultaneously. Under these conditions, there may be conflicts among priorities, especially if they are working under different project managers. To minimize such conflicts, team members should be asked to let project managers know about scheduling conflicts in advance. Team members may then be reassigned to different tasks.

Team members should be given detailed instructions, and participation should be encouraged from the beginning. Their input should be solicited. Let the members propose solutions and assist in implementation. Active participation will motivate the project team. When the ideas are good, the entire project benefits.

Conducting the Initial Meeting

Before starting the project, the project manager should meet with the team to set a positive tone and define the project's purpose. The meeting can help avoid misunderstandings, saving time and effort later. It also clarifies the nature of the assignment, as well as the authority and responsibility of each individual.

Meetings should then be scheduled at regular intervals but limited in time and frequency. If the project team spends all its time in meetings, not much else will be accomplished. At the same time, it is important to get together to review progress, resolve problems, and ensure adherence to budgets and schedules.

At the initial meeting, each team member should identify the problems he or she anticipates in working on the project. A list should be prepared of possible problems and team members should generate solutions. If additional data is needed, discuss who will research the data and from what sources. How will this information be verified? Possibly some of the data may be inaccurate, obsolete, or someone may have misinterpreted the data. Be sure to consider how much time it will take to gather additional data or to conduct research.

A list of initial tasks should be prepared and assigned to appropriate individuals. Whenever possible, let the team members volunteer; they are likely to be more motivated if they define their own roles. The entire team should gain an understanding of the scope of the entire project at the initial meeting.

For all major phases of the project, prepare an initial schedule. For each phase, as well as for the overall project, establish the anticipated start and completion dates. Some phases, of course, may overlap. Subgroups of the team may be working independently, and the work of one subgroup may not depend on the work of another subgroup. Nonlinearity in a project and its overlapping phases offer tremendous flexibility in scheduling activities.

While deadlines should be established in the initial schedule, maintaining flexibility is also important. It is highly unlikely that everything will happen according to schedule. Furthermore, as the team starts its work, the members will gain a better understanding of the problems, and the schedule and budget may have to be modified.

An initial financial budget should be prepared for each phase of the project after considering human, financial, and information resources. For capital expenditures, consider both purchasing and leasing, as appropriate. Variance analysis should be conducted at the end of each phase by comparing the actual to budget figures for costs, time, and productivity. This allows you to monitor actual expenditures and time, and to take corrective action, if necessary, to keep the project within budget.

Assembling the Project Team

The project team is a major determinant of the success or failure of a project. As the team increases in size, its diversity increases, the managing tasks become more difficult and complex, and the potential for conflict increases. There might be misunderstandings in communication. Different individuals have different motives and goals.

Team Assignment

As a project manager, you may or may not have control over the staff members assigned to the project team. If a team is being imposed, you should communicate with senior management employees and request that they allow you involvement in the selection process. For example, you could give them a list of individuals with whom you have worked successfully in the past. Emphasize the importance of having a cohesive project team and that such a team is critical to a project's success.

Of course, sometimes it is just not possible to put together a team of your choice and you have to do the best with those you are given. These individuals may be perfectly capable of doing the job. They may have been assigned to this project only because they were available. It is also possible that these individuals were assigned because of their interest or talent. In any event, you should give each employee a chance to do the best possible work—you may be pleasantly surprised.

It is important to inspire and motivate team members. Your aim should be to help team members understand how the success of the project will affect their success. Primarily interested in themselves, team members will not commit to the project if they do not anticipate personal gain. You need to specifically identify the benefits to the team members to motivate them and to focus their energies on the project. An ideal team member understands the desired result and is committed to making it happen.

Job Assignment

It is generally best to break a large project into several phases and each phase into distinct tasks. Each team member should then be assigned the responsibility of executing one or more of those tasks, which should not be highly structured. To motivate team members, assign them the responsibility for a given job and let them approach it the way they believe is best. This, of course, does not mean that you should not supervise them or give them guidance. Coordinate the activities and make sure the team members understand the goals and aims of the task. However, by providing team members with responsibility for certain tasks, you give them an incentive to put in their best efforts. This also lets them know that you trust them and that you have confidence in their abilities.

Delegating Duties

If you are too assertive and too controlling, you may stifle the freedom of your project team and impede its creativity. An effective project manager knows how to delegate the work. You should not insist that the project be done your way. Your role should be to monitor the team's work and coordinate its efforts, while watching the budget and the time schedule of each phase of the project. Of course, you should be available to help your team members, especially if they come to you with a problem.

Conflict Resolution

Conflicts sometimes develop among team members or groups of team members. For example, individuals may differ as to how to approach the project or to solve a problem, or groups may compete for credit for some work. As the project manager, your aim is to resolve conflicts and to make sure they do not destroy the project. Emphasize to your team that the success of the project is more important than the success of any individual. Stress that everyone benefits from the project's success and everyone loses from its failure.

Self-Directed Work Teams

The self-directed team structure is an alternate to the traditional team structure and has become popular. A self-directed team is a group of well-trained workers with full responsibility for completing a well-defined segment of work, which may be the entire finished product or an intermediate part of the whole. Every member of the team shares equal responsibility for the entire segment of work. Conceptually, self-directed teams are the opposite of traditional teams that work in an assembly-line manner. In an assembly line, each worker assumes responsibility for only a narrow technical function. In self-directed teams, each worker is equally responsible for the entire segment. This, of course, requires that the team members receive extensive training in administrative, technical, and interpersonal skills to maintain a self-managing group. Self-directed teams have many more resources available to them compared with traditional teams.

Traditional teams assign a narrow function to each member. Since a large number of people contribute to the finished product, individual workers see little relationship between their efforts and the finished product. This leads to apathy and alienation. All members in self-directed teams receive extensive cross-training, and they share in the challenging as well as routine activities for their segment of work.

Obtaining Senior Management Buy-in

Obtaining the cooperation of senior management is essential. Senior management's involvement and attitude toward projects differ from company to company and from person to person. Senior management might be very supportive of the project or could not care less about it. Senior management's attitudes may be classified as follows:

- "It is your project. You have to solve your own problems. I don't want to be bothered until it is completed."
- "I would be happy to work with you and resolve any problem you encounter."
- "Although I would like to help, there is nothing I can do. You will have to resolve this problem on your own."
- "Keep me apprised of the situation and any problems you encounter."

Regardless of senior management's attitude, you should be prepared to complete the project without any help. Frequently, you will have no choice but to do the best you can with available resources.

Developing a Feasible Budget

The budgeting process may be a source of confusion and frustration for many project managers. There may be a great deal of pressure to remain within the budget. A budget is simply an estimate of the sources and uses of cash and other resources. Since the budget is an estimate, it is unlikely that the final expenditures will be exactly equal to the budget.

Preparing the budget at a realistic level is important. Agreeing to an inadequate budget is unwise. While it may be convenient at the formation stage to reduce or minimize conflict, you and your project will eventually suffer. You will be expected to explain unfavorable variances to senior management. Moreover, you will be perceived negatively when your project goes over budget.

The budget should always be developed by the project manager. It is unrealistic to work with an imposed budget. The project manager is generally in the best position to know what the project should cost and is responsible for explaining any resulting variances. Accordingly, you should always insist on developing your own budget and should not settle for an inadequate budget simply to minimize conflict at the outset. Otherwise, both you and your project will suffer in the long run.

Project budgets are typically more difficult to prepare and adjust than departmental budgets. Projects typically consist of nonroutine activities. Departmental budgets are generally prepared annually and are often revised quarterly or semiannually. In contrast, project budgets are generally for the life of the project and are not related to a fiscal year. Revisions to project budgets are uncommon in the absence of a mistake in the original budget or a major change in the scope of the project. Unfavorable variances in a project usually are noticed more than unfavorable variances in a departmental budget. At the departmental level, variances are often accepted as being inevitable, but similar variances in a project are often frowned upon. In general, a project manager is typically held to a higher level of accountability than a department manager.

The major expense in most projects is likely to be for human resources. When estimating labor expense, consider both the labor hours and the skill levels needed to complete each phase of the project. Multiplying the hours by the labor rate at each level will give the total labor cost.

Also for each phase of the project, prepare a detailed budget listing the materials, supplies, and equipment requirements, which vary widely. Some projects consist essentially of administrative tasks and do not require any special materials or supplies. Other projects may require considerable expenditures on property, plant, or equipment.

Fixed and variable overhead is another major category of expenses for most projects. Companies differ in how they allocate fixed overhead, but it is usually by formula. Overhead may be allocated based on labor hours, labor cost, machine hours, square feet, and so on. Variable overhead is allocated to the project like other project-specific expenses. In general, overhead is more likely to be allocated for longer-term projects. For shorter-term projects, senior management may decide not to allocate overhead expenses. It is essential to identify significant variances from budgeted amounts. Most companies require formal variance analysis at the end of the project. You should do variance analysis at each phase of the project and take corrective action. If a phase is long, consider doing monthly variance analyses. All significant variances, whether favorable or unfavorable, should be investigated.

If actual expenses exceed budgeted expenses, investigate the cause. Budgets are closely tied to work schedules. Certain phases might be taking longer than estimated. You may have no choice but to demand more work from your team members. Also, your original assumptions and estimates might be wrong or a significant change might have occurred in the scope of the project. You could request senior management to revise the project budget. It is sometimes possible to absorb unfavorable variances from one phase into the next phase. Your personal involvement in future phases of the project might also enhance productivity. You may need to initiate budgetary controls to curb spending.

It is important to investigate all significant variances, not just the unfavorable ones. Sometimes expenses turn out to be less than budgeted. Examine why you are under budget. Is your team more productive than anticipated? Was there a significant decline in the price of materials, supplies, or equipment? Were your original estimates accurate? Is quality being sacrificed in any way to obtain cost savings? Do you expect to incur expenses in later phases that might wipe out any savings from the earlier stages?

Detailed Time-Schedule Preparation

Prepare a schedule for each phase of the project. You will be unable to complete your project on time without planning and controlling the time budget. Even a small delay in one phase of a project can have a significant effect on the overall completion time. Many tasks in a project are interdependent. A small isolated delay might not be a problem. However, when activities are interdependent, a small delay might throw off the entire schedule.

The schedule should be reasonable and realistic. Some projects are plagued by delays. If you have been unable to complete the initial phases on time, it is unlikely that you will complete the project on time. An effective project manager knows how to set up a realistic time budget and how to follow through on it. Time management skills are essential for a good project manager.

When planning the initial schedule, budget a little slack. However, project deadlines are often imposed and you may have no choice but to work within the imposed guidelines. Sometimes a delay in one phase of the project simply has to be overcome in a later phase.

As the project manager, you are responsible for staying on schedule and meeting the deadline. It does not matter what caused the delay. You are personally responsible for controlling the activities, monitoring progress, anticipating problems, and taking corrective actions before delays cause you to miss the final project deadline.

Although your goal should be to meet the project deadline, it is unwise to let the quality of the project suffer. Your final results should be accurate and of high quality, even if it means that you need to request an extension. You should try, of course, to work faster, put in overtime, or modify your original plan to meet the deadline. However, if the trade-off is between meeting the deadline and doing quality work, the project's quality must not be sacrificed.

Project Scorecard

A project scorecard measures the characteristics of the deliverables produced by a project. It also measures the progress of the internal project processes that create those deliverables. The following table provides examples of the types of metrics that could be reported. This information is not exhaustive by any means but may help provide additional ideas for you.

Balance Category	Sample Metrics
Cost	Actual cost vs. budget (variance) for project, for phase, for activity, etc. Total support costs for X months after solution is completed Total labor costs vs. nonlabor (vs. budget) Total cost of employees vs. cost of contract vs. cost of consultant (vs. budget) Cost associated with building components for reuse Total cost per transaction Ideas for cost reductions implemented and cost savings realized
Effort	Actual effort vs. budget (variance) Amount of project manager time vs. overall effort hours
Duration	Actual duration vs. budget (variance)
Productivity (Difficult to measure accurately unless function points are counted)	Effort hours per unit of work/function point Work units/function points produced per effort hour Effort hours reduced from standard project processes Effort hours saved through reuse of previous deliverables, models, components, etc. Number of process improvement ideas implemented Number of hours/dollars saved from process improvements
Quality of deliverables	Percentage of deliverables going through quality reviews Percentage of deliverable reviews resulting in acceptance the first time Number of defects discovered after initial acceptance Percentage of deliverables that comply 100% with organization standards Percentage of deliverables that comply with organization architectural standards Number of customer change requests to revise scope Number of hours of rework to previously completed deliverables Number of best practices identified and applied to the project Number of successfully mitigated risks

Balance Category	Sample Metrics
Customer satisfaction with deliverables	Overall customer satisfaction with deliverables in terms of (survey) Reliability Minimal defects Usability Response time Ease of use Availability Flexibility Intuitiveness Security Meets customer needs Easy-to-understand messages User documentation Application response time (calculated by the system) Number of approved business requirements satisfied by the project
Customer satisfaction with project team	Overall customer satisfaction with the project team in terms of (survey) Responsiveness Competence Accessibility Courteous Good communication Credibility Knowledge of the customer Reliable/follows through on commitments Professionalism Training provided Overall customer satisfaction Turnaround time required to answer customer queries and problems Average time required to resolve issues Number of scope change requests satisfied within original project budget and duration
Business value	Based on the cost-benefit analysis or the value proposition that was created when the project was approved and funded

Scheduling Tools and Techniques

Presenting the schedule information in a visual form helps you and your team understand the project work flow and time requirements.

Gantt Charts

A Gantt chart is a tool to monitor progress. Showing both planned and actual outcomes for each phase, a Gantt chart allows you to isolate and solve scheduling problems in a methodical manner. While the project as a whole might be overwhelming, a Gantt chart helps in managing a large project by breaking the project into a series of smaller phases. As each phase is completed, you can see if the final deadline is likely to be met. If you are behind schedule, you can attempt to get back on track by absorbing the delay in one phase and making it up in another phase. This tool should be used not only by the project manager but by the entire team.

A Gantt chart may be constructed using several techniques involving different combinations of lines and symbols. The actual and planned beginning and ending points for each phase are plotted along a timeline. The first phase is plotted at the top and the last phase is plotted at the bottom. Gantt charts may be constructed by hand or through computer software packages.

Exhibit 19.1 shows a Gantt chart of IT project planning. Project activities are listed down the page and time across the page. The heavy lines show how much of each activity has already been done. You can use this chart to visualize the progress and to adjust your project activities. As you can see, one of the strengths of project scheduling with Gantt charts is the simplicity of the schematic model.

Networks

Most large projects can be represented by a network of activities. PERT (program evaluation and review technique) and CPM (critical path method) network techniques are used extensively to aid in the planning and scheduling of large projects. PERT and CPM are probably the most commonly used of all quantitative techniques in management. Many extensions and modifications have been made to these tools to increase their usefulness and application.

PERT is a useful tool for planning and scheduling large projects involving a large number of activities with uncertainty about completion time. The activities are independent of each other and must be completed in a certain order. CPM is closely related to PERT. Its focus is on the trade-off between cost and completion time for large projects. CPM considers the relationship between the cost of using additional resources and their effect on reducing the completion time of jobs within a project.

Unlike PERT, CPM assumes that the time to complete a job is known with certainty. It also assumes that the relationship between the amount of resources utilized and the amount of time needed to complete the project is known. CPM is concerned simply with the time–cost trade-offs.

The differences in the two techniques make them suitable for different applications. PERT is used more extensively in research and development projects, where completion times are uncertain. CPM is used more widely in projects where the organization has experience in similar projects. Both techniques, however, require the project to consist of a set of independent activities that must be performed in a specific order.

PERT

Gathering and analyzing data are familiar tasks for the IS professional. Assume you are gathering and analyzing data and your project consists of five independent activities, or jobs. The project starts with determining the aim and scope

PROJECT PLANNING CHART

Project Number 01 - 650
Project Name Labor Cost Anaylsis Module
Project Leader J. Flaherty

Page 1 **of** 1
Prepared by S. Doe
Date 12 / 8.

ACTIVITY		WEEK STARTING																			
No.	**Name**	11/17	11/24	12/1	12/8	12/15	12/22	12/29	1/5	1/12	1/19	1/26	2/2	2/9	2/16	2/23	3/2	3/9	3/16	3/23	3/30
1-1	Organize implementation team																				
1-2	Prepare system support procedures																				
1-3	Develop conversion plan																				
1-4	Develop testing plan																				
2-1	Prepare program specifications																				
2-2	Revise system documentation																				
2-3	Perform programming tasks																				
3-1	System test																				
4-1	Install system support procedures																				
5-1	Acceptance test																				
6-1	Conversion																				

Exhibit 19.1 GANTT CHART FOR PROJECT SCHEDULING

Activity Name	Description	Immediate Predecessors	Time (Weeks)
a	Define the aim and scope of project.	—	2
b	Identify participants and prepare a mailing list.	a	4
c	Prepare a survey questionnaire.	a	5
d	Do pilot-testing and fix flaws in questionnaire.	c	7
e	Mail survey; collect and analyze data.	b, d	10

Exhibit 19.2 PERT ACTIVITIES AND FLOW

of the project. Next, you prepare a mailing list of people to be surveyed. Note that you can start preparing the survey instrument while obtaining the mailing list. Neither activity is dependent on the other. After preparing the survey, you pilot-test the survey and correct the flaws. Finally, surveys are mailed and data is collected and analyzed.

Exhibit 19.2 shows the activities and describes their flow. The immediate predecessor activity or group of activities is also shown. Note that each activity is represented by a letter. The table shows the amount of time needed to complete each one. A PERT network may be generated from this information, as shown in Exhibit 19.3.

The minimum time required for completion of the whole project is given by the longest path in the network and is known as the critical path. As Exhibit 19.3 shows, there are two paths in this project: a-b-e and a-c-d-e. The completion time for a-b-e is 16 weeks and the completion time for a-c-d-e is 24 weeks. The path a-c-d-e is the critical path because it is the longer path in the network. Slack is determined by subtracting the completion time for the noncritical paths from the completion time for the critical path. Therefore, the slack for path a-b-e is 8 weeks. Slack information is extremely useful to project managers. It tells how much flexibility you have in scheduling various activities.

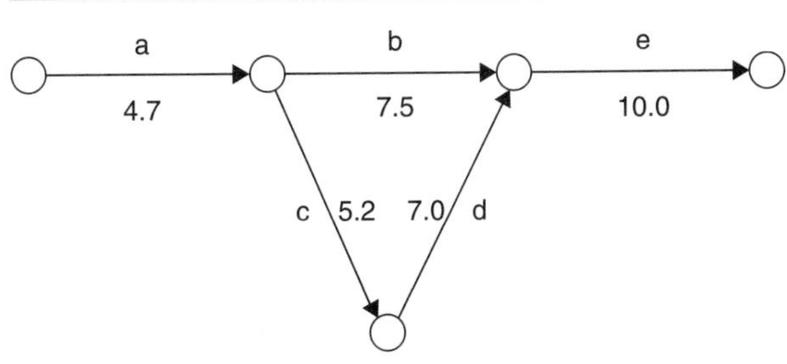

Exhibit 19.3 SAMPLE PERT NETWORK

More complex projects can have multiple critical paths. If there are two critical paths with no common activities, then at least two activities, one on each path, must be shortened to reduce the project's completion time. If the critical paths share one or more of the activities, shortening that activity reduces the entire project's completion time.

PERT specifically takes into account uncertainties inherent in completing activities. An estimate is made of the most likely, pessimistic, and optimistic completion times by a knowledgeable individual. The pessimistic estimate is based on a familiar assumption: Everything that can go wrong will go wrong. However, this estimate does not include the effect of catastrophic or highly unusual events such as earthquakes or fires. The optimistic estimate is based on the assumption that everything goes right, and it represents the shortest possible time for the completion of the activity.

While not always easy to prepare, the three estimates give important information about the expected uncertainties. The three estimates will be close together for some activities and cover a narrow range; the estimates may be over a wide range for other activities. These estimates may or may not be symmetrical around the mean.

The expected completion time for each activity is calculated using the beta distribution, which is not based on empirical data. Since many projects occur only once, it is not possible to use historical data to empirically determine probabilities. Under these conditions, using the beta distribution is generally the best possible option.

The beta distribution assumes that the pessimistic and optimistic activity times occur with equal frequency. The most likely estimate occurs with a probability four times more likely than either the pessimistic or the optimistic. Applying these weights,

$$t_e = \frac{t_o + t_m + t_p}{6}$$

The expected completion time t_e is equal to the sum of the optimistic time estimate t_o, the pessimistic time estimate t_p and four times the most likely time estimate t_m divided by 6.

Continuing with our earlier example, assume the estimates shown in Exhibit 19.4 were obtained for the optimistic

Activity	t_o	t_m	t_p	t_e	S_t	V_t
a	2	4	10	4.7	1.3	1.8
b	2	8	11	7.5	1.5	2.3
c	4	5	7	5.2	0.5	0.3
d	6	6	12	7.0	1.0	1.0
e	4	10	16	10.0	2.0	4.0

EXHIBIT 19.4 NEW DISTRIBUTION ESTIMATES

t_o, most likely t_m, and pessimistic t_p times. Based on the beta distribution, the expected completion time t_e has been calculated. The standard deviation S_t and variance V_t are also shown. The network based on these new time estimates is shown in Exhibit 19.5.

Standard deviation and variance are commonly used as measures of variability. The variance is the average squared difference of all the numbers from their mean, and standard deviation is simply the square root of variance. The calculation of standard deviation and variance in PERT are even simpler because the beta distribution is represented by only three values. Standard deviation S_t can be estimated as follows:

$$S_t = \frac{t_p - t_o}{6}$$

In other words, S_t is one-sixth of the difference between the pessimistic and optimistic time estimates. The greater the uncertainty, the greater the range and the higher the S_t. A high standard deviation means that there is a great likelihood that the time to complete the activity will differ significantly from the expected completion time t_e. Variance V is the square of standard deviation.

The expected completion time and variance for a sequence of independent activities is the sum of their separate times and the sum of individual variances. The critical path and the expected completion time and variance for the project may be calculated by adding the time and variance for each activity along the path. If a project has more than one critical path, select the one with the largest variance.

CPM

CPM was developed to solve scheduling problems, and it is less concerned with the uncertainty problems of PERT. CPM is concerned with minimizing the costs of project scheduling. It is a deterministic model, unlike PERT, which is a probabilistic model. CPM recognizes that most activities can be completed in a shorter time by utilizing additional

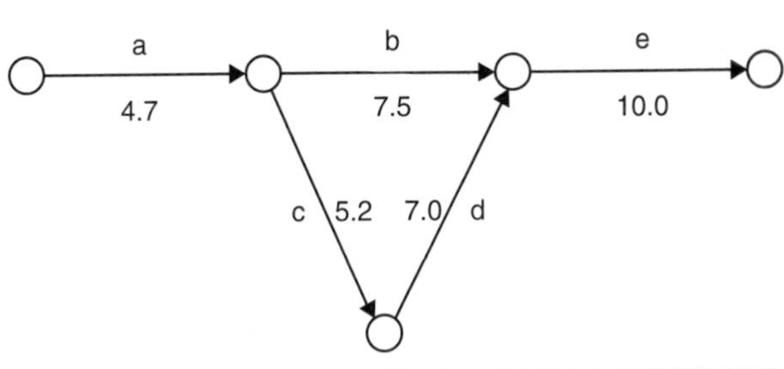

Exhibit 19.5 NETWORK BASED ON NEW TIME ESTIMATES

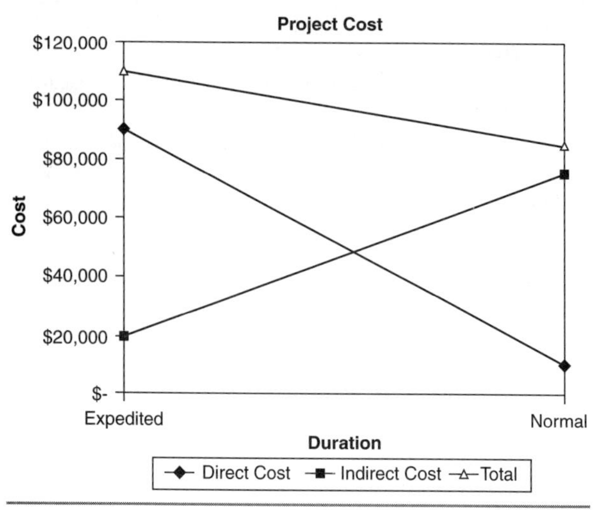

Exhibit 19.6 DIRECT AND INDIRECT COSTS VERSUS DURATION

resources, thus increasing the cost of the project. If the advantages outweigh the incremental costs, a job should be expedited, or "crashed." In contrast, if a job has significant slack and there is no reason to shorten it, the job should proceed at its normal or most efficient pace with fewer resources. Thus, only critical jobs should be expedited or crashed, and CPM is used to determine which jobs to crash and by how much.

Project costs may be classified into two categories. Direct costs are associated with individual activities in a project. Indirect costs are overhead items and fixed expenses. If a project's duration is shortened, direct costs increase and indirect costs decrease. This relationship is illustrated in Exhibit 19.6.

To illustrate the concept, assume that the time–cost trade-off is linear and that the relationship can be represented by a straight line. Exhibit 19.7 shows the time–cost trade-off for a typical job. The slope of the line gives us the cost of expediting an activity: the steeper the slope, the higher the cost. A vertical line represents an activity that cannot be shortened regardless of the extra resources. The vertical line in Exhibit 19.7 suggests that it is not possible to shorten the activity, no matter what additional resources are expended. A horizontal line indicates that shortening or expediting a job would require no extra resources. The horizontal line in Exhibit 19.7 indicates that slowing down the activity would decrease the direct costs only up to a certain extent beyond which no additional savings would be obtained. Costs may even start to increase if the activity is slowed excessively. Typically, we expect a line to slope

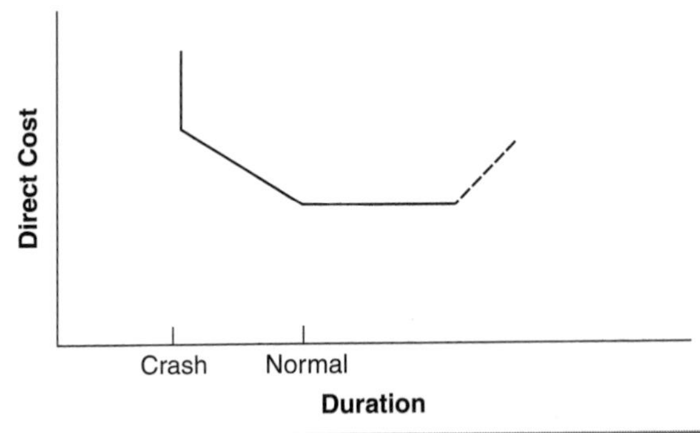

Exhibit 19.7 TIME–COST TRADE-OFF

downward to the right. The negative slope of the line indicates that there is a negative association between cost and time; costs go up as duration is shortened.

Using CPM, we can determine the optimum project length, striking a balance between shortening jobs and not shortening them to minimize the direct and indirect costs. A preliminary schedule with maximum time length and normal resources is generated. This schedule is reduced by expediting one or more activities at an additional cost. If these additional costs are less than the savings in indirect costs from expediting the project, then the activities should be expedited. A new schedule is then generated and additional activities are expedited. This continues while net savings are realized in total cost. Improvements continue to be made using a stepwise method.

Only activities along the critical path affect a project's length, and thus only these activities are considered for crashing. The cost–time slope for each activity along the critical path is examined, and the one with the smallest slope is selected because it can be shortened with the least expenditure. Cost-benefit analysis is conducted to determine if net savings exist. This process is repeated until either no activity on the critical path can be shortened or the cost of shortening would exceed the resultant savings from shortening the project duration.

Consider a basic project with four activities, as shown in Exhibit 19.8. The normal and crash duration times, as well as the cost to crash, is given in Exhibit 19.9 for each activity. The activity's normal time represents the number of weeks needed to complete the activity at an efficient pace. The crash time represents the minimum time that results from the use of additional resources. It is possible to have other times between the normal and crash durations. However, reducing the project time beyond the crash duration is not possible. The cost of crashing is the cost of the additional resources needed to shorten the activity completion time by

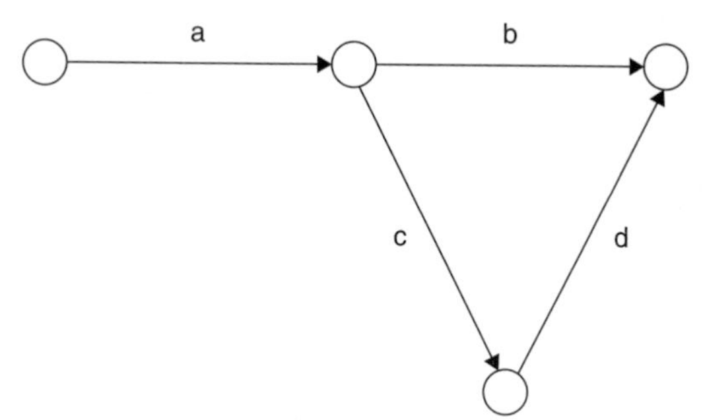

Exhibit 19.8 BASIC PROJECT DIAGRAM

1 week. Exhibit 19.10 shows the cost–time trade-off for each activity. Recall that it is more expensive to crash activities with steeper slopes. As Exhibit 19.10 shows, activity a has the steepest slope, followed by activity c, activity d, and activity b.

The critical path is represented by a-c-d. It takes 15 weeks to complete this project. Assume that the time-related indirect expenses for this project are $6,500 per week. If we do not expedite the project, total relevant cost is:

Total relevant cost = Cost of crashing + Cost of overhead
= $0 + $6,500 × 15 weeks
= $97,500

The total relevant cost is not necessarily the same as total cost. When considering the relevant cost for decision-making purposes, we can ignore the base cost of the project. The base cost has to be paid regardless of whether the project is expedited and is thus irrelevant.

The critical path is a-c-d, and since activity d has the smallest slope on the critical path, it is the least expensive to shorten. Activity b has 2 weeks of slack; therefore, d can be shortened by 2 weeks before activity b becomes critical. By shortening d by 2 weeks, the project can now be completed in 13 weeks and its cost is as follows:

Total relevant cost = Cost of crashing + Cost of overhead
= $3,000 × 2 weeks + $6,500 × 13 weeks
= $90,500

Activity	Normal	Crash	Cost of Crashing
a	4	2	$6,000
b	9	4	$2,000
c	5	2	$5,000
d	6	3	$3,000

Exhibit 19.9 CRASH AND DURATION TIMES

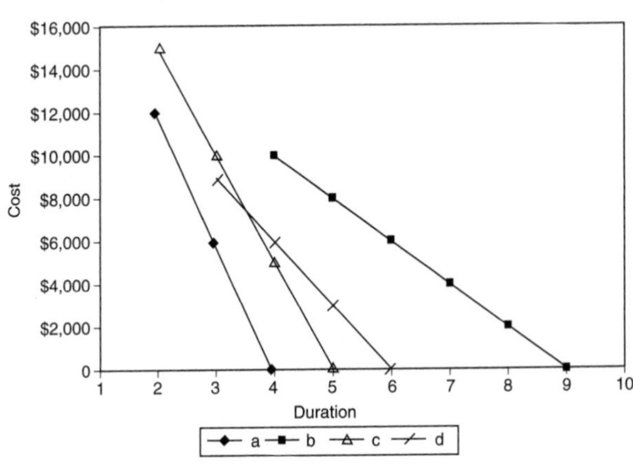

Exhibit 19.10 COST-TIME TRADE-OFF FOR EACH ACTIVITY

Although we incurred $6,000 for crashing activity d, we saved $13,000 by reducing overhead costs and realized a net savings of $7,000 ($90,500 versus $97,500).

Now we have two critical paths, a-b and a-c-d. Both paths must be reduced if we want to shorten our schedule. We have several choices, as shown in Exhibit 19.11. Activity a is common to both paths, and reducing it will shorten the overall project. Alternatively, we can reduce activities b and c or activities b and d. Clearly, the best alternative is to crash activities b and d; they have the lowest combined cost of crashing. Keep in mind that d can be crashed only 1 additional week, since d cannot be less than 3 weeks and we have previously reduced it by 2 weeks. The total relevant cost for crashing b and d by 1 week is:

Total relevant cost

= Cost of crashing b and d + Cost of overhead

= b → $2,000 × 1 week + $6,500 × 12 weeks

d → $3,000 × 3 weeks

= ($2,000 + $9,000) + $78,000

= $89,500

Crash Activity	Cost of Crashing (Per Week)
a	$6,000
b and c	$2,000 + $5,000 = $7,000
b and d	$2,000 + $3,000 = $5,000

EXHIBIT 19.11 ACTIVITY VERSUS COST

Crash Activity	Cost of Crashing (Per Week)
a	\$6,000
b and c	\$2,000 + \$5,000 = \$7,000

EXHIBIT 19.12 RELEVANT ACTIVITY VERSUS COST

As shown in Exhibit 19.12, we now have two choices. Activity a can be shortened from four to two weeks:

Total relevant cost

= Cost of crashing a, b, and d + Cost of overhead
= b → \$2,000 × 1 week + \$6,500 × 10 weeks
d → \$3,000 × 3 weeks
a → \$6,000 × 2 weeks
= (\$2,000 + \$9,000 + \$12,000) + \$65,000
= \$88,000

The only alternative left is to shorten b and c. Recall b has already been shortened by 1 week, but it can be shortened by another 4 weeks. Activity c, however, can be shortened by only 3 weeks. If we reduce b and c by 3 weeks, then:

Total relevant cost

= Cost of crashing a, b, c, and d + Cost of overhead
= b → \$2,000 × 4 week + \$6,500 × 7 weeks
d → \$3,000 × 3 weeks
a → \$6,000 × 2 weeks
c → \$5,000 × 3 weeks
= (\$8,000 + \$9,000 + \$12,000+15,000) + \$45,000
= \$89,500

It does not make sense to crash b and c, since the cost exceeds the benefit. Hence, our final schedule consists of 10 weeks and requires crashing activities a, b, and d. The total relevant cost for the project is \$88,000.

COMPUTER SOFTWARE FOR PROJECT MANAGEMENT

Most project management applications today use computers extensively. The management of projects is enhanced by tools such as Gantt charting, the program evaluation and review technique (PERT), and the critical path method (CPM). These tools are easily computerized and indeed there are dozens of commercial packages on the market. The user inputs activity time estimates and procedure information, program output slack for each activity, duration and variance for critical paths, and other useful project management information. Many project management software packages, such as Microsoft Project, let planners enter defined activities, events, and times only once, then present either a Gantt or a PERT chart—or both—on the computer's monitor. The project manager can then see how changing parameters will alter the charts and completion times. Some managers prefer using Gantt charts, some prefer PERT charts, and others use both for the same projects. The preference depends on the personality of the manager and on presentation needs rather than on the nature of the project. The types of project management software are described below:

- *Project- and resource-tracking software:* With these applications, you enter each task and subtask of the project as well as each subproject, then define resources, such as employees and contractors, and assign them. Most of these tools let you define priorities and set the order in which subprojects or individual parts of the project must be done. Many good specialized project-tracking tools are available, but remember that spreadsheets and even text editors can do the job in a pinch. The quality of your project management depends more on your skill and attentiveness than on the tools you choose to use.
- *Time-tracking software:* These applications let you track in detail the amount of time it takes to implement your project. Keeping abreast of this information over time will help you improve your estimating skills.
- *Bug-tracking and source-code version-control software:* These applications are not just for software development projects. You can use these products to control changes to documentation, keep on top of the versions of vendor software that are in your standard desktop image, and track problems with every portion of your project.

Below is a list of project management software:

Artemis International Solutions Corporation
http://www.artemisintl.com
Artemis Views 5

Computer Associates International
http://www.cai.com
AllFusion Process Management Suite

Integrated Strategic Information Systems Pvt. Ltd.
http://www.iPlanEnterprise.com
iPlan Enterprise 4.3; iPlan Web 1.3

Microsoft Corp.
http://www.microsoft.com
Microsoft Project 2000
Microsoft Visio Standard 2002

Pacific Edge Software
http://www.pacificedge.com
The Edge Solution w/Portfolio Edge & Project Office

PlanView
http://www.myplanview.com
PlanView

Primavera Systems
http://www.primavera.com
Primavera TeamPlay

Welcom
http://www.welcom.com
Cobra 3.5
Open Plan 2.6
WelcomHome 2.5

APPENDIX A

COMPLIANCE SOFTWARE BUYER'S GUIDE

Below is a comparison of 16 vendors now offering software to help companies meet the requirements of Sarbanes-Oxley Section 404.

	Click Commerce	**Documentum (EMC)**	**Hyperion Solutions**	**IBM**
	$18 million revenues Founded 1996	$227 million revenues Founded 1990	$610 million revenues Founded 1981 (as IMRS)	$81 billion revenues Founded 1911
Sarbox/404 program	Allegis eBusiness Suite (v. 7.0)	eRoom Financial Compliance Workplace; Enterprise Controls Repository	Hyperion Financial Management (v. 3.4)	IBM Lotus Workplace for Business Controls & Reporting
Program description	E-business suite enables companies to automate sell-side processes which serve as process documentation and evidence of control. Applications include marketing funds management, ordering, claims management, and returns.	Web-based Workplace one of several templates used to manage 404 and 302. Program provides capability to manage testing, document findings, and report/ manage remediation. Integrates with Enterprise Controls Repository, a records manager and storage offering.	Packaged program that consolidates financial results from multiple ERP or GL systems. Assists with risk assessment, information and communication, and monitoring during monthly and quarterly close and reporting cycle.	Designed to help users manage processes, controls, and information subject to 404. Created in tandem with KPMG, app intended to provide foundation for financial-reporting processes and organized approach to gathering information about internal controls.
Financial controls documentation	Yes	No	No	Yes
Financial controls attestation	No	Yes	Yes	Yes
Integrates with ERP	Yes	Yes	Yes	No

	Click Commerce	**Documentum (EMC)**	**Hyperion Solutions**	**IBM**
XBRL enabled	No	No	Yes	No
Monitor operational systems	No	No	No	Yes
Size of business targeted	M, L	All	M, L	All
Price	Varies	Varies	Contact vendor	$1,150 per user @ list price

	Microsoft	**Movaris**	**Nth Orbit**	**onProject**
	$32.2 billion revenues Founded 1975	Revenues NA Founded 1988	Revenues NA Founded 2001	$5 million revenues Founded 1989
Sarbox/404 program	Office Solution Accelerator for Sarbanes-Oxley	Movaris Certainty (v. 6.5)	Certus (v. 1.3)	S-O Comply (v. 1.41)
Program description	Helps organizations manage compliance initiatives related to 302 and 404. Program facilitates regulatory compliance and sustainable corporate governance by enhancing visibility over financial processes and internal controls.	Created specificaly for Sarbox. App based on business process-management platform that manages company's entire Sarbox obligation, from documentation and risk assessment to ongoing monitoring and attestation preparation.	Certus, which addresses full range of Sarbox Compliance (including 302 and 404), is designed to help users implement full compliance from risk assessment, controls documentation, gap management, remediation, testing, and ongoing monitoring.	S-O Comply functionality includes a flexible and secure framework, ability to import and centrally document internal control data, assign and manage tasks or issues, and document disclosure activity.
Financial controls documentation	Yes	Yes	Yes	Yes
Financial controls attestation	Yes	Yes	Yes	Yes
Integrates with ERP	Must be customized	Yes	Yes	Yes
XBRL enabled	No	No	Yes	No

	Microsoft	Movaris	Nth Orbit	onProject
Monitor operational systems	Through SQL Server 2000	Yes	Yes	No
Size of business targeted	All	M, L	L	All
Price	Contact vendor	Contact vendor	$50,000 – $500,000	Starts at $9,900

	OpenPages	Open Text	Oracle	Paisley Consulting
	Revenues NA Founded 1996	$178 million revenues Founded 1991	$9.5 billion revenues Founded 1977	$10 million revenues Founded 1995
Sarbox/404 program	OpenPages Sarbanes-Oxley Express (V. 2.0)	Livelink for Corporate Governance	Oracle Internal Controls Manager	Risk Navigator (v. 1.3), Focus Control Assurance (v. 1.2)
Program description	Enterprise compliance-management program designed to reduce time, resource costs of compliance for 404 and 302. Combines document and process management with flexible reporting capabilities. App intended to help managers enforce internal controls.	Tracks, reports, manages processes and info for corporate governance Features: auditable process workflows based on COSO; integrated records, document, and content management; secure collaborative tools; integrated online training, training audits. Open architecture.	Comprehensive tool for executives, controllers, internal-audit departments, business-unit managers, business-process owners, and public accounting firms. Programs documents and tests internal controls, and monitors ongoing compliance.	Risk Navigator includes documentation and testing, control self-asssessment surveys, and operational risk assessments; also features executive dashboard. Focus documents financial process risks/ controls, tracks issues and action plans. Includes pre-populated process, risk, and control templates.
Financial controls documentation	Yes	Yes	Yes	Yes (both)
Financial controls attestation	Yes	Yes	Yes	Yes (both)

	OpenPages	Open Text	Oracle	Paisley Consulting
Integrates with ERP	Yes	Yes	Yes	Yes (Risk Navigator); No (Focus)
XBRL enabled	Yes	No	Yes	No (both)
Monitor operational systems	Yes	Yes	Yes	No (both)
Size of business targeted	All	L	M, SMB, L	S (Focus), M (both), L (Risk Navigator)
Price	$65,000 and up (minimum 25 users)	$125,000 (must also have core product suite, which starts at $100K for first 100 users)	Price available online	See footnote[1]

[1]Risk Navigator installation package: $150,000, plus annual user fees (based on number of users) starting at $150 per user.

Focus: Per-user license fees start at $700 per user, plus 20 percent maintenance charge.

	PeopleSoft	Providus Software Solutions	SAP	SAS
	$1.9 billion revenues Founded 1987	Under $5 million revenues Founded 2002	$9.5 billion revenues Founded 1972	$1.2 billion revenues Founded 1976
Sarbox/404 program	PeopleSoft Enterprises Internal Controls Enforcer	RiskResolve 3.0 for Sarbanes-Oxley for financial services industry	SAP Compliance Management for Sarbanes-Oxley Act	SAS Corporate Compliance for Sarbanes-Oxley (v. 2.1)
Program description	Designed to automate and enforce internal controls required under 404. Enables users to streamline documentation and continuously monitor internal controls. Diagnostic capabilitites intended to help companies reduce the cost of compliance.	Software provides financial institutions with single Active Risk Management Console, enabling a top-down view of risk and potential risk across all lines of business.	Addresses internal-control requirements of 404 via comprehensive management of rols. Helps document/model business processes, document existing controls, test results, and suggest improvements. Also provides status reports to management according to law's provisions.	Targets all relevant Sarbox provisions. Software provides tracking and auditing of internal controls, rapid consolidation of financial data, validation/ verification of financial reports, and dashboard monitoring, as well as risk-impact assessment and alerts.
Financial controls documentation	Yes	Yes	Yes	Yes
Financial controls attestation	Yes	Yes	Yes	Yes

	PeopleSoft	Providus Software Solutions	SAP	SAS
Integrates with ERP	Yes	Yes	Yes	Yes
XBRL enabled	No	No	Yes	No
Monitor operational systems	Yes	No	Yes	Yes
Size of business targeted	SMB, L	All	All	All
Price	Varies	Varies, ranging from $120,000 to $350,000 and up for large-scale enterprisewide deployments	Contact vendor	Base price for software license, plus per-user cost

Source: From CFO.com © CFO Publishing Corporation 2004. All rights reserved. Reprinted by permission.

APPENDIX B

CRM SOFTWARE PROVIDERS

Provider	ACCPAC Pleasanton, CA (800) 945-8007	Aspect Communications San Jose, CA (800) 391-2341	Baan Golden, CO (800) 967-6730	Best Software (CRM division) Scottsdale, AZ (800) 643-6400	Blue Martini Software San Mateo, CA (800) 258-3627
Sales/Marketing Contact	ACCPAC Client Care (800) 873-7282	Lakshmi Bakshi (408) 325-2623	Lailla Matthews (303) 274-3112	Bob Neeser (800) 643-6400	Laurent Pacalin (650) 356-4000
Product Name	ACCPAC CRM	Aspect Enterprise Contact Server	iBaan for CRM	SalesLogix	Blue Martini 4
Provider	BroadVision Redwood City, CA (866) 287-6669	Chordiant Software Cupertino, CA (888) 246-7342	Computer Associates International Islandia, NY (800) 225-5224	Dendrite Morristown, NJ (973) 425-1200	E.piphany San Mateo, CA (877) 764-4163
Sales/Marketing Contact	Stephanie Mello (214) 224-5969	Jonathan Miller (888) 246-7342	Robert Sterbens (631) 342-3307	Mark Maffei (908) 541-5877	Mike Trigg (650) 356-3800
Product Name	BroadVision One-to-One Enterprise	Chordiant 5 Selling and Servicing	Intelligent CRM Suite	WebForce	E.piphany E.5
Provider	eGain Communications Sunnyvale, CA (888) 603-4246	Firepond Waltham, MA (800) 396-0663	FrontRange Solutions Colorado Springs, CO (800) 776-7889	Genesys Daly City, CA (888) 436-3797	Group 1 Software Lanham, MD (800) 368-5806
Sales/Marketing Contact	Max Fiszer (408) 212-3400	Eric Snow (781) 487-8400	Michele Reser (719) 278-7102	Dana Dye (415) 437-1100	Linda Flynn (301) 918-0727

Product Name	eGain eService Enterprise	SalesPerformer Suite, eService Performer Suite	GoldMine, HEAT	Genesys Suite 6	Data Quality, Marketing Automation
Provider	Intershop Communications San Francisco (877) 644-5534	eGain Communications Sunnyvale, CA (888) 603-4246	Jeeves Solutions Emeryville, CA (877) 453-3837	Kefta San Francisco (415) 391-6881	Motive Communications Austin, TX (877) 466-8483
Sales/Marketing Contact	Jonathan Durnin (415) 844-2138	Joel Reed (800) 727-5333	Mike Fenn (510) 985-7930	Michael Oiknine (415) 391-6881	Lauren Short (415) 856-5126
Product Name	eGain eService Enterprise	SalesPerformer Suite, eService Performer Suite	GoldMine, HEAT	Interaction Manager, Customer Acquisition Optimizer, Customer Retention Optimizer, Customer Service Tools	Data Quality, Marketing Automation
Provider	Maximizer Software Vancouver (800) 804-6299	Net Perceptions Edina, MN (800) 466-0711	Onyx Software Bellevue, WA (888) 275-6699	Oracle Redwood Shores, CA (800) 672-2531	PeopleSoft Pleasanton, CA (800) 380-7638
Sales/Marketing Contact	Gary Vollhoffer (800) 804-6299	Terri Reden (952) 842-5000	Robin Rees (425) 451-8060	Mark Jarvis (800) 672-2531	Robb Eklund (925) 694-3000
Product Name	Maximizer, Maximizer Enterprise	NetP 7.0	Onyx Enterprise	Oracle E-Business Suite	PeopleSoft CRM

Provider	Rainmaker Systems Scotts Valley, CA (800) 631-1545	Remedy Mountain View, CA (650) 903-5200	Responsys Palo Alto, CA (888) 219-7150	SafeHarbor Technology Seattle (800) 480-5777	Salesforce.com San Francisco (800) 667-6389
Sales/Marketing Contact	Kerry Benoit (831) 430-3800	Steve Balentine (650) 919-5717	Mike Romley (650) 858-7434	Sue Cummings (206) 922-5003	(800) 667-6389
Product Name	Contract Renewals Plus	Remedy CRM	Responsys Interact	SafeHarbor Support Services 3.0, Online Banking Support Services 3.0	CRM
Provider	SAP America Newtown Square, PA (800) 872-1727	eGain Communications Sunnyvale, CA (888) 603-4246	SAS Cary, NC (800) 727-0025	Sento American Fork, UT (801) 492-2000	Siebel Systems San Mateo, CA (800) 647-4300
Sales/Marketing Contact	(610) 661-1000	Joe Springer (408) 558-4847	Customer Interaction Center (800) 727-0025	Jason Young (801) 492-2000	Thomas Arnold (510) 788-4518
Product Name	mySAP CRM	iAvenue	The SAS Analytical CRM Solution	Customer Choice Platform, Assist, Recite, Service Portal	Siebel eBusiness Applications V.7

Source: CFO.com© CFO Publishing Corporation 2004.

GLOSSARY

802.11 a family of specifications developed by the U.S. Institute of Electrical and Electronics Engineers (IEEE). There are currently three specifications in the family (802.11a, 802.11b, and 802.11g), with more being developed. The 802.11b standard, often referred to as Wi-Fi, is currently more widespread. However, hardware manufacturers are increasingly offering multistandard equipment that can work with various standards.

application program computer software written specifically to process data in an information system. It performs tasks and solves problems applicable to a manager's work.

artificial intelligence (AI) thinking and reasoning software based on information input into it by a human expert. The reasoning process involves self-correction. Significant data is evaluated and relevant relationships uncovered. The computer learns which kind of answers are reasonable and which are not. Artificial intelligence performs complicated strategies that determine the best or worst way to accomplish a task or avoid an undesirable result. Examples of applications of **AI** are tax planning and capital budgeting analysis.

audit software computer programs designed to examine and test a company's accounting records. Some packages aid in gathering evidence, performing analytical tests, sampling data, appraising internal control, audit scheduling, and printing exception reports. The software is used by internal auditors.

automatic programming process of using one program to prepare another program.

automatic recovery program program enabling a system to continue functioning even though equipment has failed.

background processing lower-priority programs are executed when the system is not being used by higher-priority programs.

balanced scorecard approach using multiple measures to evaluate managerial performance. These measures may be financial or nonfinancial, internal or external, and short term or long term. The scorecard allows a determination as to whether a manager is achieving certain objectives at the expense of others that may be equally or more important. There are four different perspectives: (1) financial, (2) customer, (3) process, and (4) the learning and growth.

baud serial information transfer speed with which a modem receives and sends data.

block diagram diagram using symbols to explain the interconnections and information flow between hardware and software.

budgeting models computer-based mathematical models generating all kinds of corporate budgets (e.g., cash flow, profitability). The models help managers look at a variety of what-if questions. The resultant calculations provide a basis for choice among alternatives under conditions of uncertainty.

buffer area of a computer's memory set aside to hold information temporarily.

business intelligence a business strategy that integrates and analyzes operational data from an array of internal sources to improve decision making and competitiveness.

business performance management (BPM) the use of business intelligence-derived operational metrics, ranging from ad hoc yardsticks to Six Sigma or balanced scorecard, to measure company performance.

business process reengineering (BPR) approach aiming at making revolutionary changes as opposed to evolutionary changes by eliminating nonvalue-added steps in a business process and computerizing the remaining steps to achieve desired outcomes.

catalog directory of locations of files.

chain links series of linked data items.

corporate planning model computer-based integrated business planning model in which production and marketing models are linked to the financial model. It is a description, explanation, and interrelation of functional areas of a business (accounting, finance and investments, marketing, production, management, economics) expressed in terms of mathematical and logical equations so as to generate a variety of reports including financial forecasts. Corporate planning models may also be used for risk analysis and what-if experimentation. The goals of the model include improving the quality of planning and decision making, reducing the decision risk, and favorably influencing the future corporate environment.

customer relationship management (CRM) software. software that automates customer service and support. It also provides for customer data analysis and supports e-commerce storefronts.

cyber investing investing through telecommunications, such as online trading on the Internet.

cyberspace originally used in *Neuromancer,* William Gibson's novel of direct brain-computer networking, refers to the collective realms of computer-aided communication.

data interchange format (DIF) file system to transfer computer files from one program to another.

data warehouse a database structured to tactical information that can be used to answer specific questions about transactional company history.

database management software computer programs used to manage data in a database. It is a set of programs that provide for defining, controlling, and accessing the database. The software allows managers to enter, manipulate, retrieve, display, select, sort, edit, and index data.

debug process of tracing and correcting flaws in a software program or hardware device. Computerized routines may be used to find bugs.

decision support system (DSS) branch of a management information system that provides answers to management problems and that integrates the decision maker into the system as a component. DSS software provides support to the manager in the decision-making process. It analyzes a specific situation and can be modified as the manager desires. Examples of applications include planning and forecasting.

enterprise resource planning (ERP) software system that grew out of material requirements planning (MRP) systems to computerize inventory control and production planning. Key features include an ability to prepare a master production schedule, a bill of materials, and purchase orders.

expert systems computer software involving stored reasoning schemes and containing decision-making processes of business experts in their specialized areas. The software mimics the way human experts make decisions. The expert system appraises and solves business problems requiring human intelligence and imagination that involve known and unknown information. The components of the expert system include a knowledge base, inference engine, user interface, and knowledge acquisition facility.

Extensible Business Reporting Language (XBRL) formerly code named XFRML, a freely available electronic language for financial reporting. It is an XML-based framework that provides the financial community with a standards-based method to prepare, publish in a variety of formats, reliably extract, and automatically exchange financial statements of publicly held companies and the information they contain.

file server computer providing access to files for remote users.

financial analysis software software capable of taking financial data (e.g., online information on the World Wide Web) and performing trend and ratio calculations. Investment and credit decisions are based on the analysis results.

financial model a functional branch of a general corporate planning model. It is essentially used to generate pro forma financial statements and financial ratios. A financial model is a mathematical model describing the interrelationships among financial variables of the firm. It is the basic tool for budgeting and budget planning. Also, it is used for risk analysis and what-if experiments. Many financial models of today are built using special modeling languages such as IFPS or spreadsheet programs such as Excel.

gateway application specific node that connects incompatible networks.

gopher browser and searching program for the Internet.

graphic software program showing business information in graphic form, including charts and diagrams. This enhances the understanding of the information in terms of trends and relationships.

hotspot provides high-speed wireless Internet access in convenient public locations or at home. Using either a laptop or PDA that is 802.11 wirelessly enabled, people can download their e-mail attachments, watch a live Webcast, or listen to streaming audio.

hyperlink a connection between different information sources.

hypertext database approach linking related data, programs, and pictures.

integrated software software package that combines many applications in one program. Integrated packages can move data among several programs utilizing common commands and file structures. An integrated package is recommended when identical source information is used for varying managerial purposes and activities.

intelligent agents personal assistant software enabling a manager to work more efficiently and productively, reduce costs, and save time. The software learns from instruction, examples, and practices. Intelligent agents can interact with each other. A workstation management agent conducts desktop activities such as reviewing and replying to e-mail messages, managing schedules and calendars, and making notes from meetings. A task coordinator agent simplifies and organizes complicated functions. It aids in planning, coordinating, and managing resources. A teacher/peer agent explains complex information. An information overhead agent handles users' problems and answers questions.

interface means of interaction between two computer devices or systems that handle data (e.g., formats, codes) differently. An interface is a device that converts signals from one device into signals that the other device needs.

Internet international network connecting smaller networks linking computers of different entities.

Intranet internal company Web sites. It is developed by the company itself.

knowledgement managenent a broad strategic approach to identifying and using a company's knowledge to improve its efficiency. One subset of knowledge, structured data, can be managed using business intelligence tools.

local area network (LAN) linking of computers and other devices for intersite and intercompany applications in a small geographic area.

management information system (MIS) a computer-based or manual system that transforms data into information useful in the support of decision making.

material requirements planning (MRP) computerized data processing system whose function is to schedule production and control the level of inventory for components with dependent demand.

multitasking simultaneous execution of two or more computer functions.

network (1) interconnected nodes (points) where working units interreact (link) with others. (2) connection of computers and devices.

neural networks a technology in which computers actually try to learn from the database and operator what the right answer is to a question. The system gets positive or negative response to output from the operator and stores that data so that it will make a better decision the next time. While still in its infancy, this technology shows promise for use in fraud detection, accounting, economic forecasting, and risk appraisals.

online analytical processing (OLAP) powerful tools that take a complex, multidimensional view of aggregated data to quickly yield strategic information. The power of OLAP tools is predictive in answering why? and what-if questions.

online searching using a computer retrieval system to obtain information from a database such as on the Internet.

optical character recognition computer tool that recognizes typed or printed characters on paper so that they can be recorded on disk.

real time computer processing of data in connection with another process outside the computer.

relational database a database consisting of relationships between data items.

simulation an attempt to represent a real-life system via a model to determine how a change in one or more variables affects the rest of the system, also called what-if analysis.

speech recognition software program in which verbal commands activate the computer to perform functions.

spreadsheet table of numbers arranged in rows and columns to make accounting, finance, marketing, and other business calculations. Spreadsheets facilitate end-result summary numbers, what-if experimentations, and projections.

statistical software computer program making quantitative calculations such as standard deviation, coefficient of variation, regression analysis, correlation, and variance analysis.

structured data subset of a company's data that is stored electronically in databases and thus can be accessed by data field.

supply-chain management management of the integration of the functions, information, and materials that flow across multiple firms in a supply chain—i.e., buying materials, transforming materials, and shipping to customers.

tag a command inserted in a document that specifies how the document or a portion of the document should be formatted. Tags are used by all format specifications that store documents as text files. This HTML.

tax software tax modules preparing federal and state income tax returns. Tax planning modules exist to examine tax options and alternatives to minimize the company's tax liability in current and future years. What-if tax situation scenarios may be evaluated.

template computer-based worksheet that includes the relevant formulas for a particular application but not the data. It is a blank worksheet on which data is saved and filled in as needed for a future business application and to solve problems. Templates are predefined files, including cell formulas and row and column labels for specific spreadsheet applications, or style sheets and macros in word processing. Templates allow for the referencing of cells and formulations of interrelated formulas and functions. They are reused to analyze similar transactions.

terminal input-output device allowing a user to communicate directly with a computer.

thinking software computer programs used by managers to prepare written reports, including specialized analyses of corporate operations. The software contains aids to improve writing skills and idea formulation so that managers can better create an outline and written report. The information is labeled, organized, and structured.

time software computer program that tracks hours worked by employees by function, operation, or activity. It prepares an analysis of the variance between budgeted and actual hours as well as prepares trends in actual hours over a stated time period (e.g., quarterly comparisons).

utility program program supporting the processing of a computer such as diagnostic and tracing programs.

wide area network (WAN) network connecting sites in a large geographic area.

Wi-Fi short for "wireless fidelity," the popular term for a high-frequency wireless local area network. The Wi-Fi technology is rapidly gaining acceptance in many companies as an alternative to a wired LAN. It can also be installed for a home network.

wireless technology a variety of technologies to communicate without wires, namely radio transmissions. Examples are cellular, microwave, infrared, and satellite.

W-LAN enables a mobile user to connect to a local area network (LAN) through a wireless (radio) connection. A standard, 802.11, specifies the technologies for wireless LANs.

World Wide Web (WWW) Internet system for worldwide hypertext linking of multimedia documents, making the relationship of information that is common between documents easily accessible and completely independent of physical location.

XBRL *see* Extensible Business Reporting Language (XBRL)

XML a general-purpose markup (tagging) standard for creating languages to standardize the data exchange between different computing platforms and applications. XML uses tags (markup) to identify pieces of data, and leaves the interpretation of the data to the user, such as one who is reviewing the financial numbers and their significance for a database management application.

INDEX

S